DIVIDED

FIVE COLLIDING
WORLDVIEWS

AND HOW TO NAVIGATE THEM

Dr. Denise R. Ames

ISBN 978-1-94384107-3

Cover design by Mia Beurskens
Cover graphic by by Bedneyimages / Freepik
Interior design by J. McGann

Printed in the United States of America
Global Awareness Books, Albuquerque, New Mexico, USA
www.global-awareness.org

For Lilly, Hahr, and Sevrien, may your future be less divided and more sustainable, joyous, and harmonious than it is today.

Also by the author

Global Awareness Books www.global-awareness.org

Waves of Global Change: A Holistic World History (two editions)

Waves of Global Change: An Educator's Handbook for Teaching a Holistic World History

The Global Economy: Connecting the Roots of a Holistic System

Connecting the Roots of the Global Economy: A Holistic Approach, Brief Edition

Financial Literacy: Wall Street and How it Works

Human Rights: Towards a Global Values System

Five Worldviews: The Way We See the World

Acknowledgments

This book has evolved over several stages and drafts. There are people I would like to thank at every stage.

I first thought of the idea of worldviews when I was writing my dissertation on a holistic world history in the 1990s. At that time, I found that the Global Wave, a fifth wave of world history from the 1990s onward, contained many different ways of seeing the world. I would like to thank my mentor, colleague, and advisor, Professor Joseph Grabill for working with me on these ideas.

In the 2000s, I resurrected my idea of worldviews and did several workshops on the topic. I also thought it would be a good concept to include in a graduate school curriculum that was weaving in native and modern ways of thinking and living. Thanks to Glenn Parry for his work on trying to make the graduate school a reality. Although the graduate school faltered, the idea stayed with me.

During the 2010s, I adapted the idea of worldviews into professional development workshops for teachers through my non-profit organization, the Center for Global Awareness. It brought context to the fierce debates that were intensifying at this time. I also wrote a book on the worldviews called *Five Worldviews: How We See the World*. I would like to thank my partner at the Center for Global Awareness, Nancy Harmon, for her many years of furthering the goals of CGA and helping me with editing and commenting on the *Five Worldviews* book.

From 2016 onward, my interest in the five worldviews intensified, especially in light of the 2016 presidential election. The election revealed that there were multiple worldviews, and we weren't very good at understanding those who were different from us. I felt a calling to revamp my original five worldviews and start teaching some classes on this controversial topic.

At this stage, I would like to thank the hundreds of people who partici- pated in my workshops on the five worldviews and read my book on the Five Worldviews, mainly at Osher Lifelong Learning Institute and Oasis Institute. Special thanks to Maralie Waterman, program supervisor at Osher Lifelong Learning Institute (OLLI) and Katherine Raskob, executive director at Oa- sis Institute, for allowing me to present these workshops Also, thanks to all those who bought my book on Five Worldviews, and for the many educators who have used it in their classrooms.

The interest and support of many people inspired me to write *Divided: Five Colliding Worldviews and How to Navigate Them*. Again, I would like to thank Nancy Harmon for her first round of editing the book and her always thoughtful comments.

Jeanine McGann, as usual, has done a superb job of formatting the book for publication and copy edit/proofreading. Jeanine is one of those rare people who is accomplished in many facets of book production from suggesting the right word, getting the exact layout, and even designing websites and technical issues, she does it all. Also, thanks to Mia Beurskens for her design of the book cover.

Thanks to those who have offered comments, edits, and suggestions. In particular, I would like to thank Moonsun Choi, who commented on several chapters and also helped develop educational resources for the book *Five Worldviews*. Many of the resources are also appropriate for *Divided*. Several workshop participants also offered to make suggestions about the book. The efforts of Ira Bolnick and Laurel Anderson are greatly appreciated.

Finally, a thank you to my partner of 20 years, Jim Knutson. His support and kind thoughts have made it possible for me to continue with the project despite times I wanted to throw in the towel and call it quits. I am very grate- ful for his love and support.

Kind regards,
Denise Ames

TABLE OF CONTENTS

PART II. FIVE COLLIDING WORLDVIEWS

For educator resources see www.global-awareness.org/books/divided.html

Reflections on the Coronavirus, March 23, 2020

As I ready this book for publication, I find it necessary to make a few comments about the deadly virus spreading across the United States and the world. The coronavirus is upending our lives, overturning our daily routines, but it also affects the way we look at the world. Seeing the world through corona eyes is such a rapid and far-reaching change that it is overwhelming to us. We are all struggling with our new way of life.

Releasing a new nonfiction book for publication at the start of such an earth-shattering event is probably not the best timing. I thought about shelving the whole project, but then I had second thoughts. I find that the book and its theme of seeing our way of life through five worldviews is very relevant to what is going on today!

We have been polarized as a nation for many years, especially since the 2016 election. Even how the coronavirus is being managed reflects a particular worldview: traditionalists emphasize the business or religious side, progressives stress the average person, globalists promote the global economy, and transformers say look at it holistically.

To solve this health crisis, and save as many lives as possible, all the worldviews need to be recognized. They are all vital in guiding us through this most devastating crisis since World War II. I talk about a tipping point that can shift us to a different worldview. The coronavirus may prove to be that tipping point. My hope is that the tip will be to the transformative worldview.

Perhaps, on a pessimistic note, the transformative worldview will not take hold, instead, a darker and more brutal worldview will emerge that brings out the more competitive and vicious side of humanity. The future is unknown.

Whatever our worldview, one thing is clear—we are all in this together. Everyone is vulnerable, a kind of equalizing mechanism. My hope is that the coronavirus will bring out the best in humankind, in which we are kind, thoughtful, and reasonable. Also, I hope we are grateful that we live in a time when our government (city, state, and federal), whether we agree with their worldview or not, has the recourses available to put an end to this deadly scourge. I wish all of you well.

Kind regards,
Denise Ames

Follow my blog at https://thecenterforglobalawareness.wordpress.com/ where I blog about the cultural divide and the new world through corona eyes.

Facebook https://www.facebook.com/centerforglobalawareness/

Twitter https://twitter.com/CGAorg

LinkedIn https://www.linkedin.com/company/center-for-global-awareness/

Preface

My Political Story: Moving to the Center

THE 2016 PRESIDENTIAL ELECTION

I knew the upcoming presidential election in 2016 would be a rough one. I knew this not because of watching CNN or Fox News or reading the *New York Times*, but because in a phone conversation in August 2016 with my cousin Joyce, she told me that her sister Sally was voting for Donald Trump for president. I was stunned! Sally had consistently voted Democratic for many years; she was an Obama and Bill Clinton fan.

I was still reeling from the Sally shocker when Joyce told me that her other sister, Cindy, also a reliable Democrat, was voting for Trump as well. Joyce and Sally live in my hometown of Rockford, Illinois, once an industrial powerhouse, but now part of the crumbling rust belt. What was going on here? Why the sudden switch from Democrat to Trump? This seemed to be a bigger story than a few of my cousins going rogue.

Ever since I cast my first ballot in the 1972 presidential election I have been a consistent Democratic voter. Although I tend to support moderate Democratic candidates, I always liked the fact that they seemed to be more in favor of the ordinary person than the business elites. Also, I have been an educator in various capacities since my first teaching job in 1972, and Democrats usually support public education and teachers more than Republicans. In the 2016 presidential election, I was firmly in the Hillary Clinton camp.

I watched the presidential debates with keen interest. Surely, voters would be offended by Trump's prowling around behind Clinton during one of the debates. But his favorability ratings held firm. Certainly voters, especially women, would be aghast at his use of abusive language directed towards women and allegations of sexual misconduct revealed in the *Hollywood Access* tapes. However, the outrage seemed to blow over and he escaped largely unscathed among his supporters.

Just presenting a laundry-list of inappropriate behaviors that Trump committed only seemed to spark a collective yawn among his supporters. There was a deeper connection that Trump was able to make with his base that transcended inappropriate behavior and unethical business practices. What was it? I still couldn't figure it out.

I wasn't too worried about the nomination of Trump to the Republican ticket, since I thought it was a political aberration and would soon go away once common sense was restored to the American public. After all, Clinton was ahead in the polls, and the pollsters seemed confident to have the pulse of the American public statistically calculated down to the last electoral vote.

ELECTION DAY, NOVEMBER 8, 2016

Election Day, November 8, 2016, dawned bright and sunny. The promise of electing the first female U.S. President promoted an optimistic feeling that floated through the air. I even got wind of it in the middle of the Adriatic Sea where I just finished a two-week lecture series on a cruise ship line. I arranged my evening to watch all the election returns in my room, as the ship I was on steamed its way to its final docking port in Venice, Italy.

As I settled into my viewing, I was disturbed to find that some early election returns were not going the Democrats' way, as I confidently assumed would happen. As my French fries grew cold on my tray, North Carolina and then Florida fell early on to Donald Trump. I was a proud Illinois native for 50 years, and I felt confident that the "Big Blue Wall," the Midwestern states that had been strongholds for Democrats for the past several decades, would come through. But the Midwest did not hold for Clinton. As several Midwestern stalwarts fell into the red column—Pennsylvania, Michigan, Ohio, and even Wisconsin—the electoral map looked like it was hemorrhaging red. Although my new home state of New Mexico fell faithfully into the Democratic column, its five electoral votes didn't make a dent in Trump's electoral juggernaut.

I could not believe what was happening. The MSNBC commentators were equally stunned, with a pained look of disbelief etched onto their tired faces. The Fox News channel journalists (I could only get two news channels on the ship) were equally stunned, but understandably jubilant at the prospect of President Trump. Their candidate had beat all odds and emerged victorious.

The surreal concession speech by Hillary Clinton was painful to watch, as her sobbing supporters huddled together for comfort. Clinton's purple pantsuit evoked a sad reminder that uniting the nation would not happen under her watch. Trump's acceptance speech was equally surreal; the dazed family perhaps wondered what they had gotten themselves into. My beliefs and hopes were collapsing around me. I was eager for a woman around my age to be President of the United States. This was not going to happen in 2016.

Hillary Clinton was smart, competent, experienced, and thoughtful. Although not a charismatic leader, and saddled with baggage from her and her husband's past actions, I thought her considerable strengths outweighed her considerable weaknesses. Her lack of an overall, unifying vision for the country was troublesome, but I thought she would be a good transition president to a future that was uncertain and in the process of being defined. Now we had a president with no political or military experience, and he appeared to be more determined to wreak havoc rather than build and preserve enduring institutions.

ELECTION DAY 2016: THE AFTERMATH

With no sleep, I stumbled through breakfast. Everything seemed to be normal. Even the breakfast server seemed unfazed and a bit baffled by my passionate declaration of dire consequences awaiting the world because of the election. All of the pessimistic warnings came to naught, but I was in an emotional and irrational frenzy. I gathered my luggage and took the bus to the airport. I chatted with several people, some of whom were as stunned as I was while others said they thought Trump would be a good president with sorely needed new ideas. I thought they must be delusional and not know that dangers lurked below the surface.

My son, a political junkie, called me at the Venice airport to hear my thoughts on the election and rant a bit—well, rant a lot—about the events. He attended an election viewing party with his neighbors near Arizona State University in Tempe, and they all staggered home in disbelief. He hoped I didn't have any trouble getting home from Europe to the U.S., as if perhaps Europeans would seek revenge on an average American citizen who could have possibly voted for Trump. Actually, I made it home safely and without incident.

As I made my way back to the United States, my depression intensified as the political reality sunk in. What could have happened? I read everything I could about the election to see why the key Rust Belt states went for Trump, although by a narrow margin. What was his appeal? I started to realize that I had missed, along with many other people, an important trend in American culture: an intense dissatisfaction with the prevailing powers by a large swath of the American public. I was fascinated with this shift and I made a pledge to understand more about it.

My investigation into the question of the cultural divide would, however, have to wait several months; more immediate events were at hand. My daughter in Brooklyn, New York gave birth to premature twins, a boy and girl. Thanks to their excellent health care, they had a good chance of survival and leading normal lives. But for the next two months their home was to be the neo-natal unit of the hospital. I gladly agreed to help out with my four-year-old granddaughter as much as needed and then help care for the twins when they arrived home from the hospital in early January. I happily switched my attention from politics to grandmotherly duties.

THE ETHOS OF PROGRESS

Even in the throes of helping my daughter and son-in-law care for their burgeoning family, I continued to think about the fierce divisions in this country that have intensified over the decades. In between diaper changes, I contemplated the divisions that had always simmered between different constituencies in the U.S.

But despite differences, the key uniting story that has always knitted this country together is the ethos of progress. We could all get ahead economically if we worked hard and played by the rules.

This ethos of progress has been the story in the United States since its founding. Americans followed this guiding purpose in conquering the frontier and building a concrete jungle that is our current way of life. We did so without thought of the social consequences, the rights of native peoples, or our own well-being, let alone environmental repercussions. This ethos embraces continuous material change, exploration, and scientific investigation. In fact, Americans have found that this ethos is so wonderful that we have exported it around the world to some who have eagerly embraced it, while others have been more skeptical and resistant.

This ethos of progress is enticing but dangerous, since the chances of its continuing unabated are slim. Also, the meaning of progress has been changing, especially among rural/urban, college/non-college educated, white/people of color, and religious/non-religious citizenry. Our political leaders (right and left) continued to preach the same ethos, but it was not resonating with a large chunk of voters.

Trump was able to speak to the disaffected voters, the white, rural, working class, religious, and non-college educated voters in ways the college-educated citizenry were unable to understand. Instead, they wrote him off as ignorant, racist, misogynist, homophobic, and other judgmental attacks that fed into more divisiveness. The spiral of anger, distrust, and misunderstanding entered a more intense and divisive level.

EXPERIENCING THE CULTURAL DIVIDE: MY STORY

To get a better understanding of a Trump supporter and the cultural divide in this country, I would like to share with you a brief description of the cultural outlook of white, non-college educated people in the Midwest through the prism of my experiences growing up in a white, working class, extended family in Rockford, Illinois.

After World War II, most members of my extended paternal family, including my father, moved from the rural swamplands of central Wisconsin to the growing, industrial city of Rockford in northern Illinois, just 90 miles west of Chicago. They settled into decent-paying factory jobs, or in the case of my father, he formed a small business building houses.

I grew up in a working class world, my father and extended family firmly held working class cultural values, expectations, and traditions. Although my mother was raised in a middle class family and her values gradually influenced me the most, the sway of the large extended family imprinted its values upon the formation of my character. Even though I went on to earn a doctorate in world history education, my Midwestern, working class roots are still with me at a deep level.

Our family's cultural values were a mix of tribal affiliations, reliance on one's own gut insticts, and a fierce pride. "Book learnin" as my father scoffed, wasn't all that useful; rely on "your gut" to make decisions. I heard repeatedly that you learned the most from the "school of hard knocks," rather than learning from books. Trump repeatedly said he followed his gut; he didn't rely on experts or data to inform his decisions. Conversely, the Clinton campaign employed a squad of experts and data crunchers to analyze trends. Trump's gut instincts won him the admiration of the working class who processed information the same way.

My family communicated with each other through story, hyperbole, and humor. We still tell long stories with vivid descriptions of long ago events or relatives living and departed, punctuated frequently by humor and laughter. Trump's exaggerations and vivid symbolism, such as building the wall, would resonate with my family. Our stories were always laced with exaggerations, even outright lies, but we didn't take these literally. A journalist for the *Atlantic* magazine, Salena Zito, stated: "The people who were against Mr. Trump took him literally but not seriously. His supporters took him seriously but not literally."[1] I remember once I corrected my father, who was the master of clever tales, that a particular part of his story was untrue. He jeered, "You just read too many books."

I was appalled at Trump's scandals. But in my family, scandal was part of the colorful stories we told. Since so many of us made mistakes and exhibited scandalous behavior at one time or another, it was largely considered part of life. We didn't judge these behaviors as reason for rejection of the accused from the extended family, since few (if any) of us escaped episodes of inappropriate behavior. Even though Trump's scandals were condemned by many of the voters, they still voted for him.

I was also dismayed at Trump's treatment of women. Although our family followed the typical social practices of the day in which men were "in charge" of their families, it was plain to see that my grandmother was the real matriarch. I was lucky to learn from many "strong" women in the family, including my mother and grandmothers. Even though many male members of my family talked about "ruling the roost," women, in their quiet and non-confrontational way, acknowledged these proud but empty declarations of male supremacy, all the while knowing who really was "ruling the roost" behind the scenes. Because of their experiences, Trump's treatment of women would not have been as abhorrent to my family as to those who held progressive views.

Our extended family was tribal. We stuck together, helped each other, and distrusted outsiders. As a youngster, my friends were my cousins, and I didn't venture outside that cocoon until high school. Even today when I travel to my family reunions in Tomah, Wisconsin, where the family cemetery is located, I feel instantly at home with all my relatives despite our political and cultural differences. Trump was able to create a virtual family with his bright red baseball caps and assorted political paraphernalia proclaiming tribal allegiance and membership in the Trump family.

Many pundits were perplexed about how Trump, a New York billionaire, could resonate with white working class people. My family admired those who made lots of money but were "still one of them." One of my cousins, a multi-millionaire, comes to funerals and family reunions and is greeted with comments such as "see, he is still family." Trump wore expensive suits, but still fit in. His language and demeanor, according to his supporters, didn't have an air of elitism and resonated with his "common man" appeal. Trump welcomed his supporters into his community of wealth, glamour, prestige, accomplishment, and belonging. They were part of "Trumpland."

UNDERSTANDING PEOPLE DIFFERENT FROM US

Something surprising happened to me as I dove into learning more about the cultural divide after the 2016 election: I moved to the center. Although I have always had centrist tendencies, I find that now I am much more comfortable residing at the center point. The center is not where most people are located; polarization and virtuous ideals on both sides are the norm. But I have found that it is beneficial to have someone pointing out what the other side may think and feel about controversial issues. I find that at the center spot on the political spectrum I can more accurately see all sides of different issues. I can see why some people so fervently support the right to life or why some people may venture to the Mexican-American border to care for recently arrived asylum seekers. Although I still hold to my principles, I understand why others may hold so dearly to the ones they do. In the cultural divide workshops that I lead, I am constantly taking the side of conservatives (traditionalists), since most of the participants are on the left. The center is not always a popular position; I have been accused more than once of going over to the "dark side."

I find the few cultural characteristics that I described in this preface separating Americans to be fascinating. For years, college-educated people, myself included, have wanted mainstream white America to understand those from "other" cultures and minorities. Usually this understanding meant people from outside the U.S. and minority populations, but rarely was there an effort to understand the many different people who eventually voted for Trump. Perhaps it is now time to reverse roles and have college-educated "elites" be the students and learn about white, non-college-educated America, Trump America. Even if Trump fails in his reelection bid, the millions of Trump voters are still part of America. They are not going to disappear even if Trump disappears.

Trump-American culture is different, varied, and worth learning more about. In order to connect with people outside our inner circle, we need to be "culturally flexible" and be able to reach out and understand "the other." If we are to get past throwing disparaging judgments at groups of people and more deeply understand who they are, then we have a better chance of advancing an agenda of greater economic justice, peace, sustainability, and inclusiveness. This book, *Divided*, is dedicated to this goal. For the future of our country, it is worth trying.

Chapter 1
Why Are We So Divided?

Out beyond ideas of Rightdoing and Wrongdoing there is a field—I will meet you there. ... Rumi

WHY CAN'T WE GET ALONG?

Do you feel that the country is irretrievably divided along political and cultural lines? Do you feel that there are so many different ways of interpreting the same events or information that it can be overwhelming? Sometimes when another person voices an opinion on a controversial topic, such as gun control, do you think "This person is from another planet! Why do they think the way they do?" Do you have difficulty expressing yourself at a family gathering because you are afraid you will get so angry that you will offend someone?

Why does an experience or situation, such as building a wall between Mexico and the United States, elicit so many different responses? Police often find that different eye witnesses can have such wildly different interpretations of the same crime that their testimonies are virtually worthless in determining the outcome of a case. Proposals to demolish a decrepit building in the middle of a town can create a firestorm of reactions, or the building of a Wal-Mart on the outskirts of town can raise the blood pressure of the entire community. Even harmless leash laws about restricting dogs from romping through the park can let loose a torrent of emotion.

I am perplexed when evangelical Christians lament the passing of family values and the disruption of small town life, yet embrace free-market capitalism, which has contributed significantly to these changes. I am bewildered when evidence showing that children raised in two-parent households have a better chance of success than those who are raised in single-parent households is largely dismissed by those on the left. I am confused when people from the Louisiana bayous, who have witnessed deadly pollution from nearby industries, reject EPA efforts to clean-up the toxic stew. I am baffled when mothers refuse to vaccinate their children when studies have shown them to be more beneficial than harmful. And I am puzzled when many people still claim that former President Obama is a Muslim born in Kenya, when the facts have been proven otherwise. I am also concerned about scientists rapidly developing Artificial Intelligence (AI) when many people want to think about the consequences more carefully first.

The 2016 presidential election was a turning point for me. Like many other liberal voters, I woke up to the fact that I was living in a "bubble." I was stunned when there was a backlash among half of the voters against Hillary Clinton's liberal worldview. This dramatic and far-reaching electoral backlash exemplified the opposing ways in which half of the electorate saw issues through one lens while the other half saw them very differently. Obviously, there is more to understanding these differences than is seen at a superficial level. Our national narrative gives us clues about why we are not getting along.

NATIONAL NARRATIVES

Everyone loves a good story, and our nation is no exception. For many years Americans have had a cohesive narrative about "we the people" and where the nation is heading—a narrative called the American Dream. National narratives are usually simplified and selective stories of the past that are woven together to explain an idealized vision of the nation. They are not necessarily factually true. Even though these narratives are in part fabrications, they still influence citizens' confidence, behavior, and aspirations.[1] Our national story is one of those intangible things that helps to unite a disparate country like the U.S.

THE AMERICAN DREAM: A NATIONAL NARRATIVE

The American Dream is a national ethos that characterizes the United States. Its set of guiding ideals includes democracy, human rights, liberty, opportunity, and equality. Each American is instilled with the ideals of freedom to pursue opportunity and success through hard work, while breaking through the few barriers hindering that success. Upward social mobility and prosperity are the rewards for that hard work. James Truslow Adams stated in 1931 that in the American Dream "life should be better and richer and fuller for everyone, with opportunity for each according to ability or achievement regardless of social class or circumstances of birth."[2] The American Dream is rooted in the Declaration of Independence, which proclaims that "all men are created equal" with the right to "life, liberty and the pursuit of happiness."

The American Dream motivated many Americans to work hard and pursue material riches and to achieve a standard of living that met and often exceeded basic needs. Although it didn't work for everyone, it worked well for my aunt who grew up in poverty in the hills of Tennessee during the Great Depression without a father, running water, electricity, or enough food. She married my uncle who worked for 40 years in a factory in Rockford, Illinois, and they raised four children in a small house. She was proud of her home and she kept it immaculate. Although there continues to be poverty, very few Americans live as my aunt did many decades ago.

The American Dream is an implicit contract with all Americans in which each generation makes steady progress and becomes more prosperous than the previous one. The fruits of American society—a comfortable, middle class way of life—await those who "work hard and play by the rules," according to the words of former President Bill Clinton. But the promise of the American Dream has proven to be more difficult to attain for the current generation and has been disrupted as a unifying national narrative.

Actually, the American Dream has always been unsustainable and untenable. It has been achievable for some, but not all. Periodically, the disparity between the different economic groups to achieve the American Dream reaches a point where confidence in its realization is called into doubt, if not shattered. We have reached that point in recent years; confidence among those subscribing to it has crumbled and it can no longer pay out the riches it has implicitly pledged. Those who have fallen to the back of the line of achieving the American Dream are now suspicious of those who are succeeding or those they perceive as succeeding. The result is a feeling of suspicion, distrust, and despair among many.

Can the American Dream be resurrected? Can it once again be melded into our national narrative, as a goal that unites us in the common pursuit of a way of living that is distinctly American? In my estimation, the American Dream, as fantasized in popular imagination, is no longer a possibility. And I believe that its usefulness as a national narrative is now past. The question is: What should replace it. The current narrative is embedded in progress, which implies economic growth and expansion. There is always something more to be obtained—a bigger TV or the latest technological gadget. But this narrative is unsustainable economically and psychologically. The bonds of community have frayed in many places, contributing to a cultural divide and a consumer lifestyle that has contributed to environmental degradation.

In the absence of a strong and realizable national narrative, the stories of different "tribal" groups in the United States have gained traction and attention. Different groups of people—white working class, people of color, the poor (lower 30 percent of incomes), recent immigrants, LGBTQ groups, the middle class, the upper 20 percent, the upper one percent, liberals (left) and conservatives (right)—have all asserted their own values and narratives. These narratives are often in conflict with each other and are fraying America even further.

Weaving together a new national narrative is essential to renewing our shaken democracy. But what shall the new national narrative be? One has not yet coalesced. Unlike Donald Trump in the 2016 presidential campaign, whose "Make America Great Again" narrative was subscribed to by a minority of voters, Democratic candidate Hillary Clinton was unable to come up with an engaging national narrative, hindering her presidential bid. Therefore, we are left with fragmented narratives from different groups that reflect our tribal mentality. As you progress through this book, think about what new national narrative we could create to bind together all Americans.

Keeping our focus primarily on the cultural divide between liberals and conservatives, the following are their respective alternative narratives to the American Dream. The Liberal Narrative, which the sociologist Christian Smith calls the "liberal progress narrative," organizes much of the moral matrix of the American academic left. The liberal narrative differs from the conservative narrative, which clinical psychologist Drew Westen in his book *The Political Brain* extracts from the major speeches of President Ronald Reagan in the 1980s.[3]

LIBERALISM: AN ALTERNATIVE NARRATIVE

At one time, the vast majority of humans lived in societies that were unjust, corrupt, repressive, and oppressive. These traditional societies were unacceptable to liberals because of their entrenched inequality, exploitation, and superstitious traditions. Humans have always yearned to be free, equal, autonomous, and prosperous, and they have struggled against the forces of despair and tyranny. Eventually, and with great sacrifice, humans succeeded in founding modern, liberal, democratic, capitalist, and social-welfare societies. While modern societies hold the possibility to make best use of the mechanisms to assure individual freedom and pleasure, there is still much work remaining to undo the entrenchment of the powerful ones who perpetuate inequality, exploitation, and repression for their own benefit. Dedicating one's life to achieving this mission of a good society in which individuals are equal and free to follow their self-defined, individual happiness is a noble and worthwhile struggle. This heroic narrative, with slight variations according to regions, is a recognizable story to those on the left around the world. It's a courageous and epic liberation narrative that calls for the victims of oppression to break the chains of tradition, authority, power, and hierarchy in order to free their noble aspirations.[4]

CONSERVATISM: AN ALTERNATIVE NARRATIVE

America was once a shining beacon on a hill. It was a land of freedom, industry, personal responsibility, and achievement. Then liberals decided to intervene and built a colossal federal bureaucracy that shackled the invisible hand of the free market. They undermined our traditional American values and besmirched God and faith in the process. Instead of valuing the act of working for a living, they took money from hardworking Americans and gave it to the undeserving poor who used it recklessly. Instead of following traditional American values of family, loyalty, and personal responsibility, they encouraged a feminist agenda that weakened the traditional family. Instead of saluting America's strength and goodness around the world, they cut military budgets, belittled soldiers, disrespected the flag, and chose negotiation and multilateralism. Conservatives have had enough and are taking back our country from those who seek to demean and emasculate it.[5]

CONFLICTING ALTERNATIVE NARRATIVES

These alternative narratives illustrate deep division between liberals and conservatives. Each tells a conflicting narrative, one that demonizes the other side instead of uniting all groups under one American umbrella. According to moral psychologist Jonathan Haidt, liberals have a harder time understanding the conservative narrative than conservatives have understanding the liberal narrative. Liberals see loyalty to a group as a basis of racism and exclusion. To them, authority is oppression and religion is used to suppress female sexuality and justify homophobia. Haidt sees the song "Imagine," written by John Lennon of the Beatles as capturing the liberal dream. "Imagine there's no countries/It isn't hard to do/Nothing to kill or die for/And no religion, too…I hope someday you'll join us/And the world will be as one." Liberals see this vision as heaven, but conservatives believe these ideas would be hell.[6]

The unifying national narrative, the promise of American progress and prosperity for all those who work hard and play by the rules is considered obsolete and unattainable by many Americans. Yet, a new unifying national narrative has not emerged to enfold Americans into a coalescing awareness. Instead, a diversity of narratives has emerged that make sense to a particular group, but not to Americans as a whole. These various narratives have conflicting messages and contribute to the divisiveness at play in the world today.

UNDERSTANDING THE CULTURAL DIVIDE

We know there is a cultural divide in the United States. It is apparent every time a mass shooting occurs, immigration reform is discussed, appropriations for Planned Parenthood come up, or any other issue, important or insignificant, comes up for national debate. But what is a cultural divide?

I define a cultural divide as a boundary in society that splits groups of people whose economic class, social conventions, religious affiliation, geographic location, lifestyle, psychological outlook, and/or educational attainment are very different. This divide hinders communications, interactions, and civil exchanges between different groups of people. For example, both Planned Parenthood and the National Rifle Association (NRA) play an outsized role in our nation's politics. Planned Parenthood spent $45 million on the 2016 election, all to support Democrats, and $175 million in 2017 on programs like "movement building" and "engaging communities."[7] The NRA poured more than $54 million into electing Republican candidates up and down the ballot in 2016, according to the Center for Responsive Politics, with a focus on supporting Donald Trump and a slate of Republicans running for the U.S. House of Representatives and Senate.[8] Thus, issues such as abortion rights and gun rights contribute to the cultural divide.

Understanding the multifaceted reasons for our deep cultural divide in the United States is a vital step in reconciling that divide. What is driving us apart instead of together as a nation? This divide threatens our democracy and the strength of our country. It leads to hostility, incivility, and intractable stalemate in our government.

Why do we need to be aware of others' perspectives? It is more comfortable to reside in our own bubble with people around us who think the same, so our ideas and actions go unchallenged. But large, multi-ethnic, multi-cultural, and diverse countries like the United States, and increasingly many other countries around the world, are not homogenous entities, and this requires their citizens to engage with others to uphold democratic processes and peaceful co-existence. Citizens cannot remain in their own insulated bubble and still have a vibrant democracy. We all need to make an effort to gain understanding and skills to navigate a more diverse world, which includes people from different lands as well as those who are our fellow citizens but live in different states or zip codes.

A problem I see today is that many of us live in a bubble, surrounded by people who have similar views on issues and comparable lifestyles, and who read the same books and listen to media that support our views. When we have a conversation about a controversial topic, we rarely hear conflicting views, which reinforces the notion that we are obviously right. Many of us rarely step outside our bubble to see other people's views. Even on some college campuses, the obvious place for voicing conflicting ideas, the speech of opposing voices is sometimes stifled because it is considered hostile and offensive to some, or it can trigger unpleasant emotions. This pattern of restricting speech is detrimental to a democracy and hampers the interaction of different people in sustaining institutions that support a vibrant nation and economy.

We recognize that there is an intractable cultural divide increasingly intensifying in the United States and throughout the Western world. The big question is: What can we do about it? Although there are many well-meaning groups that have sprouted up to encourage people to have conversations with people unlike themselves, I believe we need to go deeper than conversations alone. I have found, and it is the purpose of this book, that before meaningful conversations can take place, we need an understanding of ourselves as well as those who are different from us. What are the values that guide us— our experiences, our traditions, upbringing, geographic location, and basic personality? What makes each group feel the way they do about various issues, events, and the future direction of this country? We can't assume that in a conversation with someone different from us we will be able to persuade them to think as we do just because we feel confident that we have the moral high ground. We are bound to be disappointed if this is our approach.

Effective understanding, communication, and empathy are essential if both sides of the divide wish to broaden their base beyond those who share similar cultural values, or even to function effectively in working with others to get something done in a political, educational, business, or other setting. For many years, I have worked to promote cross-cultural understanding among different cultural, ethnic, and national groups around the world. However, I now feel that these cross-cultural skills and knowledge are desperately needed at home.

Since it is my contention that the foremost step in navigating the cultural divide is to deeply understand those with whom we disagree, this book tries to make sense of the multiple perspectives, values, and attitudes that different groups of people express. Although the different perspectives presented here cannot possibly give a complete picture of our disparate realities, my purpose is to give an overview of different lenses through which reality is perceived and acted upon. These lenses help us in understanding people different from us, as well as ourselves, and hopefully this greater understanding will help ease the tensions arising from our cultural divide.

One of the lenses through which we see reality is one I call worldviews. The five worldviews—indigenous, traditionalist, progressive, globalized, and transformative—that I define and present in this book are not the only way that we can see differences, but they are lenses that help shape our perception of reality. I do not aim to neatly categorize all people into one of the worldviews; you may find that you or others you know identify with two or more. But the five worldviews together give a range of beliefs that are firmly held by a wide variety of people in the U.S. and the world.

The second lens draws on the work of moral psychologist Jonathan Haidt and his work in developing six moral foundations: care/harm, fairness/cheating, liberty/oppression, loyalty/betrayal, authority/subversion, and sanctity/degradation. I integrate the six moral foundations and five worldviews to facilitate greater understanding of, and empathy towards, our differences.

These two approaches to the understanding of others can help us become more aware of the diversity of thoughts and opinions that seem to be more prevalent today than in the past and to look into each other's perspectives without necessarily trying to change them. Since individuals are very resistant to changing their perspectives and resent those who try to make them do so, the point of learning about other perspectives is not to gain the tools to change others' perspectives but to become aware of the existence of different perspectives and understand those holding them. If we are aware of different perspectives, we may stop expecting the other to change their perspective and realize instead that "the other" makes sense of the world from their own perspective. In other words, we may find that the other side's outrageous or nonsensical ideas actually become reasonable and sensible when seen from their point of view.

I am not on a mission to change your political party or your opinions about issues. I am merely presenting information for readers to understand people who hold different ideas and positions on issues. I hope to do so in a non-judgmental way, in which all perspectives are respected and appreciated. Some of the information may be uncomfortable because it may challenge your long-held beliefs. I know it was uncomfortable for me. Some of you may want to forget this whole project and continue to hold to your treasured beliefs and find fault with the other side. That is certainly your prerogative. However, if you are intent on deeply uncovering what is causing this cultural divide and navigating ways to remedy it, I encourage you to engage with this material with an open mind.

Becoming more aware of different worldviews, and learning about those who hold a different worldview or have different moral foundations without trying to change them, is a difficult task. The attempt at dialogue or discussion often descends into a shouting match, hateful language, vile stereotypes, bullying, and other forms of conflict. Yet, it is possible to uncover shared values, or shared aspects of values, without fundamentally changing one's perspective. Developing approaches to uncover shared values is an important area for development in conflict analysis and resolution. It is also one of the hoped-for end results of reading and discussing this book.

In presenting information about different perspectives, my goal is not only to convey information but also to encourage readers to appreciate the different ways in which individuals see the world. This approach helps readers evolve their own capacity for understanding others and encourages engagement in creating positive change.

STEERING CLEAR OF THE JUDGING GAME

The third-century Persian prophet Mani preached an elaborate dualistic cosmology depicting an epic battle between the forces of absolute goodness and the forces of absolute evil. His preaching developed into Manichaeism, a religion that spread throughout the Middle East and influenced Western thinking. Our politicians and colliding liberal and conservative factions in the United States have, unfortunately, fulfilled the prophecy of Mani, turning our country into a political battleground of rancor and polarization. Many on each side have seized the banner of absolute goodness and are confident of their virtue, while determining that compromise with the enemy is a sin. Goodness must prevail, although which side is good and which one is evil is impossible to determine.[9]

When studying worldviews, it is helpful to realize that no one experiences reality directly. We all experience reality through our perceptual filters or our own lenses. We assign meaning to our experiences as they happen, and the meanings we give to our experiences are influenced by our attitudes and past experiences. It pays to remember that when we judge a situation—or when we assume something about someone else—we are doing this according to our perceptions of the event, not the actual event itself. Our perspectives may be hidden to us, but they are always active.

When worldviews are not in our awareness or acknowledged, stronger parties in a conflict may advertently or inadvertently try to impose their world-views on us. For example, judgments are one way in which one party tries to impose its perspective on another. Judgmental people who criticize and spread negative energy do this from the overflow of negativity that they have within them. When a person labels others as racist, bigoted, hateful, igno-rant, homophobic, misogynists, baby-killers, murderers, white trash, or oth-er hateful terms, the accuser is asserting that she has the moral high-ground and her values prevail. Those accused feel judged, demeaned, humiliated, and stripped of their dignity.

When attacking those who are perceived to be in the wrong, the attacker must be aware that this assault is likely to make the situation worse. Using judgmental language to attack people we disagree with will not change their behavior. Thus, the attacker's real purpose in using judgmental language is to shame the target population while rationalizing that the attacker is morally superior. Thus, wisdom tells us to steer clear of judging others.

TEN REASONS FOR THE CULTURAL DIVIDE

You might wonder why the cultural divide seems so intense at this particular moment in history. I see that a number of threads are coming together to create an explosive and divisive atmosphere. Which one is more important is hard to determine and there are others that are important as well, but the fusion of these ten threads has sparked a toxic brew of divisiveness. Here are my top ten reasons (not necessarily arranged in order of importance):

1. Neoliberal Economic Policy
Economic policies that were put in place during the Great Depression and World War II promoted fairness and opportunity for many ordinary Ameri-cans. But these policies have been steadily dismantled since the early 1980s and current government policy promotes a neoliberal economic model that favors large corporations and the wealthy, while ordinary workers experience stagnant wages and fewer benefits. Preference has been granted to behemoth corporations, while anti-trust actions have been sidelined and small business formation has been given less attention. Great economic and social inequal-ity has resulted.

2. Economic Globalization

The government has pushed economic globalization, in which American workers compete with workers around the world, and companies have outsourced jobs to lower-wage countries. Although about 20 percent of Americans have profited from this move and the one percent at the top of the wealth scale has done exceedingly well, the remaining 80 percent of Americans have lagged behind. While the global economy has lifted many people around the world out of poverty, it has also resulted in approximately 80 percent of the citizens of Western nations experiencing a decline or stagnation in their wages, increased working hours, fewer benefits, and fewer comparable opportunities than in the past. This has caused anger and discontent among this group directed at the upper 20 percent and upper one percent.

3. Economic Inequality

Economic globalization has reduced global inequality between nations, but it has also increased inequality within nations. There are many detrimental results of higher income inequality within nations, including reduced social, cultural, and civic participation among the less wealthy. Researchers have found a link between increased economic inequality and higher rates of health and social problems, such as obesity, mental illness, homicides, drug use, and incarcerations. Research has also shown that in more equal societies, people are more likely to trust each other and measures of social capital, such as goodwill, fellowship, and mutual sympathy, increase.

4. Sweeping Technological Changes

Sweeping technological changes have disrupted traditional workplaces and companies, again resulting in skewed income distribution to the top earners. Many workers have not kept up with the changing skills and mindset needed in a highly sophisticated technological world and have fallen by the wayside. Rapid technological changes have also created an atmosphere of anxiety, tension, and unease, while stabilizing traditions of the past—family, religion, workplace, community, and neighborhood—have been displaced by the disquieting marketplace and a divisive media.

5. Changing Social Values

Distressing social changes have left many people alienated, depressed, and prone to addictive and destructive behaviors. The social fabric of American life that gave people stability and order for decades—churches, extended and nuclear families, neighbors, civic organizations, and workplace connections—has frayed, with disastrous results. The epidemics of opioid addiction, depression, and homelessness are a visible reminder of a tattered social fabric.

Increasingly, traditional values of family, religion, and personal responsibility have been disparaged by those on the extreme left. For example, at some universities, angry students have prevented speakers with different political beliefs from giving speeches. Protesters have shouted down those with whom they disagree. The American principles of free speech and rational discourse—the cornerstones of universities—are being challenged. These principles have been under assault by some people at universities for several decades, as some proponents believe they reinforce white privilege and existing power structures.

6. Partisan Media Outlets

Highly partisan media outlets, on the left and right, have given voice to angry citizens, whose rantings have created a spiral of anger, disenchantment, and demand for change. Conspiracy theories go uncontested on national media platforms and are believed to be true by gullible followers. In many venues the principles of reasonable inquiry, civil discourse, and the hearing of all sides of issues have been eroded and replaced with "alternative facts," vulgar language, and outright lies.

7. Consumer Culture

The consumer culture implicitly promises to bring happiness and fulfillment to those who willingly participate in the ritual of consumption. Yet after decades of copious amounts of consumption, the promise of happiness has not been fulfilled. Since the American economy runs primarily on consumerism, this is a paradox that is not easily reconciled.

8. Identity Linked to Political Parties

As traditional ties to family, religion, and community have unraveled, ties to political parties have emerged as a source for connection and a way to express one's identity and ideas. One's identity has been linked to political engagement. Partisan in-group preferences are powerful. For example, the fervor with which some young people on the left support traditionally oppressed groups, such as the LGBTQ community, women, African-Americans, Muslims, and immigrants, leads to the conclusion that they are finding meaning in these activities, meaning that was formerly part of a religious organization, school, extended family, or community.[10]

9. Lifestyle Bubbles
As a result of technological, economic, and social changes, residential patterns have allowed each of us to isolate ourselves within bubbles of like-minded individuals. We surround ourselves by people who think and act like we do. Our counties and towns are becoming increasingly segregated into "lifestyle enclaves," in which ways of voting, eating, working, and worshipping are increasingly aligned. Haidt notes, "If you find yourself in a Whole Foods store, there's an 89 percent chance that the county surrounding you voted for Barack Obama. If you want to find Republicans, go to a county that contains a Cracker Barrel restaurant (62 percent of these counties went for Senator John McCain)."[11]

10. A Search for Meaning
We are at a critical juncture in our history. The modern worldview and its ways of being are unraveling, while the traditions of the past are being systematically chipped away. What are Americans today left with to give their lives meaning? Political identification and identity politics have stepped in as meaning-making substitutes for traditions of the past. But these are proving shallow, while real meaning is proving elusive and ever harder to grasp. This has contributed to growing unease in America, which can trigger cultural eruptions that vent increasing exasperation. It is an unsettling time in our history.

CONCLUDING INSIGHTS: WHY WE ARE SO DIVIDED

Why does it have to be so nasty? Our polarized country seems to be slipping to the point of dysfunction, if it isn't already at that point. Since 2000, Americans have increasingly moved further apart. What will it take to bring us back together? Progressives often boil down the divide into economic issues, while conservatives emphasize social reasons such as the decline of family values. Until we are able to more effectively communicate and understand each other, distrust, hatred, and further divisions will continue and intensify.

Chapter 2
Worldviews: Our Windows to the World

...[I]t seemed a part of her life, to step from the ancient to the modern, back and forth. She felt rather sorry for those who knew only one and not the other. It was better, she thought, to be able to select from the whole menu of human achievements than to be bound within one narrow range. ... Orson Scott Card, Children of the Mind

WORLDVIEWS: AN INTRODUCTION

Worldviews have always fascinated me. Even when I hadn't yet conceptualized the idea I found instances in my life where there was a clear clash between peoples' perceptions of and reactions to events.

My father, a World War II veteran, and I, a rebellious college student, experienced heated clashes over opposing views of the Vietnam War in the late 1960s. While living in Mississippi for two years in the 1970s, a friendly neighbor came by my house to introduce herself and asked me what Baptist church I went to. She assumed I was a Baptist, since that religion was the most predominant in the area and the church influenced her worldview. When I visited the Native American pueblo of Acoma in New Mexico in the 1980s, I was surprised to hear one of the visitors criticize the pueblo's system of collective land-ownership. He grumbled that more money could be made dividing the land into individual plots and selling them off to the highest bidder. During the 1990s when globalization was heralded as the savior of the Western world, I found most people in the business community thought it was an inevitable process and could not be stopped, even though I and others had some misgivings about it. While visiting Iran in the 2000s, I was disturbed to find out that the "culture police" could arrest me or any other woman for not dressing in the traditional way and looking too Western. All of these events and many others gave me glimpses into the different worldviews that people hold.

I first started to think about developing the concept of worldviews during the writing, teaching and researching for my world history college course and the writing of my book, *Waves of Global Change: A Holistic World History*. In my teaching, and writing, I organized world history according to five waves of human development: communal, agricultural, urban, modern, and global. This was different from the traditional chronological format that organized world history according to the progression of time rather than the holistic approach, which emphasized a less-sequential way of human development. But I also found that within each wave there was uneven development, and not everyone in each of the waves marched along to the same beat. I found this especially true of the Global Wave, which I had approximated starting around the year 2000.

I find that during the Global Wave, there are many contentious and conflicting ways of living and seeing the world. Iranian fundamentalists established a theocracy in Iran after a revolution in 1979 (which continues today), while fundamentalists such as Pat Robertson were drawing many followers in the U.S. into the fold, mostly through television programming. The nationalistic fervor characteristic of the Modern Wave (see next chapter), which was supposed to decline with the upswing in globalization, was continuing and intensifying in the U.S. and other countries, even as the world was becoming more interconnected and global in scope.

The traditions of the Communal and Agricultural Waves were being reasserted during this time, as many indigenous people resisted the pressure to modernize or allow resources on their lands be exploited for extraction by multi-national corporations. The push for globalization, both economic and cultural, by the U.S. and other countries was a growing phenomenon that was supported politically, economically, and by the media. It appeared as an "inevitable" process, and we'd better jump on its bullet train of untold progress and riches or get left behind. Yet, there were those who resisted fundamentalism, modernism, and globalization and took actions to create a different way of life. Although globalization supporters were garnering the most attention and putting forth an optimistic vision of the future, many other people were voicing different views. But each individual has different ways of "seeing" events, facts, situations, people, movements, information, evidence, spectacles, and ways of living, which make the world an unpredictable and confusing place.

I decided that the Global Wave was not an all-encompassing, homogenous view of the world, but that many differing views within it needed to be heard and recognized.

As a result of my research, observations, and experiences, I decided to organize the Global Wave into five worldviews—indigenous, traditionalist, progressive, globalized, and transformative. I thought it would be unwieldly to have more worldviews and I wanted people to remember them. Also, the five worldviews coincided nicely with the five waves in my holistic world history. I would use the term worldview since it most closely described the phenomena that I was identifying.

WORLDVIEWS: A DEFINITION

Worldview is a term that has multiple meanings and is often used inconsistently. It comes from the German word *Weltanschauung: welt* means world and *anschauung* means outlook or view. A worldview is a way of understanding or a lens through which one explains events, phenomena, and actions that happen in our everyday lives. It refers to the framework of ideas and beliefs through which an individual interprets the world and interacts with it. A person's worldview includes basic assumptions and images that provide a more or less coherent, though not necessarily accurate, way of thinking about the world. Worldviews are those systems or structures within which our values, beliefs, and conventions lie. They influence how we see ourselves and others and how we form relationships. Worldviews keep our lives coherent by giving us a sense of meaning, purpose, and connection.

A pair of glasses is a useful way to think of how a worldview shapes our reality. We can see through the glasses without actually being aware of them, yet the glasses' prescription is focusing the world for us. So too are worldviews. Every book read, policy statement enacted, vote cast, problem solved, Congressional bill passed, religious sermon preached, as well as the way children are raised and even the approach used to write this book are shaped as much, if not more, by our worldview as by any objective data or analysis.[1]

Worldviews are rarely brought out into the light of day, so people are not usually aware of them. They are hidden deep in our human consciousness, all the while quietly shaping our reactions to new ideas and information, guiding our decisions, and ordering expectations for the future. Worldviews deeply influence the kind of political, economic, cultural, and social patterns we build, and those, in turn, reinforce the events that occur around the world. For example, our worldview guides us in answering questions such as: Is free trade good for the economy? Is universal health care a human right? or Does land always have a monetary value?

An iceberg serves as a way to understand worldviews. At the tip of the iceberg, the 10-20 percent seen above the surface represents events that occur around the world. These events are reported on the television news, headlined in the newspaper, or featured on the internet. But beneath the surface level of the iceberg's events are episodes.[2] For example, we see the event of a category five Hurricane Katrina on the news, but the hurricane is not an isolated event; it is part of larger episodes of hurricanes that are wreaking havoc along coastlines. And if we look further below the surface of the iceberg's events and episodes, we see that a society's political, economic, technological, social, environmental, and cultural patterns have an impact on the events and episodes. Many scientists attribute violent and extreme weather conditions to climate change, which is caused by burning fossil fuels. The modern economic system, the pattern, is based on the burning of fossil fuels for the energy consumption that drives a modern way of life, while the environmental impact of burning fossil fuels is considered an unfortunate but necessary by-product.

Farther down towards the base of the iceberg are worldviews, which, in turn, influence the events, episodes, and patterns. Our worldview extols the idea that unlimited economic growth is the path to prosperity and well-being. However, environmental repercussions of this worldview are revealing the unintended consequences of this belief in unlimited growth. Finally, at the very base of the iceberg we see the great mass of ice supporting the whole iceberg; these are our human behaviors, the universal human commonalities that shape who we are. Therefore, if we want to change events, episodes, and patterns we need to change the worldview that created them in the first place.

These worldviews are not merely the latest psychological profile fad but deeply entrenched mental constructs of how we see the world. They are the lens through which we make sense of reality, arrive at solutions to problems, create a way of living, or structure government and other institutions. In other words, we make both big decisions and little decisions through the lens of our worldview.

DEVELOPING AND PERPETUATING A WORLDVIEW

A person's worldview is socially constructed, largely shaped by her culture and upbringing. Although infants have instincts that shape their behaviors, infants do not have a worldview. Each person's worldview takes shape over time as they grow, develop, gain new experiences, interact with others, and express their instinctual preferences.

Those involved in the early formation of a child's worldview vary across cultures, such as those in either a nuclear or extended family. In the United States, those who facilitate the formation of a youngster's worldview are usually parents and/or close members of a nuclear family. Their influence is powerful during formative years. Other influences in modern society, such as television, social media, and pop culture, have an increased bearing on worldview formulation and outcome. Youngsters often hold to their early worldviews into adulthood, with varying degrees of firmness.[3]

Those involved in shaping a youngster's worldview hope to produce a preferred outcome by exposing the child to selected experiences and providing instruction by way of narratives, rituals, and behaviors. This indoctrination process may involve screening out alternative worldview narratives and experiences, or at least carefully managing a youngster's interaction with them. Even a broad-minded approach, one which does not seek to restrict exposure to alternate worldviews, involves instilling certain interpretations and offering guidelines that direct youngsters to accept a particular worldview. These guidelines may be regarded as helpful for general well-being and meaning-making, but the unconscious intent is to frame the youngster's worldview.

The process of education, by its very nature when conducted in public and private schools, instills a particular worldview. Public education in the U.S. interprets the world in a secular way according to authenticated, scientific standards of knowledge, while molding conduct around common values of society and a respect for individualism. The authentication process involves training experts in the peer-accepted standards of scientific knowledge and research. Religious schools may accept some of the scientific standards of knowledge found in the public schools but also infuse religious ways of knowing that may conflict with scientific standards. Even progres-

21

sive schools that teach a social justice curriculum are promoting a particular worldview.

For those instilling a worldview, the picture is more complicated than in the past. No longer can a family easily control all the child's interactions with the outside world. The complexity and rapid changes within today's culture are bringing many more factors to bear on the child's worldview formation. Technological developments and ubiquitous commercial advertisement also shape a youngster's worldview. The contemporary situation presents intense conflicts for parents who seek a high degree of control in shaping their child's worldview. Even the most open parents may be challenged by obstacles hindering what they intend as the preferred outcome.

FIVE CONTEMPORARY WORLDVIEWS

A unique period of human history is occurring at this time, a fifth turning—what I have called the Global Wave—that is transforming our human story as this new millennium unfolds. The Global Wave is characterized by rapid technological, intellectual, psychological, spiritual, economic, social, cultural, political, and ecological changes that are profoundly altering familiar patterns of the past. As is often the case when deep changes occur, there is a great deal of anxiety, tension, conflict, and disruption as well. Deep transformations are not new in our human history, for punctuations of human rhythms have shifted the flow of history in the past as well. Periods of discontinuity alter the balance of continuity and create change. Now, once again, is a time of ground-breaking change.

Within the Global Wave there is not one all-pervasive way of thinking and seeing reality. Instead I have identified five often contentious and conflicting worldviews with contradictory ways of knowing and understanding the world, each promoting dissimilar visions for the present and future. In the United States and throughout the world, most people identify with one or another of these worldviews or hold a combination of ideas from these five worldviews. The following is a brief summary of the five major worldviews: indigenous, traditional, progressive, globalized, and transformative. A more detailed description is found in the following chapters.

1. An Indigenous Worldview

Very few people today hold an indigenous worldview. Indigenous peoples share a similar ethnic identity and usually inhabit a geographic region with which they have had an early historical connection. "Indigenous" means "from" or "of the original origin." Indigenous peoples today live in groups ranging from only a few dozen to hundreds of thousands or more. Many groups have declined in numbers and some no longer exist, while others are threatened. Modern populations have assimilated some indigenous groups, while in other cases they are recovering or expanding their numbers. In many cases, indigenous groups are losing or have lost their language, lands, and traditional ways, and have experienced intrusion and pollution of their lands by exploitative industries.

2. A Traditional Worldview

A traditional worldview encompasses those with different beliefs bound together by a unifying adherence to traditions, either political, religious, economic, or social in nature. Different traditional groups include political conservatives, religious fundamentalists, the populist right, and those on the extreme right. Traditional political conservativism is a political philosophy emphasizing the bonds of social order over hyper-individualism and the defense of ancestral institutions, customs, traditions, and religion. Fundamentalism is a strict belief in a set of principles that are often religious. Many adherents strive to defend what they see as traditional religious beliefs of the past. Traditionalists rely on their traditional values, which give them a sense of comfort and security in a rapidly changing and complex world. The populist right spouts an anti-establishment rhetoric denouncing elites, while purporting to speak for the common people. Those on the extreme right fall into the margins of this worldview, and use violence and hate to further their agenda of white racial superiority.

3. A Progressive Worldview

Progressive implies progress, the foundational belief of the progressive worldview. I have placed different groups on a progressive spectrum: classic liberals, progressives, populist left, and the extreme left. The progressive label aptly fits their central belief in the perfectibility of humankind through education and developing government programs and institutions to support progressive causes. To achieve this perfectibility, progressives believe people must cast off the chains of religion, family hierarchies, and traditions, which, to them, have hindered humans from reaching their full potential. Thus, progressives embrace continuous change, reinvention, and left-wing extremists even advocate for revolution to reformulate society into their ideal version. One of progressivism's central tenets is social equality and egalitarianism, which is in opposition to social hierarchy and class distinctions.

4. A Globalized Worldview
In a globalized worldview the rapid pace of growth and development has spread to the farthest reaches of the Earth. A globalized worldview affects all aspects of society and individuals' daily lives. In this worldview, global capitalism is the dominant economic system. It is governed by capitalist principles and it has enveloped national and local economies that national governments have regulated and protected in the past. A global economic marketplace conducts business, currency exchanges, and trade policies that ignore national boundaries. Global multinational corporations and state-owned or partially-owned corporations make many of the economic rules and conduct the business of the world marketplace. They promote a consumer-focused economy and support a powerful financial sector. The globalization process has both negative and beneficial aspects.

5. A Transformative Worldview
At this point in time, diverse people say a different worldview or a different story is needed to make sure our human species and life as we know it on Earth continues. Leaders from diverse fields are contributing to the creation of what I call a transformative worldview. Critics say that none of the other worldviews alone are able to meet the challenges of the twenty-first century. Some transformers want to draw on the beneficial qualities of the others worldviews, such as the traditionalist support of community and family; indigenous connection with local place, the environment, and spirituality; the progressives' support of human rights and concern for the environment; and the globalizers' sense of global citizenship and technological advances. They also recognize that our human nature needs to be understood and contemplated as we go forth in tack-

ling the biggest challenges that we have yet faced as a species: living on a densely populated and environmentally compromised planet.

THE RISE OF POPULISM

A growing political phenomenon, populism, is making headway in many countries around the world today, including western democracies. I have added a description of populism after the five worldviews because it is a worldwide phenomenon with far-reaching ramifications that spills over into both the traditional and progressive worldviews. The term was coined in the late nineteenth century, and the movement has resurfaced at various times in modern history. Populism is a political stance that appeals to ordinary people who feel that their concerns are overlooked by the established elite. Populism sets in on the left and right side of the political spectrum but it currently appears to be advancing more on the right. Although I describe populism as a separate movement within the traditional and progressive worldviews in later chapters, at this point I will describe seven general characteristics of the phenomenon to give an introductory overview of this significant trend.

SEVEN CHARACTERISTICS OF POPULISM

1. A Thin Ideology
Populists call for ousting the political establishment, but they don't identify what should replace it. According to Cas Mudde, populism is a thin ideology, one which, on its own, is not substantive enough to offer a comprehensive ideology for governance. It differs from "thick-centered" ideologies such as liberalism, socialism, federalism, nationalism, conservatism, or fascism that have developed more comprehensive views on the relationship of politics, economics, society, and religion. As a thin-centered ideology, populism is flexible and populist politicians attach it to thick-centered ideologies. It is a complementary ideology that spreads itself through thicker ideologies in order to facilitate political rule.[4]

2. Appeals to Common People
Populists are dividers, not uniters. Although populism means "for the peo-

ple," it splits society into two hostile groups: "the pure (or common) people" and "the corrupt elite." Populists purport to speak to the common people, who feel that the political establishment overlooks or degrades their concerns and anxieties. In keeping with the flexibility of populism, the concept of "the people" is vague.

According to populists, the pure people share a sense of identity that distinguishes them from different groups within society. The pure people are also considered virtuous and their selection of populist leaders is self-legitimatizing. While a liberal democracy is a political system based on pluralism in which different groups with different interests and values are all legitimate, populism is just the opposite.[5]

Populists tend to define the common people as those who are with them. They separate the world into warring camps. The common people may be connected according to their socioeconomic status or class, in which they share certain cultural traditions and popular values. Populists make the case that the dominant elite belittle or devalue those peoples' values, tastes, character, and judgments. Therefore, it is the duty of the people to retaliate against this disparagement.[6]

Populists often employ the common people as a synonym for the whole nation, whether that national community is conceived in ethnic or civic terms. In such a framework, all individuals are regarded as being "common" to a particular state either by birth or by ethnicity.[7]

3. The Common People are the Underdogs

Populists morally frame the common people as the underdogs, oppressed by evil elites. The way of life of the common people is good and rooted in the country's "real" history and its traditions, which is regarded as being beneficial to the public good. Populists' leaders claim that they alone represent the common people. Even though they may lack majority support, they claim the polls are rigged or the questions on the survey favor the elites. Populists reason that they only lose an election if the common people have not had a chance to express their views. For example, Bernie Sanders' supporters in his bid for the Democratic party nomination in 2016 blamed his loss on a "rigged" system that elected the more establishment candidate Hillary Clinton, despite the fact that he lost by thousands of votes. Hence, populists frequently invoke conspiracy theories or elaborate rationalizations for political losses; the elites are still manipulating events behind the scenes in order to benefit them and keep the common person compliant. Therefore, if the populist politician doesn't win, there must be something wrong with the system.[8]

Logically, this argument would seem to fail once populists enter government and become the establishment. But a primary appeal of populism is its underdog status, so they continue to portray themselves as victims even at the height of their power in an incessant game of blaming others for their shortcomings or mistakes.

4. Populist Leaders Are Usually Elite Men

Anti-elitism is a key feature of populism. Populist leaders often present themselves as representatives of the people, but they often come from the upper echelons of society, either through wealth or elite education. Leaders get around this contradiction by distinguishing their elite status as "self-made," a qualifying mark of their leadership abilities. They vigorously claim that they are not the despised established political elites. In fact, they are fighting against the established elites for the ordinary person. Populists often condemn not only the political establishment, but also economic, academic, cultural, and media leaders, which they present as one uniform, corrupt group. For example, President Donald Trump does not consider himself to be in the category of the elites; instead he frames himself as a self-made businessman who has sacrificed his position of power and wealth in order to battle against the corrupting elites who are oppressing the common person. A populist leader who gets into power is in a perpetual crusade to prove to the people that he is not an establishment figure and never will be.

The overwhelming majority of populist leaders have been men. They often present themselves as men of action and images rather than men of words, talking of the need for bold action and common sense solutions to issues which they call crises. Male populist leaders often express themselves using simple and sometimes vulgar language in an attempt to present themselves as the common man or "one of the boys" to add to their populist appeal. Overstepping traditional political boundaries, they may use language that draws attention to their virility and sexual prowess.

27

5. Populists as Disrupters

Populists typically show their distrust of the establishment by transgressing normative rules of behavior, language, and ethics. One example is behaving in a way that is not typical of politicians, such as using bad manners. Stylistically, populists often use short, simple slogans and direct language, and engage in coarse behavior, which makes them appear like real people. They use this colorful and crass language to distinguish themselves from the establishment. News coverage of populists often follows a tabloid format, emphasizing their preference and tendency toward melodrama, gossip, infotainment, and scattered and confusing narratives.

6. Authoritarian Tendencies

Some populists have authoritarian tendencies. According to political psychologist Karen Stenner, "Authoritarianism is an individual predisposition to intolerance of difference that brings together certain traits: obedience to authority, moral absolutism, intolerance and punitiveness toward dissidents and deviants, and racial and ethnic prejudice."[9] Among authoritarians individual autonomy gives ways to group authority. Stenner concludes that authoritarian tendencies are mostly latent when there is political consensus, little strife, and authority figures are trusted. However, the authoritarian tendency may be triggered or activated when people feel leaders are unworthy of trust and respect, and normative beliefs are no longer shared across the community or nation. Authoritarians are boundary-maintainers, norm-enforcers, and cheerleaders for authority figures. The loss or perceived loss of these boundaries, norms, and authority is a catalyst for activating their latent authoritarian predispositions.[10]

Authoritarians do not necessarily strive to preserve the status quo and are in favor of social change when that change entails shifting together in support of common goals. They are not opposed to government intervention to enhance oneness and sameness. Unlike libertarians, they are not necessarily supportive of laissez-faire economics.

Authoritarians are not open to new experiences, instead they have difficulty handling complexity, freedom, and difference. Conservatives grow more attracted to authoritarianism when public opinion is fragmented and fractious, and major institutions fail to inspire confidence. But when confidence in societal institutions is at a reasonable level, they are disinclined to adopt authoritarian stances. The prospect of some wholesale overthrow of the system in pursuit of greater unity is appealing to many authoritarians. An example of this sentiment was when Trump supporters in the 2016 presidential campaign claimed that they wanted someone to "shake things up." The consequences of this shake up were vague, but the mere act of "doing something" to right the wrongs of the perceived corruption and chaos was appealing to his supporters. As a result, liberal democracy is least secure when authoritarians believe that another type of government is better able to grant them the oneness and sameness they crave.[11]

Mocking, belittling, and patronizing authoritarians are triggers that further aggravate their anger and insecurity. Stenner found that to ease their distress, there needs to be greater consensus on issues, leaders capable of inspiring confidence, and rhetoric far more focused on the power of unity than the joys of diversity. Authoritarians are malleable in their positions; for example, the boundaries of "us" and "them" can be shifted as long as there is a common in-group identity.[12]

7. Populism and Democracy

The relationship between populism and democracy has sparked intense debates. Some critics see populism as dangerous to democracy, while populists often present themselves as the only true democrats. On the positive side, populism can serve to give status and recognition to some social groups who feel excluded and marginalized from the political process. It also directs negative attention to the elites of society, whom the populist perceives as usurping power, privilege, and wealth from the common person.

Populist leaders tend to dislike a complicated democratic system. When populism takes the authoritarian track, it is at odds with liberal democracy. As mentioned above, populists who have an authoritarian predisposition undermine the tenets of liberal democracy by rejecting notions of pluralism and the idea that constitutional limits should constrain the "general will" of the people.[13] Populists tend to view democratic institutions such as Congress as alienating, rambunctious, and full of conflict; instead, they prefer direct democracy like referendums or executive orders that settle issues in a clear-cut manner. Ultimately, populist leaders make decisions in a way that typically isn't possible in traditional democracies.

Populists who live in liberal democracies often criticize the independent institutions designed to protect the fundamental rights of minorities, particularly the judiciary and the media. Mudde notes, "Populists in power tend to undermine countervailing powers, which are courts, which are media, which are other parties. And they tend to do that through a variety of mostly legal means, but not classic repression."[14] Fearful of this type of governance, liberal philosopher John Stuart Mill described it as the "tyranny of the majority."

WORLDVIEWS:
A TOOL FOR UNDERSTANDING DIFFERENT PERSPECTIVES

Most people dislike being categorized and put into boxes for analysis—I am one of them. But in this book a useful heuristic device is needed to understand the diversity of thought and ways of looking at the world. Therefore, if we can forego the uncomfortable feeling of categorization and being placed in a pigeonhole, we can gain valuable insights into understanding people different from us.

When worldviews are not in our awareness nor acknowledged, stronger parties with more dominant worldviews may advertently or inadvertently try to impose their worldviews on others. Understanding worldviews can be a tool for recognizing and analyzing conflicts when fundamental differences divide groups of people. When each side of a conflict is understood according to a group's particular worldview, then places of connection and divergence may become clearer, leading to a better understanding and promoting reconciliation.

Worldviews, with their embedded meanings, can be a seedbed from which new shared meanings may emerge. By looking at the stories, rituals, myths, and metaphors used by a group of people holding a similar worldview, we can learn efficiently and deeply about their worldview and what matters to them and how they make meaning. These shared meanings may arise as people co-create new stories, design new rituals, establish shared values, and find inclusive metaphors. In any given contentious debate or conflict, established societal values, such as security, family, and responsibility, will emerge. Because people relate to these values differently according to their worldview, misunderstandings and negative judgments about those who differ may follow. As one becomes aware of the existence of different worldviews, she may stop expecting "the other" to make sense of the way she perceives the world, and realize instead that "the other" makes sense of the problem from his own worldview. In other words, the other side's perceived outrageous or nonsensical ideas may actually become reasonable and sensible when seen from their point of view.[15]

ALTERING A WORLDVIEW

Worldviews influence how we see ourselves and others and how we make meaning of our lives and relationships. Since resolving conflict and negotiating through a multi-cultural, complex world necessarily involves some kind of change or accommodation, it is essential to understand the operation of worldviews. When people are asked to change their worldview, identity, or what they find meaningful, they will often resist. Worldviews keep our lives coherent and give us a sense of meaning, purpose, and connection. When engaged in conversations, problem-solving situations, or conflict resolution processes, we need to help people look into each other's worldviews without trying to change them. It is possible to uncover shared values without forcing fundamental change.

An adult's worldview may, but need not, remain consistent. As a person goes through life there may be events that compel a radically different outlook. For example, exposure to new ways of thinking through education may prompt a changed perspective. Vivid experiences or persuasive encounters may cause a dramatic shift in outlook. Exposure to different cultural practices, mores, geography, living circumstances, or significant tragedy or success, may modify one's way of thinking about life and meaning.[16]

Purposeful attempts to alter another person's worldview may not be successful. Stress and internal conflict (for the one who is the target) may arise. For example, when an educator teaches about evolution, this subject may test the worldview of a student who believes in creationism and the student may resist the imposition. Presenting facts that reinforce a particular worldview does little to persuade others to change their worldview to the one that is perhaps more factually accurate. Even a person intimidated or persecuted to change their worldview may resist doing so.[17]

BOUNDED ASSUMPTIONS IN THE FIVE WORLDVIEWS

Each worldview has many unquantifiable, bounded assumptions or finite reference points. I use this term, bounded assumptions, to mean a supposition
that is accepted as true with or without actual proof. The assumption or finite
reference point is bounded within the meaning, definitions, and actions of the
group perpetuating the worldview and gives them guidance in ordering their
decision-making. I take the position that each worldview has many bounded
assumptions that followers unconsciously cling to and perpetuate. Although
many will deny this fact, many of us cleave to our bounded assumptions that
underlie and give meaning to our worldview. All of us presuppose certain
things to be true without absolute proof, and arguments fall back on this point
or points when they exhaust other evidence supporting them. Below are a few
of the many bounded assumptions that people in each of the five worldviews
unconsciously promote:

1. **Indigenous Worldview**

- Mother Earth is a powerful force in which spirits permeate all material and
  nonmaterial elements.
- The Universe is omniscient and beyond the knowing of ordinary humans.
- Communal ownership is better than private property and is a reflection
  of the notion that the community is more important than the individual.
- Loyalty to the tribe or group is indisputable, while outsiders are viewed
  with caution.

2. **Traditional Worldview**

- Christians believe in a personal God and faith in Jesus. They have unques-
  tionable absolute truths, such as good and evil.
- Scripture in the Bible is derived from God and is the ultimate Truth.
- The populist right reveres a strong authority figure (usually male) who
  makes decisions for them.
- Science and facts can be manipulated and have limited value at times.
- Stories, with lots of hyperbole and even falsehoods, are a way to communi-

cate in a nonliteral way.
- Patriotism to the tribe or nation is a virtue.
- The educated elites and science cannot be trusted all the time.
- Liberty, loyalty, freedom, sacredness, and individual choice are cherished.
- The individual bears responsibility for success or failure, not society.
- Customs, traditions, and rituals of the past (often religious) are to be honored.
- Hierarchical authority structures work best and are the most efficient.
- The human body, unborn children, and family are sacred entities.
- The unborn child belongs to God, it is not the property of an individual woman's body.
- Place, land, and community are sacrosanct.
- Laws, order, rules should be obeyed; borders and boundaries mark clear demarcations.

3. Progressive Worldview

- Classic liberals believe that science is neutral and facts should validate ideas.
- Literal, factual, and scientific interpretation of events.
- Humans are basically good and can become better through education and government help.
- Educated elites are morally superior and have the best ideas for non-elites.
- Education (including college) is a basic requirement and much needed in today's world.
- Religious beliefs are superstitious and delusionary (many progressives are atheists).
- Almost all foreign problems are attributable to negative effects of U.S. imperial actions.
- See oppressed groups—women, people of color, LGBTQ, immigrants, Muslims—as victims who should receive preferential treatment.
- White males have wielded power for centuries and now this should be reversed.
- Structural change is necessary, and progressives will enact change since they know the best strategies and can "help" others succeed.

- Cosmopolitan and urban life are trendy and upscale.
- Society, not the individual, bears ultimate responsibility for success and failure.
- Compassion extends to those around the world, many advocate for open borders.
- Equity, not just equality, should be enacted.
- The environment is in crisis.
- The centralized state, run by progressives, should enact and enforce a paternalistic agenda.
- Display one's status by professing a set of "luxury beliefs" that show one is awakened to progressive ideology.

4. Globalized Worldview

- Competition leads to the best outcomes if left to the free-market.
- Economic growth and consumer choice are the highest goals and pursued at all costs.
- Individuals are responsible for their own luck and hard work will lead to success.
- Consumer choice and an array of material goods lead to happiness and fulfillment.
- Indulge all desires through the market place of consumer goods and services.
- Bigger, faster, better are to be pursued.

5. Transformative Worldview

- Compassion, love, and kindness are the highest ideals.
- Diversity of people and thoughts is to be valued, and all worldviews appreciated without judgment.
- Human behaviors are rooted in our evolutionary past, and are not always rational or benign, but we do our best to overcome negative behaviors and appreciate positive ones.
- Communicating in a civil manner in which all parties' needs are met is ideal.
- Earth is our home and must be treated with reverence for the continuation of the human species.

- Individuals have responsibilities as well as rights.
- Connection with family, community, and spirituality (although not necessarily religious) are paths to happiness.

I have concluded that no worldview has gained dominance at this time. If this is so, it means that it will behoove us all to understand and learn to negotiate with people holding different worldviews in order to have a more peaceful, tolerant, and viable future. We all have a voice and a critical stake in the outcome.

Chapter 3
The Modern Worldview

What could be more fundamental to our sense of meaning and purpose than a conception of whether the strivings of the human race over long stretches of time have left us better or worse off? How, in particular, are we to make sense of modernity—of the erosion of family, tribe, tradition, and religion by the forces of individualism, cosmopolitanism, reason, and science? ... Steven Pinker, The Better Angels of Our Nature: Why Violence Has Declined

THE MODERN WORLDVIEW: AN INTRODUCTION

The ushering in of modernization around the year 1500 was a monumental shift in how people saw and acted in the world. Over this 500 year period modernization magnified and grew to spread its tentacles around the world. I have called this profound turning point in my holistic world history the Modern Wave. From 1500 onward a modern worldview took shape that eventually dominated across the world. It is a profound occurrence, yet we are unaware that we are shaped by its impact.

A worldview is an overall perspective from which one sees and interprets the world, a set of simplifying suppositions about how the world works and what is seen and not seen. It is an internal collection of assumptions held by an individual or a group that is firmly believed to be self-evident truth. These assumptions shape an individual's beliefs, ideas, attitudes, and values, which, in turn, affect behaviors and actions. A worldview is a paradigm, a fundamental way of looking at reality which functions as a filter. When people look out through a filter, such as a pane of colored glass, they usually see through it, rather than seeing it—so as with worldviews. They admit information that is consistent with our deeply held expectations about the world while guiding us to disregard information that challenges or disproves these expectations.[1] A worldview acts as a built-in "operating system."

Each of us has a worldview. It develops in part because we seek some understanding of our own significance. People desire certitude by which to live their lives. Through the lens of a worldview an individual is able to answer universal queries. These include notions of the existence or nonexistence of the supernatural and a deity or deities; the origins of the universe and of human life; the source of morality and values and identification of what is good or evil; how to live one's life; the meaning of life and of death; and so on. To a greater or lesser degree, people are able to obtain reassurances from worldview coherence.

The five worldviews that I introduced in Chapter 2—indigenous, traditionalist, progressive, globalized, and transformative—have emerged from or have been influenced by the worldview of the Modern Wave. Before going further into explaining the five worldviews, it will be helpful to describe the Modern Wave and the worldview that accompanies this profound shift in world history.

The modern worldview traces its historical origins back more than 500 years to the expansion of Western European power and its influence and ultimate dominance around the world. This view has been especially powerful over the last two centuries and has expanded to the farthest reaches of the globe. ("Modern" means relating to the present and recent time and not ancient, remote, or obsolete). The modern worldview has ushered in a host of astonishing human achievements, such as the equality of women, medical breakthroughs, educational progress, and advancement of human rights. However it has also introduced appalling failures, such as rampant consumerism, cut-throat competition, unlimited economic growth, the disintegration of community, military force to resolve conflict, and subjugation of nature. One of the challenges of the twenty-first century is how to draw on the achievements coming from a modern worldview and rethink or discard the darker elements.

Around the watershed date of 1500, a number of interrelated factors started shaping a modern worldview: the Renaissance, European exploration, the unleashing of capitalism, the Scientific Revolution, family structures, and the Protestant Reformation. From these origins, the modern worldview evolved and morphed as different factors continued to shape its characteristics, ideology, and traditions. As a result of the coalescing of these various factors, powerful forces emerged that sparked changes in the way of life for people in Western Europe. These changes were then unevenly diffused at various times and places around the world. Of course, the introduction of a modern worldview was not uniformly assimilated by those it encountered, but was shaped by cultural differences, geography, and many other factors. Some people exposed to the modern worldview eagerly accepted the changes while others violently resisted it.

Let's next turn to look at the ideological, philosophical, scientific, religious, political, environmental, and economic characteristics of the modern worldview in more depth.

MODERN THOUGHT

The European Renaissance ushered in changes in European consciousness. Roughly encompassing the dates 1400-1600, a new spirit called the Renaissance swept across Europe among the educated, urban elite. Actually, there were two distinct Renaissances: first, a change in political, economic, social, and religious conditions, and second, an artistic and cultural movement. Renaissance, meaning "rebirth," began in Italy and was a renewal of Greco-Roman civilization. Above all, the Renaissance was an age of recovery from the disasters of fourteenth century Europe such as the effects of the Black Death, political disorder, and economic recession. The Renaissance celebrated a new attitude: the individual was extolled. A high regard for human dignity and worth and a realization of individual potentiality created a new social ideal of the well-rounded or universal person who was capable of achievements in many areas of life. Renaissance enthusiasts despised the Christian tradition of humility and encouraged a new pride in human improvement. An individual's thirst for fame and a strong desire to put his imprint upon the contemporary world were at the heart of the Renaissance.

Secularism and a focus on the here-and-now affected a person's acts and thoughts. Early Christians upheld a simple and humble way of life in keeping with the life and the teachings of Jesus, but this view shifted to one in which wealth and the acquisition of riches was respectable. Increasingly, people viewed life as an opportunity for glory and pleasure rather than as a transitory stop on the way to eternal bliss or everlasting damnation.

Man was the measure of what life had to offer. Renaissance entrepreneurs endorsed new business techniques in banking, bookkeeping, trade, and commerce. Highly valued was the pursuit of profit, a departure from

Christian values of the Middle Ages. Unlike in earlier Christianity, the merchant was elevated in status to reflect the growing impact of commerce. These Renaissance ideas would pave the way for further intellectual, scientific, political, economic, and religious changes in the sixteenth century and beyond.

Starting in 1517 with Martin Luther's break from the Catholic Church, several fervent Protestant religious sects broke away from the all-powerful Catholic Church during the Protestant Reformation. These new religious sects set up their own denominations and celebrated religious beliefs that, in part, justified an emphasis on wealth acquisition. Protestants rejected traditional Catholic beliefs, which, at least in theory, regarded poverty as akin to the life of Jesus. Instead, many Protestants, especially Calvinists, preached that material wealth was a favorable sign from God and should be embraced and not shunned. These new beliefs justified the new attitude that wealth and its accumulation were respectable and in accord with Christian principles. These new ideas accompanied the expansion and lure of the beginning of a capitalist economic system.

Around the 1500 time frame, scientific findings and the subsequent Enlightenment challenged the religious thinking of the time and, instead, celebrated the wonders of the scientific method and reason. The modern worldview is often called the Newtonian or mechanistic worldview, since many of its characteristics are derived from the famed English scientist Sir Isaac Newton. He depicted the universe as a giant machine operating in a predictable, orderly mode; once the parts of the machine were individually analyzed, the whole machine could be explained. In Newton's universe, definable laws acted uniformly on objects that behaved predictably and consistently. Scientists busily set about classifying, dividing, and analyzing everything from plants and animals to human behavior. Nothing escaped their curious reach to scientifically examine and explain the planet.

Nineteenth century scientists continued their quest for scientific certainty. The French philosopher Auguste Comte postulated that all intellectual activity progressed through predictable stages: first, the theological or fictitious; second, the metaphysical or abstract; and finally the highest stage, the scientific or positive. One of the most famous scientists of the modern age, Charles Darwin, theorized that humans were not divinely created, as the Christian world had confidently assumed for centuries, but had evolved from simple to complex organisms through stages of natural selection.

The advancement of science contributed immensely to the formation of the modern worldview. Scientific discoveries ushered in a change in values from religious values based on faith and miracles to scientific values based on evidence, reason, efficiency, rationality, order, and analysis. Although the vast majority of Europeans, including many scientists, held to their religious faith during the Scientific Revolution, religious beliefs were starting to be devalued as unscientific, irrational, and superstitious.

THE MODERN ECONOMY

European exploration or exploitation (depending upon your point of view) contributed to the formation of a modern worldview. The Renaissance era of excitement and possibilities translated into more explorations by famed early explorers, such as Christopher Columbus, Amerigo Vespuci, Ferdinand Magellan, Francis Drake, Hernán Cortés, and many others. One of the reasons for this explosion of exploration was the relative poverty of Western Europe at the time compared to other regions of the world, especially Asia and the Middle East. Material poverty stimulated expansion by way of their only option: the sea. Europeans imported more goods from Asia than they exported to them; therefore, they had a trade imbalance that needed to be remedied. Asians were quite self-sufficient and did not want or need any of the poor quality goods Europeans made. But Europeans coveted China's luxury imports and spices from Southeast Asia. Exploration also signaled prestige, glory, and strength, attributes that Western Europeans craved. Hence, they invented or adapted from others' technologically sophisticated weaponry which propelled them to become "gunpowder empires." These new technological inventions gave the West an edge in killing and intimidation around the world.

Accompanying Western exploration was the expansion of a capitalist economic system, another important force in shaping the modern worldview. Wealth poured into Western European banks in London and Amsterdam from the production of cash crops, such as sugar, tobacco, and cotton, as well as the fur trade, the mining of silver and gold, and the slave trade. African slaves, indigenous peoples, and indentured servants provided cheap and coerced labor necessary for conversion of these raw materials into valuable commodities traded on the world market. An emerging middle class or *bourgeoisie* of bankers, merchants, financiers, and entrepreneurs secured this new-found wealth for themselves. They acquired a taste for sugar, furs, and many other luxury products that spurred a consumer frenzy. With the modern worldview, two main economic forms developed: capitalism (managed and free trade) and socialism/communism.

In a modern capitalist system private parties make their goods and services available in an open market and seek to make a profit on their activities. Private parties own the means of production. There are two variations of capitalism: free market capitalism, often called *laissez faire*, and managed or regulated capitalism. Adam Smith is credited as the founder of free market economics, in which the "invisible hand" of the open marketplace would set prices according to the principles of supply and demand. This economic thinking emerged out of the liberal political traditions discussed below. Generally, Smith and free market capitalists are against the government's interference in the marketplace and argue that property should be privately or individually owned. They believe that tariffs (taxes on imported goods) should be eliminated in order to foster efficiency and competition in trade. Managed or regulated capitalism came about with the Great Depression in the 1930s and continued into the 1970s in the U.S. and other European countries. Supporters say that government should play an active role in regulating the economy in order for wealth to be more equally distributed to a greater number of people than under free market capitalism in which wealth tends to concentrate in the hands of a few.

Under managed capitalism, the government erects protective tariffs to shield national or local industries from cheaper competition abroad. For example, the United States had protective tariffs on steel imported from other countries in order to have a profitable steel industry that provided jobs for thousands of U.S. workers. If the tariff was added to imported steel, say from low-wage China, that steel would be priced higher than steel made in the U.S. Therefore, the industries manufacturing such things as cars and appliances would pay a bit more for the steel used in production than if there were no tariffs. Of course, there are always many sides to any issue. Continuing with our steel example, with protective tariffs the price of goods manufactured in the U.S. would be slightly higher than if "free trade" (no tariffs) were allowed but, on the other hand, more workers would be employed in well-paid jobs in the U.S. to make products from U.S. steel. In the U.S., the managed version of capitalism prevailed from the 1930s into the 1970s.

In 1980, the U.S. economic policy shifted to a version of capitalism called *laissez faire* capitalism, also called neoliberalism or free market capitalism. In this version of capitalism, government regulations and tariffs were lifted. The result has been lower prices for imported goods in the U.S., since many of the products are now made in China, which has a lower cost of labor and production. But it has also resulted in a decline in the number of well-paid American manufacturing jobs, since many of these jobs have gone to nations where labor costs are low.

Communism and socialism are also economic systems of the modern worldview. Karl Marx, a nineteenth century economic theorist, reasoned that human history advanced through stages of development from a feudalistic past, to the middle stage of capitalism, and then finally to communism, the pinnacle of human achievement. Under a communist economic system or command economy, there is no private ownership. Instead of private ownership, the state collectively owns property for all. In theory, this economic form avoids the exploitation of the common person by the elite who have amassed wealth in a capitalist system. The communist system was implemented in the Soviet Union in 1917 and continued for over seventy years, but in the end it failed miserably. Instead of a capitalist wealthy elite, a communist wealthy elite emerged who wielded governmental power and controlled the collective property of the citizenry.

Socialism is a modern economic system in which the government owns and operates large industries, such as military, education, transportation, health care, utilities, and others, while small businesses are privately owned and operated and citizens can own private property. Many Europeans employed a socialist/capitalist mixed economy after the end of World War II and it still operates in many European countries today. In fact, the United States is seeing the popularity of democratic socialism in its politics with the candidacy of Bernie Sanders in the 2016 and 2020 elections and several notable congressional members.

Placing the different economic systems on a continuum, the differences of each system become apparent. Communism is considered on the far left of the continuum, while *laissez faire*, free market capitalism (neoliberalism) is considered to be on the far right. Socialism is placed to the immediate left of center, while managed capitalism is placed to the immediate right of center. Many different economies around the world fall at some point on this continuum.

MODERN POLITICAL CHANGES

The Enlightenment of the late sixteenth and early seventeenth centuries contributed to shaping the political features of the modern worldview. It was an intellectual movement that created the concept of political liberalism, celebrated the wonders of the scientific method and reason, challenged the religious thinking of the time, extolled the dignity of the individual, and defied the notion of absolute political authority. The Enlightenment *philosophes* argued for rational, written constitutions to limit monarchs' power and to ensure certain individual rights and equality before the law. They revered, above all else, reason, progress, objective thinking, and the optimistic idea that humans could be perfected through state-sponsored education and a rational society. Some *philosophes,* such as John Locke, advanced the merits of private property and the improvement of that property for monetary gain. The *philosophes'* ideas were particularly popular among the rising Western middle class who profited from their ideas, especially the concept of private property.

The Enlightenment *philosophes* posited the concept of political liberalism and rejected the absolute authority of the church and monarchs. As a result, by the nineteenth century many countries in Western Europe and the United States had adopted some form of representative government guided by a written constitution. Although these were not direct democracies, this was a marked change from the days of absolute monarchical rule. Those represented in government expanded over the years from the common man—as long as he was male, white, over 21, and a property holder—to all individuals over the age of maturity. With this move to a more inclusive political system, the idea of freedom and liberty for the individual, in the political sense, emerged. The idea of individualism and human rights became a new political value.

Another political change in the modern worldview was the reconfiguration of political rule. For thousands of years, people lived in large empires, small states or city-states, or in decentralized territories ruled by feudal lords. With the modern worldview, there was a shift from those kinds of political rule to the nation-state as the preferred political structure. Great Britain, the United States, Netherlands, and later France pioneered this new political entity. As new nation-states were formed in the nineteenth and twentieth centuries, the question remained: what kind of government would they embrace?

As mentioned above, the liberal form of government, (not to be confused with the liberal/conservative division in the U.S. today) which advanced written constitutions and representative government, was adopted as a preferred form of political structure by many nations. But not all nation-states in the modern era developed a liberal, representative type of government. Some nations have held to the monarchy as a form of political rule; some have ceremonial monarchs such as in the United Kingdom, and others have active monarchs such as in Saudi Arabia, Jordan, Morocco, and Kuwait.

Also part of the modern worldview, some nations turned to authoritarian types of government, most dramatically in the twentieth century. For simplicity there are three main types of authoritarian rule found in the modern era: communism, fascism, and dictatorships. The values held by authoritarian regimes are obedience to authority, protection of the "mother land," strong masculine images, and patriarchal attitudes. Men defend the family against outside aggression, while women remain in the home. Honor, resolve, courage, valor, obedience, and vindictiveness are commonly held values.

Emerging out of the modern worldview is communism. It is a form of authoritarian rule based on a theory of social organization in which all property is held in common by the state. The Soviet Union, the first communist nation, was formed in 1917, when a revolution led by Vladimir Lenin overthrew the Russian monarchy. The Soviet Union continued as a communist form of government until its collapse in 1991. Pockets of communist rule still exist around the world, although mostly in a hybrid form in China, Cuba, Vietnam, and North Korea. Fascism is a radical and authoritarian nationalist political ideology that demands an extreme loyalty to the state by subservient citizens. Germany (Nazis), Italy, Spain, and Japan were fascist governments leading up to and during World War II. Dictatorships are often established through a military coup after which the government is ruled by an individual dictator. Dictatorships have been common throughout the twentieth century but are now outnumbered by republican forms of government.

The twentieth century also witnessed the darker side of the modern worldview. Two horrific world wars, fought over national competition, colonial acquisitions, and the struggle for world supremacy, exalted armed conflict as the chosen method for resolving differences. The Soviet Union and the United States challenged each other's ideologies in a Cold War (1945-1991). Although the two nations never came to blows, numerous proxy wars were fought, such as in Korea, Nicaragua, Vietnam, Afghanistan, and others. Although still severe, these Cold War battles were smaller in scope and saw fewer people killed than in World War II, perhaps reflecting the acknowledgment that our planet cannot survive the nuclear, environmental, and human devastation of another world war.

Even though the lessons of the two world wars are readily apparent, some people today still cling to an authoritarian stance reminiscent of the oppressive rule imposed by many empires of the past and the totalitarian regimes of the twentieth century. Forms of authoritarian rule—dictatorships, monarchies, neo-fascist movements, and communist rule—continue to survive, while pockets of militia activity are found in parts of Europe and the United States. Although a controversial addition, some people argue that large multi-national corporations, run by corporate oligarchies, are a form of authoritarian rule, since they extend their non-democratic reach into every corner of the world.

THE ENVIRONMENT IN THE MODERN WORLDVIEW

The big problem of our modern society is that we feel that we are separated from nature. But it's just the opposite. We are interrelated and our DNA is the same....
Marina Abramovic

With the modern worldview, the capitalist system calculated an economic price for nature's bounty. This economic thinking meant that nature was not regarded as a sacred source of beauty, awe, inspiration, and reverence but used as a supplier of resources, an economic commodity. Although probably unintentionally, but certainly carelessly, Westerners tampered with the world's ecosystem by introducing new species into colonial areas and by over-hunting, overgrazing, and deforesting vast stretches of land, which reduced, altered or

46

exterminated the diversity of life.

Today's environmental devastation is largely a result of seeing the environment through the modern worldview lens. Resources are extracted from what is seen as inanimate nature in a detached and mechanistic way. Nature is an object, separate and inferior to human extractors. Often environmental damage is not experienced immediately but at some time in the future, yet the unseen, long-term consequences are conveniently ignored or postponed to a vague future date. Nature's purpose in this worldview is to provide the materials necessary for "progress" to be achieved by human beings.

MODERN SOCIETY

One of the most destructive things that's happening in modern society is that we are losing our sense of the bonds that bind people together - which can lead to nightmares of social collapse. ... Alexander McCall Smith

The modern worldview profoundly changed society and family patterns. The section below highlights changes that have occurred in middle class, modern families from the nineteenth century onward.

In many middle class homes in the nineteenth century, a small nuclear family became the expected norm. The economic role of the middle class family shifted from one centered on production of basic necessities to one focused primarily on consumption of material goods. Along with consumption, the modern family's responsibilities included reproduction, socializing children, fulfilling psychic and emotional needs, instilling societal values, providing affection to all family members, guiding children's personality development, and encouraging and guiding school and career decisions for children.[2] However, these middle class family functions did not necessarily apply to the working class, peasants, or the elite. The nuclear family decreased in size as children were accorded greater parental affection, while incidences of divorce increased as women became more independent. The family no longer served as the center of economic activity.

Modern, middle class marriages shifted from an arranged economic or political alliance to one based on individual choice. Sexual and psychological attraction, affection, and personal satisfaction became important criteria in selecting a spouse, and more emotional interaction between middle class men and women resulted. Marriage was carried out primarily to fulfill personal desires for home and children and to enhance personal happiness. Western Europeans socially and legally disapproved of polygamy. Monogamy, the normative marriage form in the West, expressed democratic, egalitarian ideals in reaction to inequalities and hierarchies often found in polygamous marital societies.[3]

The middle class family encouraged affection. The importance of love as an ingredient in family life became a modern value. The family served as a pleasurable nurturing center that provided an emotional bond among individuals and a reliable, comfortable refuge from outside strife. With fewer children, childrearing practices among the modern middle class began to change. Parents increasingly treated children with love and respect. This practice coincided with Enlightenment beliefs, which assumed children could improve and become responsible adults through humane and supportive treatment. Harsh discipline as a means of dealing with childhood transgressions declined, although it certainly was not eliminated. Instead, it was believed that children should be afforded certain rights and protective services, and the tradition in which children were obliged to accept arbitrary parental directives decreased. Middle class parents spanked children less often and drew them more closely into the family orbit of affection. The old European practice of swaddling—wrapping infants tightly in cloth to prevent movement—began to disappear. Adult supervision increasingly replaced physically restraining children.

Parents experienced a decline in their traditional authority, especially the father's role as authoritative head of the family. Although the father's influence did not fade away completely, this subtle decline of traditional family authority and male preeminence was linked to a lessening of family members' reliance upon each other for mutual benefit and even survival. Instead, family dependency shifted towards more reliance on the outside marketplace as a source of necessities and income. In middle class families, fathers, some mothers, and children spent at least parts of the day outside the home, which meant that at least a partial transfer of family influence shifted to other institutions, such as schools or the workplace, which began to take over some of the family's traditional functions.[4]

Through the years, many people holding a modern worldview have fought for steady, incremental progress in forging a more equitable and inclusive society. Supporters of various social movements—civil rights, feminism, Native American rights, environmental protection, LGBTQ rights, people with disabilities, and others—have supported the recognition and implementation of legal, political, and other rights that have helped those historically discriminated against win greater inclusion into mainstream society. Although the results have been uneven, blatant discrimination of minorities has been tempered, and society, especially among the younger generation, is now more accepting of diversity of social norms than previous generations.

WEIRDNESS IN THE WEST

Do you think you are weird? You may think it is weird to ask this question, and you probably want to know the definition before answering. In 2010, three cultural psychologists published an important article titled "The Weirdest People in the World?" The authors showed that nearly all research in psychology is conducted on a very small subset of the human population: people from cultures who are Western, educated, industrialized (individualistic), rich (by world standards), and democratic—in other words, WEIRD. In their review of studies they found that WEIRD people are statistical outliers; they are the least representative group of people to study if you want to make generalizations about human nature. Americans are more extreme outliers than Europeans, and within the U.S., the educated upper middle class is the most extreme of all![5] In other words, if you are reading this book, you are probably WEIRD.

A WEIRD person follows the modern worldview. They see a world full of separate objects, rather than relationships. While non-modern people think holistically, as Jonathan Haidt explains "seeing the whole context of the relationships among parts, WEIRD people think more analytically, detaching the focal object from its context, assigning it to a category and then assuming what's true about the category is true about the object." Modern philosophers since Emmanuel Kant and Karl Marx, continues Haidt, "have mostly generated moral systems that are individualistic, rule-based, and universalistic. That's the morality you need to govern a society of autonomous individuals."[6]

If WEIRD people think and see the world differently from non-modern people, then it is assumed that they have different moral concerns. If you see a world of individuals, then you'll devise a morality that protects those individuals and their individual rights. Concerns about harm and fairness for individuals will be emphasized. On the other hand, if you live in a non-modern society in which people focus more on relationships, groups, and institutions, protecting individuals will not be your primary focus. The morality will be more socio-centric, which means that the needs of the group and institutions come before the needs of the individual. If you have a socio-centric morality, then morality will likely be based on more than just the concerns of harm and fairness. Additional virtues are required to bind people together.[7] These other moral virtues—sanctity, loyalty, and authority— will be discussed in Chapter 9.

Although the modern worldview continues to be fervently held by many people, it is not the only worldview at the present time. Aside from the indigenous worldview which has continued for millennia, in this time of tumultuous change, four distinct, coherent worldviews have developed that have grown out of or even rejected the modern worldview—traditional, progressive, globalized, and transformative. But first, let's look at the indigenous worldview.

Chapter 4
The Indigenous Worldview

Treat the earth well: it was not given to you by your parents, it was loaned to you by your children. ... Indigenous Proverb

THE INDIGENOUS WORLDVIEW: AN INTRODUCTION

Who should claim the rights to indigenous artifacts? Natural history museums before 1990 often had exhibits that included artifacts and possibly skeletons of Native Americans; the tribes could claim no ownership rights to artifacts that were taken from their land. Their burial grounds were dug up by archaeologists, and the findings were dispersed to museums across the country and world. Many artifacts were either purchased, often below the value of the object, or stolen, with little legal recourse for Native groups. Although these exhibits may have been informative to the museum-goer or provided scientific information to academics, many Native Americans resented these exhibits being used in this way.

This changed in 1990 when the federal government passed the Native American Graves Protection and Repatriation Act, which gave them the legal authority to reclaim artifacts from federally funded museums. Museums now are often asked to return objects that are sacred to particular groups, who use them in present-day ceremonies. Institutions also must give back artifacts that have "ongoing historical, traditional, or cultural importance central to the Native American group or culture itself." Tribes can claim ownership of the objects, and if a review determines their claim is justified, ownership of the artifact is given to the tribes. However, the question remains, "Who should own Native American artifacts?"[1] The essence of the question is also being asked globally. Should Egypt be able to request the return of their plundered antiquities from the British Museum in London or the Berlin Museum? It is not the purpose of this example to answer this question but to show that how one answers this question reflects, in part, one's particular worldview. This chapter explains the indigenous worldview.

The indigenous worldview is held by very few people today. Indigenous peoples are any ethnic group who share a similar ethnic identity and inhabit a geographic region with which they have the earliest known historical connection.[2] The adjective "indigenous" has the common meaning of "from" or of "original origin." Therefore, in a sense, any given people, ethnic group or community may be described as being indigenous in reference to some particular region or location. Indigenous peoples are usually a politically underprivileged group whose ethnic identity is different from the nation in power and who were an ethnic entity in the locality before the present ruling nation took over power.[3] Other terms used to describe indigenous peoples are aborigines, first people, native people, aboriginal, or Native Americans or Indians in the U.S. However, the preferred term, indigenous peoples, appears to be used by different international agencies, such as the United Nations, and will be used here.

Indigenous societies are found in every inhabited climate zone of the world, from small farming villages in India and Africa, to Native American pueblos in the southwestern United States, to farming and herding communities high in the Himalayas, to nomadic groups in the African savannah, and to remote groups in the far arctic reaches of Canada and Alaska. Indigenous societies range from those who have been significantly exposed to modern influences, such as the Maya peoples of Mexico and Central America, to those who as yet remain in comparative isolation from any external influence, such as the Sentinelese and Jarawa of the Andaman Islands in the Bay of Bengal to the east of India.

The total world population of indigenous peoples is hard to estimate given the difficulties of identification and inadequate census data, but estimates at the start of the twenty-first century range from 300 million to 350 million. This would be just under six percent of the total world population. This total number includes at least 5,000 distinct peoples in over seventy-two countries.[4]

Indigenous peoples today survive in populations ranging from only a few dozen to hundreds of thousands or more. Many groups have undergone a dramatic decline and some have even been entirely destroyed, while others remain threatened. Some groups have also been assimilated by modern populations, while in other cases, indigenous populations are undergoing a recovery or expansion in numbers. Some indigenous societies no longer live on the land of their ancestors because of migration, relocation, forced resettlement, or having their land taken by others. In many cases, the changes for indigenous groups are ongoing and include permanent loss of language, loss of lands, intrusion onto traditional territories, pollution of traditional lands, and disruption in traditional ways of life.

In the past and even today, many indigenous peoples have been subject to intense discrimination by Europeans or other people holding a modern worldview. The modern societies, who held superior warfare technology and immunity to many deadly diseases, derisively labeled indigenous people as primitive, inferior, savage, uncivilized, backward, undeveloped, ignorant, and other derogatory terms. Through education and greater awareness, these labels have been largely jettisoned and replaced with terms such as indigenous peoples, which do not hold an evaluative judgment of superior or inferior.

Even though their number is small and the modern perception of inferiority still continues among some, inclusion of their worldview is important since they have successfully survived for thousands of years compared to modern society that has continued for a mere 500 years. They have much wisdom to share with all of us.

Because of the systematic destruction of indigenous cultures during the Modern Wave (1500 onward), the United Nations (UN) has taken up their cause. The UN General Assembly adopted the Declaration on the Rights of Indigenous Peoples in September 2007, a process stretching back to 1982. The non-binding declaration outlines the individual and collective rights of indigenous peoples, as well as their rights to identity, culture, language, employment, health, education, and other issues. Four nations with significant indigenous populations voted against the declaration: the United States, Canada, New Zealand, and Australia. In 2004, the United Nations General Assembly declared 2005-2014 to be the Second International Decade of the World's Indigenous People. The main goal during this decade was to improve international cooperation around resolving the problems faced by indigenous peoples in areas such as culture, education, health, human rights, the environment, and social and economic development.[5]

The United Nations has not adopted any official definition of "indigenous" considering the diversity of indigenous peoples. Instead, the UN has developed an understanding of indigenous based on the characteristics below.[6]

One characteristic of indigenous people is that they reached a social and technological plateau hundreds to thousands of years ago (although many have recently adopted modern technology so this characteristic may no longer apply). Many indigenous groups rely upon subsistence-based production using pastoral (herding), horticultural (simple agriculture), and/or hunting and gathering techniques. Many live in non-urbanized societies, although this is changing as well. Indigenous societies may be either settled in a given locale or region or follow a nomadic lifestyle.

Seven Characteristics of Indigenous People

1. Self-identification as indigenous peoples at the individual level and accepted by the community as their member

2. Historical continuity with pre-colonial and/or pre-settler societies

3. Strong link to territories and surrounding natural resources

4. Distinct social, economic, or political systems

5. Distinct language, culture, and beliefs

6. Members of non-dominant groups of society

7. Protection of ancestral environments and systems as distinctive peoples and communities

---

A few indigenous people continue to observe an ancient hunting and gathering or foraging way of life in which their material possessions are few. Following a nomadic way of life, they must rely on nature for all of their material wants and needs. Their social structure is usually egalitarian with women having equal status, their kinship bonds are strong, and elders are respected as wise leaders. This way of life is practiced by people such as the !Kung in southwest Africa and Mbuti in the forest regions of the Congo who have continued their traditional ways for thousands of years. Other examples of indigenous peoples include herders who move their camps in order for their animals to feed on fresh pastures. Some still survive on the Mongolian steppes, but their way of life is also rapidly changing.

Many traditional agricultural people have historically been self-sufficient in supplying their own food and other needs, but this way of life is being eroded by the increasing commercialization and globalization of agriculture and animal husbandry. As a result, many traditional people have migrated to cities from "underdeveloped" areas of the world. Some people in villages and herding camps have been able to survive but also work at jobs that pay a wage in order to purchase basic needs in a cash economy. Even though this "hybrid" approach does not replicate agriculture or herding people of the last several thousand years, many are able to preserve their cultural traditions, close family networks, and indigenous religious traditions as much as possible in the face of mounting pressures from the "outside," globalized world.

CLASHING WORLDVIEWS: MODERN AND INDIGENOUS

The Story of a Mexican Fisherman

An American banker stood at the pier of a small coastal Mexican village when a small boat with just one fisherman docked. Inside the small boat were several large yellowfin tuna. The American complimented the Mexican on the quality of his fish and asked how long it took to catch them.

The Mexican replied, "Only a little while." The American then asked why he didn't stay out longer and catch more fish. The Mexican said he had enough to support his family's immediate needs. The American then asked, "But what do you do with the rest of your time?"

The Mexican fisherman said, "I sleep late, fish a little, play with my children, take siestas with my wife, Maria, stroll into the village each evening where I sip mezcal and play guitar with my amigos. I have a full and busy life." The American scoffed, "I have an MBA from Harvard and I could help you. You should spend more time fishing and with the proceeds buy a bigger boat. With the proceeds from the bigger boat, you could buy several boats, and eventually you would have a fleet of fishing boats. Instead of selling your catch to a middleman you would sell directly to the processor, eventually opening your own cannery. You would control the product, processing, and distribution. You would need to leave this small coastal fishing village and move to Mexico City, then L.A. and eventually New York City, where you will run your expanding enterprise."

The Mexican fisherman asked, "But, how long will this all take?"

To which the American replied, "15 to 20 years."

"But what then?" asked the Mexican.

The American laughed and said, "That's the best part. When the time is right you would announce an IPO and sell your company stock to the public and become very rich. You would make millions!"

"Millions—then what?"

The American said, "Then you would retire. Move to a small coastal fishing village where you would sleep late, fish a little, play with your kids, take siestas with your wife, stroll to the village in the evenings where you could sip mezcal and play your guitar with your amigos."[7]

Indigenous people have been under pressure over the last hundred years, and especially since the end of World War II, to change their way of life to conform to modern ways of living, a process often called modernization. On the surface this seems like a simple switch, with traditional people acquiring a few additional material possessions that would presumably make their life more comfortable. However, modernization efforts profoundly change the indigenous deep-seated way of life.

The following is a look at the economic, social, religious, political, psychological, and environmental changes that traditional people undergo when adapting a modern way of life. A comparison of the modern and indigenous worldviews highlights the stark differences between the two worldviews. With this comparison, we can better understand both the indigenous and modern ways of living and why many indigenous people have resisted modernization; for those who have accepted modernization, we will see the difficulties they face in making the transition to a different way of life.

INDIGENOUS AND MODERN ECONOMIC DIFFERENCES

Modernizers pressure indigenous people to change their economy in several ways. The use of machine power instead of animal or human power illustrates moving from the simple to the complex use of technology. Since many indigenous people are farmers, there is a push for them to substitute tractors and gas-powered machines to do the work they traditionally did through their own human labor and harnessed animal power. Modernizers want farmers to become more productive and efficient in their farming methods and produce a more abundant crop, usually a commercial crop for the world market. But for small farmers to be more productive, one of the changes they must undertake is to use modern, labor-saving machinery. However, tractors and other farm machinery need technical expertise to maintain operations; therefore, farmers must be trained as mechanics or rely on outside mechanics to maintain the machinery for them. Also, fuel for the machines and the machines themselves must be purchased at world market prices; hence, farmers must participate in the market place to obtain cash to purchase these items. Cash is usually earned by converting subsistence crops to growing cash crops. The cash crops are sold on the world market for market prices that fluctuate dramatically from year to year and even month to month.

The self-sufficient farmer does not need cash for farming and, therefore, does not borrow money from banks or other money lenders. But if the farmer participates in the global economy, cash is needed for machinery, seed, pesticides, fertilizers, and more land to expand farming operations. To borrow money the farmer needs some type of collateral for the bank loan. The only collateral available is usually the land that is probably part of collective land the group holds communally. Modernizers push traditional farmers to privatize their communal land into individual plots that have a monetary value and can be bought and sold. If a farmer uses privately-held land for collateral for a loan, he faces the risk of losing it if his crops fail to bring in the needed revenue for repayment of the loan's principal and interest. Now, the formerly self-sufficient farmer is transformed into a farmer dependent on the world market and credit system for his livelihood.

Since market farming favors economies of scale, many small farmers are not able to make a living as market farmers and end up losing their land. Without a way to make a living, many reluctantly move from their traditional rural villages to large urban centers for jobs, and, most likely, from self-sufficiency to poverty status. Other desperate small farmers seek work on large agricultural plantations that grow cash crops on a vast scale. They earn a low wage for their labor and live in housing, often squalid, provided by absentee landowners.

INDIGENOUS AND MODERN SOCIAL DIFFERENCES

Indigenous people also experience profound change in their social relations. For example, in traditional societies social relationships tend to be personal and emotional, and interaction is face-to-face. Economic negotiations are conducted with the implicit purpose of maintaining social associations, and a person's word or handshake is a ritual for an agreed-upon transaction. In modern societies social relationships are neutral, impersonal, detached, and indirect. These social relations make it possible for efficient market associations to take place, while legal, written contracts replace the handshake or a verbal agreement as a way to seal a transaction.

The indigenous family is a network of complex, multi-layered relationships and responsibilities. The family provides emotional support for all members, oversees marriage and reproduction, performs informal socialization and education, cares for the welfare of the elderly and young, and performs religious functions. The modern family is small and nuclear and has very different and reduced functions and responsibilities compared to indigenous families. Education, religion, care of the elderly, and medicine are four areas in which traditional and modern people differ.

For the modern family, care of the young is shared with specific institutions that take over the responsibility of formal education and preparing children for work in a market economy. Schools, either private or state-sponsored, provide care and education for children who are sometimes as young as a few weeks old to young adults in graduate schools who are well into their twenties and beyond. Modern, formal education practices, such as the push to eradicate illiteracy and introduce the young to scientific principles and Western values, are an effort to inculcate indigenous people with modern ideals. Indigenous education that emphasizes self-sufficiency, traditional crafts, and how to function in a traditional society has been devalued.

Indigenous families care for the elderly. The elderly are highly regarded for their wisdom and experiences and are leaders in the community. In contrast, modern societies have created the concept of retirement for the elderly. Around the age of sixty-five, the elderly retire from their work and pursue a life of leisure and hobbies if financially able. Some head off to "retirement communities," where they live with other retirees, not their children, in a cocoon separated from the outside world. For some the retirement years are banal and unfulfilling, and many yearn to be more productive members of their communities. Modern society emphasizes youth and youthful beauty, and often seniors are publicly ridiculed as senile or "out of touch." Older seniors are often separated into state or private corporate facilities designated especially for their care, often called nursing homes, where they are largely forgotten. The elders' years of experience, leadership, and wisdom go largely untapped by modern society.

INDIGENOUS AND MODERN RELIGIOUS DIFFERENCES

Religious functions in indigenous societies are integrated into all aspects of community life and serve people in closely-knit villages and families. Shaman or healers traditionally perform religious rituals and healing ceremonies and guide the practice of ancestor worship. In modern societies, religious functions are the responsibility of institutions outside the family who train religious leaders. Modernizers have often ridiculed indigenous medicines and healing practices as superstitious and unscientific, while modern medicines and practices are promoted. This mockery has been changing in recent decades, as practices such as Chinese medicine, acupuncture, massage, and shamanic healing have proven beneficial to some patients.

Modernizers have sought for hundreds of years to rid indigenous peoples of their traditional religions and impose one of their universal religions, such as one of the forms of Christianity, Islam, Judaism, or Buddhism. In order to appease their conquerors, many indigenous peoples have blended their traditional, animistic beliefs with one of the universal religions, a blending called syncretism.

INDIGENOUS AND MODERN POLITICAL DIFFERENCES

The political changes experienced by indigenous peoples as they modernize are quite disruptive. These changes involve replacing the traditional religious, family, and ethnic political authorities with a single, secular, national political leader. A decentralized, local political system is replaced with a modern, highly centralized government, complete with a large bureaucracy and written laws. Loyalty to the extended family and tribe is supposed to shift to an allegiance to state and political parties. A modern political system requires diverse social groups to come together to form working coalitions of different political parties. These parties then compete in a voting procedure for political rule with the winner selected as the elected leader.

A large centralized government requires a complex bureaucracy in order to function smoothly. Some upper-level indigenous workers in the bureaucracy are formally educated in the functions of a modern state system. Often, the education for this indigenous elite is obtained overseas in Western educational institutions, such as in the United States or Europe. The educated indigenous people return to their country of origin intent on changing the indigenous political system to what they consider the superior, modern one they learned about while in the West.

An impersonal, legal structure is typical of modern political exchanges, which is usually alien to indigenous peoples. Untold numbers of indigenous people have had their land swindled by intricate legal technicalities that they are unfamiliar with or that are not compatible with their worldview as to how agreements are conducted. In the United States in the 1890s, for example, native people known as the Five Civilized Tribes were displaced onto reservations in Oklahoma, according to the provisions of the Dawes Act of 1887. Eager white settlers rushed onto the tribes' territory to stake a proprietary claim on what they deemed "unsettled" land. Native people faced additional pressure to "give up" their land when oil was discovered on the Oklahoma parcels that were previously thought to be of no value. Lawyers descended like locusts on

Tulsa, Oklahoma, to defraud tribal people of their claim to land according to a corrupt legal system. Of course, the lawyers made a great deal of money in their deceitful endeavors.

INDIGENOUS AND MODERN PSYCHOLOGICAL DIFFERENCES

The psychological changes that accompany modernization are perhaps the most unsettling for indigenous people who must accept modern values instead of the traditional values that have served the community for generations. Probably the most significant change in values is the increased focus on self-orientation and individualism—the modern individual—rather than a focus on the collective or group orientation of indigenous peoples. The modern individual is socialized to be independent, active, and open to new experiences, interested in public policies and cultural matters, and concerned with long-term, future plans. Traditional individuals are socialized to be passive and accept traditions of the group, think in the present and short-term, defer decisions to group leaders, and stay rooted in their local place. Modern individuals have a mobile personality and readily adapt to a rapidly changing world, even if it means relocating to a different place apart from their family. Modern individuals are socialized to strive for an achieved status—through education and hard work—and understand that there is the potential to become something different in the future. Indigenous individuals, on the other hand, generally follow their ascribed status to which they are born.

An indigenous person often experiences the disruptive forces of modernization, which tend to produce alienation, anomie, and psychological disintegration. Alienation is the state in which individuals feel separated or detached from their past experiences, family, or group. They are forced or pressured to create a new modern identity which can lead to physiological stress, often resulting in an increase in violence and conflict. For example, the increased incidences, especially among indigenous men, of alcoholism, drug addiction, and abuse of family members repeatedly accompany the transition from traditional to modern societies. One source of violence in these societies is the gap between new aspirations that individuals strive for (and are told they need through advertising) and their ability to satisfy these aspirations while remaining marginalized from mainstream society.

INDIGENOUS AND MODERN ENVIRONMENTAL DIFFERENCES

The concepts of subsistence, sustainability, and land ownership are seen differently by people holding modern and indigenous worldviews. Modernizers see land as a commodity that can be bought and sold, privately owned, and valued on a monetary basis. Commodification of land is in keeping with modern economic views that apply capitalist principles to every aspect of life. Indigenous views of land are quite different. Groups own land collectively, with no individual private ownership. Although families may farm the same plot of land over the years, there is no notion that the land belongs to them. In countries with large indigenous populations, laws protect collective ownership. For example, in nine of the 12 countries of South America at least 20 percent of the land is legally in indigenous and peasant hands under a collective legal system.[8]

Sustainability or resource preservation is more compatible with the indigenous worldview than with the modern. Continuity is a practice guiding many indigenous beliefs (at least in the past). There is not an impulse to exploit resources for growth and instant gratification, rather the attitude of preserving resources for future generations. A motto among many indigenous peoples is that all actions must be guided with the well-being of future generations in mind.

GROWING UP IN AN INDIGENOUS SOCIETY: THE STORY OF RIGOBERTA MENCHU

We Indians never do anything which goes against the laws of our ancestors....
Rigoberta Menchu

The childhood story of Rigoberta Menchu, who grew up in the country of Guatemala, is an example of an indigenous culture that is quite different from modern culture. In a sense, she speaks for all indigenous peoples of the American continent. The cultural discrimination she suffered is something that all the continent's indigenous peoples have experienced since the European conquest. She has witnessed discrimination and survived violence aimed at destroying her family, community, and culture. Yet, she is determined to break the silence and to confront the extermination of her people.

Menchu belongs to the Quiche people (a branch of the Mayans), one of the largest of the 23 ethnic groups in Guatemala, each having its own language. Born on January 9, 1959 in the hamlet of Chimel on the Altiplano (highlands) to a peasant family, who lived in a village in the northwestern Guatemalan province of El Quiche, she was immersed in the Mayan culture. In her autobiography, *I, Rigoberta Menchu*, she tells the story of the Guatemalan people and her personal experiences, which are, in essence, the reality of a whole people. Colonial powers have historically oppressed her people, and she is determined that the sacrifices her family and community have made to fight this oppression will not have been in vain. She makes it clear that "Latin Americans are only too ready to denounce the unequal relations that exist between ourselves and North America, but we tend to forget that … we too are involved in relations that can only be described as colonial. In countries with a large Indian population, there is an internal colonialism which works to the detriment of the indigenous population."[9]

Rigoberta Menchu felt that living in the village of Chimel as a child was paradise. The village had no major roads and no cars. People could only reach it by foot or horseback. Her parents moved to Chimel in 1960 and began cultivating the mountainous terrain. It was a hard life but her family decided to stay. They had been forced to leave their previous hometown because *ladinos* (Guatemalans of mixed Spanish and Indian ancestry) settled there and gradually took control. Her parents spent all they earned and accumulated so much debt that finally they had to leave their house to pay the *ladinos*.

Rigoberta's father had a very hard life. His father died when he was a child, leaving his wife to raise three small boys. Rigoberta's grandmother went to work as a servant for the town's only wealthy family, while the boys did small jobs around the house, such as carrying wood and water and tending animals. As they grew into young men, her employer didn't want to keep feeding them, so her grandmother had to give away her eldest son, Rigoberta's father, to a man who fed and worked him. Her father soon left that situation and found a job on a plantation growing coffee, cotton, and sugar cane. He sent for his mother and brothers to live with him. They earned very little money but they were together and finally able to save enough to move to the high country. Shortly after the move, Rigoberta' grandmother became ill and died. The brothers decided to split up, and the army forcibly recruited her father.

After her father's discharge from the army, her parents met and soon after married. Her mother also came from a very poor family who lived in the Altiplano. The couple moved about looking for work. Then, her parents scraped together enough money to pay a fee to the government to cultivate land in the Altiplano. Since it took many long, hard years of working the land to finally produce crops, her parents had to travel down to the coast to work on the plantations for an income.

The family grew rapidly; Rigoberta was the sixth of nine children. Like other indigenous families, the children suffered from malnutrition. Most children didn't reach the age of 15 years old. When she was a little girl she remembered spending only four months in the family's home in the Altiplano and the rest of the year working on the coastal plantations. Only a few families owned the vast plantations producing cash crops that were sold abroad. Poor families like the Menchus tended the crops, a harsh life that her parents and others endured for many years.

The birth of a baby was very significant for the community, as it belonged to all, not just the parents. Her mother, a midwife, helped women give birth at home; villagers considered it a scandal to have a child in the hospital. The community baptized a newborn even before the parents took the infant to church. The newborn's hands were tied for eight days, which symbolized that one should not accumulate things the rest of the community does not have. On the eighth day the child's hands were untied; the open hands meant the baby had learned how to share and be generous. The family taught each child how to live like fellow members of its community; no one had more than others.

In Menchu's community there were highly respected elected representatives who acted as a father and mother to the whole village. Her mother and father were the village's representatives and mother and father for all the children of the village.

Rigoberta's fellow villagers were Catholic, but they saw the religion as just another channel of spiritual expression. They didn't totally trust all the priests, monks, and nuns of the church. They believed that the sun was the father, and the moon was the mother. Rigoberta felt that the Catholic Church has tried to "keep her people in their place," but as Christians they gradually acquired an understanding of their rights and dignity. She thinks "that unless a religion springs from within the people themselves, it is a weapon of the system."[10]

When the family traveled to work on the plantations, they took all the necessities for their stay—bedding, cooking utensils, and clothing. Sometimes employers paid them by the day and sometimes for the amount of work done. If a child accidentally broke a branch of a coffee bush, the worker had to work to cover the damages. Children who did not work did not earn any pay and were not fed. The little ones who worked got a ration of tortillas. Rigoberta's mother shared her ration of food with her children.

The plantation owners ran a cantina that sold food, alcohol, and sweets. The children always pestered their parents for sweets, cakes, and soft drinks. The prices were marked on an account, and at the end of the work period when the workers were paid, they had to settle their debt, which was always substantial. Workers often got drunk at the cantina and piled up huge debts. They often spent most of their wages just paying off the debt. Rigoberta sadly remembered her father and mother going to the cantina out of despair. She commented, "[H]e hurt himself twice over because his money went back to the landowner. That's why they set up the cantina anyway."[11]

When Rigoberta turned eight she started to earn money on the plantation by picking coffee, and when the family returned to their mountain home, she worked in the fields growing maize (corn). The plantation work was very hard and her parents were usually exhausted. She noted that most of the women who worked picking cotton and coffee had nine or ten children. Of these, three or four were healthy and would survive, but most of them had swollen bellies from malnutrition and the mother knew that some of her children would die. Even Rigoberta's brother died from malnutrition. Men who had been in the army often abused young girls. Many girls had no families and turned to prostitution. She was sad to see this happen since prostitution did not exist in Indian culture.

Rigoberta celebrated her tenth birthday in the Altiplano. Her parents explained her responsibilities and that soon she would be a woman who could start having children. On her twelfth birthday, it was the custom to receive a gift of a small animal to raise; her father gave her a pig. She sold weavings that she did in her spare time, after working in the fields all day, to get enough money to buy food for her pig.

Rigoberta's community respected many things connected with the natural world. Water, for example, was considered sacred to her community. She explained, "Water is pure, clean, and gives life to humans. The same is true for the earth. The earth is mother of humans, because she gives us food. Her people eat maize, beans and vegetables; they cannot eat things made with equipment or machines. That is why they ask the earth's permission to sow maize and beans."[12] Copa, the resin of a tree, was a sacred ingredient in candles for her people. The candles gave off a strong, smoky, delicious aroma when burned, and they were used in ceremonies to represent the earth, water, and maize. They prayed to their ancestors and recited ancient prayers. Their grandfathers said they must ask the sun to shine on all its children: the trees, animals, water, man, and enemies. To them, an enemy was someone who steals or goes into prostitution.

A happy moment in village life was when the farmers planted maize. They had a fiesta in which they asked the earth's permission to cultivate her. They lit candles and offered prayers and then blessed the seeds for sowing. According to the ritual, they honored the seed because they buried it in the sacred earth and by the next year it would multiply and bear fruit. They did the same with beans. When the maize started growing on their farms, they traveled down to work on the plantations. When they came back, the maize had reached maturity. Maize was the center of their culture; they believed they were made of maize. They thanked mother earth for the harvest. After they harvested their crops, they all gathered together for a feast.

Every village had a community house where all assembled to celebrate their faith, to pray, and to enjoy special ceremonies and fiestas. They all worked communally to clear bush in the mountains, and when sowing time came, the community met to discuss how to share the land, whether each one would have their own plot or if they would work it collectively. Everyone joined in the discussion. In Rigoberto's village, the villagers decided to have their own plots of land but also to keep a shared, communal piece of land. If anyone was ill or injured, they would have food to eat from the communal land. It mostly helped widows. Each day of the week, someone would work the communal land.

Rigoberta saw a stark difference between indigenous and modern education. To indigenous people, nature was the teacher. Her father was very suspicious of modern schools and said that once people learned to read and write, they weren't any use to the community anymore. They moved away and were indifferent toward their community. Rigoberta wanted to go to school to learn to read and write. Her father said she would have to learn on her own since he had no money for her education. He thought she was trying to leave the community and was concerned that she would forget her heritage. She still insisted she wanted to learn. Despite her father's misgivings, she sporadically attended a Catholic school.

As an adult, Rigoberta suffered a great deal at the hands of the government and military who wanted to suppress her work and exploit her people. In response to the suffering she witnessed she dictated her autobiography, *I, Rigoberta Menchu* (1984), to tell the world not only about her own story but also about the lives of her fellow indigenous people. Her book and her social justice campaign brought international attention to the conflict between indigenous people and the military government of Guatemala. In 1992, she was awarded the Nobel Peace Prize and used the $1.2 million cash prize to set up a foundation to continue the fight for human rights of indigenous peoples. Due to her efforts, the United Nations declared 1993 the International Year for Indigenous Populations. Menchu now serves as a UNESCO Goodwill Ambassador and is a figure in indigenous political parties.

CONCLUDING INSIGHTS: THE INDIGENOUS WORLDVIEW

Indigenous peoples often have much in common with other neglected segments of societies, such as lack of political representation and participation, poverty, lack of access to social services, and discrimination. Despite their cultural differences, indigenous peoples share common problems related to the protection of their rights. They strive for recognition of their identities, their ways of life, and their right to traditional lands, territories, and natural resources.

Indigenous peoples are the holders of unique languages, knowledge systems, and beliefs and possess invaluable knowledge of practices for the sustainable management of natural resources. They have a special relation to their land and its traditional uses. Their ancestral lands have a fundamental importance for their collective physical and cultural survival. Indigenous peoples hold their own diverse concepts of development, based on their traditional values, visions, needs, and priorities. They have much to teach.

Chapter 5
The Traditional Worldview

Tradition is a guide and not a jailer. ... W. Somerset Maugham

What do religious fundamentalists, political conservatives, and the populist right have in common? They are all part of the Traditional Worldview. A traditionalist is a person who supports the established customs and beliefs of his or her society or group and does not want to change them. While change is a major focus among progressives, continuity is a theme among traditionalists. This worldview encompasses seemingly disparate ideas that often coalesce at election time in the United States to put forth a slate of candidates who represent different elements of this worldview. Donald Trump pulled together what seemed like an incompatible coalition in the 2016 election. In this chapter, I will describe four groups who all contributed to Trump's win—traditional political conservatives, the populist right, white nationalists, and religious fundamentalists—with more emphasis on religious fundamentalists, the largest group.

TRADITIONAL POLITICAL CONSERVATISM

Conservatives believe in the ties that bind us. Society is stronger when we make vows to each other and we support each other. ... David Cameron

The forces of traditional conservatism are with us today. Although battered and diminished by the energy of progress sweeping through the nineteenth and twentieth centuries, conservatism plods along reminding people along the way that traditions and institutions are not to be haphazardly cast aside and that many contain bits of wisdom that have survived through the ages. Many conservatives do not wish to return to the past just for the sake of a return; instead they want to find out what is eternally true, eternally valid, and then restore it, regardless of whether it seems obsolete, ancient, current, or even brand new.[1]

Traditional political conservatism is about conserving society, the good sentiments that conservatives believe can be too hastily and easily destroyed. It is a political philosophy emphasizing the bonds of social order over hyper-individualism and the defense of ancestral customs, traditions, and institutions, such as the church (or other religious institutions), as unifying establishments. Traditions provide a stabilizing force to help individuals, families, communities, and the nation withstand the winds of rapid technological, economic, and social changes. They are the moral and ethical glue offering guidance and solidity for those seeking meaning in a world that often seems hollow and pointless.

The modern political philosophy of conservatism traces its ideas to the work of eighteenth century English statesmen Edmund Burke, who is widely regarded as the philosophical founder of the conservative ideology. Burke stressed the importance of underpinning virtues and manners in society as well as the importance of religious institutions for the moral stability of the state. For example, Burke articulated his support for the American colonists who were expressing grievances targeted at the government of British King George III. He proposed resolutions to peacefully settle disagreements with the colonies, but his efforts were largely unsuccessful. Burke later on staunchly rejected the French Revolution, which rocked the monarchy and Catholic Church in France from 1789-1815. He asserted that the revolution was destroying the fabric of good society and the traditional institutions of state and society. He also condemned the maltreatment of the Catholic Church that resulted from it.

Through the nineteenth century conservatism was linked to support for the monarchy, church, and nobility. After these institutions were defeated in the push to political liberalism by the rising middle class, conservatism took on a different definition. It meant preserving traditions, customs, religion, and social arrangements of the past. In the United States, it meant supporting large and small business owners who were in opposition to wage laborers working in factories. Conservatism lay dormant under the cloud of the depression years and World War II.

After the war, a group of conservatives, collectively known as the "New Conservatives," gained national attention by admonishing New Deal progressive economics, a mushrooming military-industrial complex, and rampant consumerism. A key figure of the New Conservatives, Russell Kirk, laid out conservative thought in his seminal book *The Conservative Man*. He argued that political problems were essentially religious and moral problems and highlighted the importance of tradition as a check upon human impulses. He admired traditional life as varied and colorful as opposed to what he saw as the conformity of leftist ideologies. Kirk emphasized hierarchical social classes as a necessity in maintaining order and the rule of law in a civilized society. He also recognized that change and reform were not identical, and stressed the importance that reform should be gradual.[2]

Roger Scruton was a noted conservative thinker and author on British and American conservative ideas. When asked how he became a conservative, he explained that when he looked out his apartment window while living in Paris in 1968 and saw crowds of demonstrators torching buildings and overturning cars, he vowed that he would be against whatever the protesters were for. Since that time he has held disdain for leftist ideas and violent protests. His conservative philosophy is summarized in this quote:

Conservatism starts from a sentiment that all mature people can readily share: the sentiment that good things are easily destroyed, but not easily created. This is especially true of the good things that come to us as collective assets: peace, freedom, law, civility, public spirit, the security of property and family life, in all of which we depend on the cooperation of others while having no means singlehandedly to obtain it. In respect of such things, the work of destruction is quick, easy and exhilarating; the work of creation slow, laborious and dull. That is one of the lessons of the twentieth century. It is also one reason why conservatives suffer such a disadvantage when it comes to public opinion. Their position is true but boring, that of their opponents exciting but false.[3]

Another preeminent conservative, William F. Buckley (d. 2008), established the *National Review* in 1955, a well-respected conservative journal still in operation. Buckley worked tirelessly to define conservatism as a political movement in which American religious and social traditions have a central voice and ideas have a leading role. He also sought to distance conservatism from anti-Semitism and racism, an association that unfortunately continues today. He firmly believed that all Americans should be included in upholding religious and social traditions, as well as the institutions of government as the Founding Fathers, as he believed, conceived them.[4]

Conservatives found a presidential candidate representing their core principles in the 1964 election, Senator Barry Goldwater from Arizona. To the dismay of conservatives, he was soundly defeated by Lyndon Johnson, a liberal Democrat who enacted sweeping social programs and expanded the war in Vietnam. The conservative movement went underground for the rest of the decade and into the 1970s. As the economic crisis of the 1970s worsened, liberals were stymied as to the right course of action to solve it. All the while, conservatives were building institutions, formulating ideas, and cultivating political leaders. They emerged victorious in the 1980 presidential election with the convincing victory of the affable and skilled politician, Ronald Reagan. Although not a "true" traditional conservative himself, he cemented his victory by putting in place a winning coalition of traditional political conservatives, Christian fundamentalists, a nascent populist right, and neoliberals championing free-market economics. It was a coalition that would endure for thirty-five years.

It can be argued that the last of the political conservative presidents in the U.S. was George H.W. Bush, who was elected in 1988 after serving as Ronald Reagan's vice-president for two terms. He positioned himself as an institutionalist, not an ideologue, who vowed to make government work. He reached out to Democrats in a way that now seems inconceivable, leading to the passage of the landmark Americans with Disability Act and a Clean Air Act amendment, as well as agreeing to tax increases to lower the deficit. His institutional instincts served him well in his foreign policy approach, where he dealt with monumental events such as the end of the Cold War and Iraq's invasion of Kuwait. He skillfully forged alliances and steered international organizations like NATO and the United Nations to achieve his foreign policy objectives.[5]

Conservatism today has become a defender of Western civilization against leftist critics who disparage the achievements of the Western tradition. The left takes a more negative and critical view of Western tradition, criticizing it as oppressive, colonialist, and focused on seizing and controlling power. Critics of the Western tradition derisively label traditionalists as holding ideas of "dead, white men," and dismiss their contributions as irrelevant and backward. Conservatives decry political correctness as a constraint on freedom of expression and reject its emphasis on Western guilt for past colonial exploits.[6]

Economically, many political conservatives shifted their slower growth economic stances of the 1950s-1960s to embrace neoliberal principles of a free-market, laissez-faire type of economic system that rose to dominance in the 1980s. Neoliberalism favors free trade, lower corporate taxes, and few government regulations of the economy. Although many self-styled conservatives still adhere to neoliberal policies, today many are questioning the benefits of this system and turning to other economic forms. Today, many conservatives are advancing the economic ideas of the populist right in which they speak out against the neoliberal, globalized economic system and favor a more local, regional, and national system. I will cover the global economy in Chapter 7, the Globalized Worldview.

Karen Stenner has identified three kinds of conservatism: authoritarianism, laissez-faire conservatism, and status quo conservatism. The later kind would apply to the traditional political conservatism described in this section. Status quo conservatives are averse to change, which is the reason they want to preserve customs and traditions of the past. According to Stenner, status quo conservatism is apparently partly a function of "conscientiousness." She concludes that "there is evidence that conscientiousness—associated with rigidity, orderliness, and a compulsion about being in control of one's environment—promotes conservatism to a considerable degree."[7] Often this personality type is attributable to increasing age, given that aging is generally associated with increasing rigidity, intolerance of uncertainty, and discomfort with new experiences. Stenner

73

goes on to say that "status quo conservatives and authoritarians may converge when their interests for rejection of change and intolerance/complexity collide. For status quo conservatives social stability is more important than striving for oneness and sameness, and aversion to change trumps aversion to difference."[8]

The preservation of customs and traditions is the center point of conservatism. These traditions include the importance of a two-parent family, marriage as an institution, and religious organizations that provide social norms and mores to guide moral human behaviors and curb impulsive destructive actions. Although conservatives do not reject all change, in their view it should be gradual and moderate. Scruton states that the "philosophical burden of American conservatism has been to define those customs and traditions and to show how they might endure and flourish from their own inner dynamic, outside the control of the state."[9]

The Reagan coalition held until the 2016 presidential election. In the Republican primary, Donald Trump obliterated the Reagan conservative establishment candidates and heralded a populist right form of conservatism that held few of the principles of the old traditional conservative coalition. Even the globalists, who had latched on to both the Democratic and Republican parties with a firm grip, were diminished by the populist storm. Even though Democratic candidate Hilary Clinton tried to distance herself from her globalist past and take on a new persona as a bona-fide populist on the left, Trump exploited her weakness in this area and went on to not only defeat her but also to defeat globalism, neoliberalism, and traditional conservatism in the monumental election of 2016.

The twenty-first century has witnessed a period of rapid and profound changes in which familiar institutions and traditions are under assault by forces on the political right and left. Throughout world history, after periods of intense change, there is often a return to continuity. Perhaps the promise of political conservativism will once again provide answers people are searching for today.

THE POPULIST RIGHT

The Populist Right has swept onto the global stage as a powerful political force that demands our attention. One of the key characteristics of the Populist Right is that its followers are against the established elite. For those on the right, the elite consist of globalizers, a progressive media, academics on the left, and left-leaning, highly-educated professionals. They intensely despise the upper 20 percent of the population according to income who are considered the highly educated, progressive meritocracy. Populists purportedly speak for the "common man" and have his interests at heart when devising political policies. In Chapter 2 I gave an overview of the ideas of populism on both the right and left. In this section I will concentrate on the Populist Right.

A number of factors are intertwining to create a tidal wave of discontent among many groups in the United States. These forces are in part powering the rise of the Populist Right (and the left to a lesser degree). I briefly outlined ten factors in Chapter 1 that are relevant to our discussion, but I will summarize four factors below that I have found have adversely affected those who hold a Traditional/Populist Right worldview.

Since the 1980s, the U.S. has led a globalization agenda guided by neoliberal principles. Economic globalization, in particular, has spread around the world. This globalization/neoliberal process has had wide-reaching consequences and has been characterized by four major shifts in the U.S. First, many national corporations have sent their manufacturing operations to low-wage countries, particularly in China, to increase profit margins. This shift, along with automation, has resulted in the decline of working class income. As a result, historic levels of income inequality and concentration of wealth at the very top and among the upper 20 percent—the highly-educated, professional class—have occurred. Second, the U.S. government, with corporate blessings, ignored illegal immigration and refused to pass immigration laws in order to have a supply of cheap labor at home to bolster profits and create a bulwark against unions. Unclear and confusing immigration laws, along with other factors, have adversely affected a shrinking middle and working class who have experienced stagnant wages and fewer job opportunities. Third, rapid technological changes and automation have created greater efficiencies in the workplace that have eliminated many jobs and disrupted everyday life. These technological advancements have been celebrated by Silicon Valley and the professional elites, but have disrupted jobs and the social fabric of ordinary Americans. And fourth, the changing nature of the nation-state and patriotism influenced by an influx of immigrants and an allegiance by the global elite/educated class to a global rather than local/national agenda has resulted in a disruption of shared core values revolving around a common love of country. Along with this decline in patriotism and a fraying of the social fabric that binds the country together, greater incivility among competing factions has occurred.[10]

These global and national forces have hit all of us in many ways, but arguably the group most negatively affected in the U.S. is the working class and poor who do not hold a college education and live in regions other than the city core areas. Their wages have stagnated for decades and opportunities for well-paying jobs with non-technical skills have also declined. These forces have occurred in many Western countries with results similar to those in the U.S. As the middle and working class grows in Asian countries and other emerging economies, the middle class in Western countries is shrinking.[11] Among this group of Americans, the perception is that they are "getting the shaft." This perception is what fuels their insecurity and anger, and they resent indecipherable academic analyses and statistics that discount their perceptions, since that academic analysis is conducted by the people they distrust the most: educated elites and government researchers.

The Populist Right in the U.S. has its recent roots in the Tea Party movement that started in 2009. The movement rose in response to President Barack Obama's push for universal health care. It was a fiscally conservative political movement within the Republican Party that advocated for lower taxes, a reduction of the national debt, and decreased government spending. They got part of their wish with President Trump's tax law passed in 2017, but as a result of the tax law the national debt and federal budget deficit have exploded.

With all these bubbling tensions simmering in a cauldron of discontent, along came the 2016 presidential election. The frustration of this group of Americans has been building for years, and in the 2016 presidential election it was directed at the political class for ignoring their plight. The Democratic Party, long a champion of the working class, has in recent years turned to the globalizers, technocrats, and upper 20 percent as a core constituency. It hasn't found a way to blend the working class agenda into its platform of contending constituents: young people, immigrants, people of color, LGBTQ, urban, and college-educated. The left, where many encourage immigration—even illegal immigration—has angered the working class, who has experienced competition or perceived competition from these new low-wage workers for a shrinking pool of manufacturing and well-paying but low-skilled jobs.

As indicated from the 2016 presidential election results, it is apparent that the Democratic agenda did not resonate with the needs of the working class. The Reagan Democrats, many of the white working class who switched to Republicans with the 1980 election of Reagan, often switch back and forth between the two parties depending on the candidate and agenda. They voted for Bill Clinton in 1992 and 1996 and Barack Obama in 2008 and 2012. But in a decisive move, many switched to Donald Trump in the 2016 election, especially in the critical "rust belt" states of Michigan, Pennsylvania, Ohio, and Wisconsin.

In early 2016, no one would have imagined that the forces of globalization would be challenged from both the left and right; populism was taking on a left and right variant. The Democratic and Republican parties of old were overshadowed by a new brand of politics: the populist right and left. (I will describe the left in Chapter 6).

On the right, populism had a new leader: Donald Trump. He was different ideologically, psychologically, and emotionally from the other Republican candidates. Spouting populist rhetoric, he pledged to smash through the ideological divide and to "Make America Great Again." It sounded good to enough people who believed him, catapulting a man without any political experience to the highest office in the land, despite his crass outbursts and braggadocio demeanor. At the time of this writing, Trump seems intent on dismantling the levers of liberalism and the checks and balances on his power. He is carrying out a populist agenda point by point.

During his campaign, Trump railed against free trade agreements—the cornerstone of the globalized worldview—that he claimed hurt American workers. He has nixed the Trans-Pacific Free Trade Agreement with Asian counterparts. On occasion he chastises American corporations planning to send jobs to Mexico or overseas. Populists want an end to free trade agreements, such as NAFTA, and a return to bi-lateral trade negotiations. They are in favor of levying a tariff on goods imported into the U.S. from

American firms manufacturing in countries that have taken advantage of low-wage foreign labor. Trump is also bent on righting trade imbalances and intellectual property theft by China by imposing selective tariffs on imported goods. He claims that he is fulfilling his campaign promises to his constituencies; however, the results are mixed.

Globalizers, Republicans and Democrats, have been very supportive of immigration in the last several decades. Immigration has added many pluses to American society by making it more diverse, interesting, and dynamic. The influx of immigrants has also helped the globalization agenda by providing cheap labor for its enterprises and attracting the brightest workers from around the world to the tech industry in Silicon Valley. However, the populist right is firmly against illegal immigration, especially those who breach our southern border. The left seems more ambivalent about immigration, many taking a more open-border stance and muddying the difference between illegal and legal immigration and asylum seekers.

Trump has sworn to stop illegal immigration. Populists cheer when Trump brags about building a wall to further separate Mexico and the U.S. They want to curtail illegal immigration and deport immigrants who are in the U.S. illegally, especially if they have a criminal record. This means approximately 11 million or more illegal immigrants, probably a number too large and costly for deportation efforts. Actually Democrats and Republicans have passed the immigration issue down the line for too long and are largely responsible for the current impasse. Trump appears strong and decisive in talking and acting on an issue the two parties have avoided for decades, while the Democrats' timid decisions and confusing language about immigration make them look weak and vacillating.

THE ALT-RIGHT

A marginal but vocal fringe of the conservative right is made up of loosely connected and ill-defined groups of mostly young men under the umbrella of what is most commonly called the alt-right or alternative right. Although I have found that there is a distinction between the alt-right and populist right, the dividing line is hard to see. It probably can be measured in degrees on the political spectrum with the alt-right landing at the extreme right of the spectrum. Most alt-right followers, I would argue, have authoritarian tendencies, while those on the populist right may not have as intense authoritarian tendencies or the tendencies may lie dormant until activated by destabilizing events.

The current alt-right movement began in 2008. The term was initially promoted in 2010 by white supremacist Richard B. Spencer in reference to a movement centered on white nationalism.[12] The alt-right tag was created in order to soften the image of the white nationalists and help to draw in recruits from mainstream conservatism. Many white nationalists accepted the term to escape the negative implications of "white nationalism."[13] Breitbart News became a popular outlet for alt-right views and became even more popular when Steve Bannon joined the organization in 2012. The journalist Mike Wendling termed it "the chief popular media amplifier of alt-right ideas."[14]

Along with white nationalists, the movement has attracted white supremacists, white separatists, neo-Confederates, neo-Nazis, anti-Semitists, neo-fascists, and other far-right hate groups. Those following an alt-right agenda have the following beliefs in varying degrees: antifeminism and misogyny, isolationism, homophobia, protectionism, identitarianism (anti-immigrant), nativism, xenophobia, and Islamophobia. People who identify with the alt-right regard mainstream or traditional conservatives as weak and ineffectual and prefer a leader who is a "man of action."[15]

Alt-right followers largely reject the American democratic ideal that all should have equality under the law regardless of creed, gender, ethnic origin, or race. They reject multiculturalism, since this concept threatens their notion of white supremacy, and they consistently attack identity politics, which they claim is perpetuated by liberals. The alt-right is broadly secular and many of its members are atheists, or highly skeptical of organized religion.[16]

The alt-right fervently supported the 2016 election of Donald Trump, and their support helped him win in swing states such as Michigan, Pennsylvania, Ohio, and Wisconsin. He has continued to give them at least tacit support for their beliefs, especially involving immigration.

An important alt-right event took place in August 2017, when a Unite the Right rally took place in Charlottesville, Virginia. The event brought together disparate alt-right activists from across the country. Many of them thought that the rally would mark a turning point in changing their movement from an online presence into a street-based one. However, when a right-wing protester willfully rammed his car into counter-protesters, killing one and injuring nineteen others, members on the so-called "alt-right lite" began to question the movement's violent turn. Bringing a great deal of negative publicity to the alt-right participants who attended the rally, they often found themselves facing personal and legal repercussions for their involvement. Internet service providers and mainstream social media websites consequently terminated many of their accounts and sites. The event and its aftermath proved disheartening for many in the movement.[17]

The Unite the Right rally aggravated tensions between the "alt-lite" and the movement's more extremist elements. The alt-right movement saw significant gains in 2015 and 2016, but in 2017 and 2018 it began to experience declining power and membership. The reasons for the fracturing of the movement include a backlash from the Charlottesville rally, more effective monitoring of major hateful social media sites, and widespread opposition by the American public.[18]

There are multiple reasons why the alt-right movement has grown into a noticeable phenomenon. Growing racial activism from the Black Lives Matter movement, race riots in Baltimore and Ferguson, and the shooting of police officers in Dallas and Baton Rouge have all contributed to growing tensions. Increasing social anxiety is also a likely contributing factor, in particular the belligerent actions of "social justice warriors" who shout down speakers at universities that they deem unacceptable. Trump supporters have been harassed, ridiculed as racist and homophobic, and other derogatory names by young demonstrators who carry "no more hate" signs, yet exhibit the same emotion they are intent on stamping out. The popularization of concepts such as white privilege, male privilege, and mansplaining, and increasingly using "masculinity" and "whiteness" in negative ways also contributes to the alt-right's growth. Political scientist Phillip Gray argues that it was the American left's increasing use of identity politics as the basis of its mobilization that "helped open space for increased popularity of an identity-based politics from the Right," and that the "intersectional Left's vilification of whiteness as a source of oppression created the atmosphere for a far-right response exulting whiteness as something positive."[19]

While the alt-right as a political movement is marginal, research shows that its ideas are more popular than they might seem. Large numbers of people shape their political identity around a sense of white grievance. They may not march around the streets yelling, but they are extremely receptive to a politics that positions whites as victims and a growing minority population as an existential threat. This kind of white identity politics has become more and more common in the mainstream conservative movement since Trump's ascendancy.[20]

AN INTRODUCTION TO FUNDAMENTALISM

When we respect our blood ancestors and our spiritual ancestors, we feel rooted. If we find ways to cherish and develop our spiritual heritage, we will avoid the kind of alienation that is destroying society, and we will become whole again. ... Learning to touch deeply the jewels of our own tradition will allow us to understand and appreciate the values of other traditions, and this will benefit everyone. ... Thich Nhat Hanh, Living Buddha, Living Christ

A form of religiosity, popularly known as fundamentalism, is a rejection of modernity. Fundamentalism refers to a belief in a strict obedience to a set of basic principles, often religious in nature, that is a reaction to perceived compromises with modern social, ideological, and political life.[21] Fundamentalism is a commonly used term referring to a widespread and complex phenomenon. Many fundamentalists have strong opinions about social, economic, and political issues, and some voice their opinions in a forceful and sometimes violent manner.

Fundamentalism has largely retained its religious references, but the term has more recently been generalized to mean strong obedience to any set of beliefs in the face of criticism or unpopularity. Some writers refer to any literal-minded philosophy with the pretense of being the sole source of objective truth as fundamentalist, regardless of whether it is called a religion.

For example, some people hold the belief—called market fundamentalism—that market capitalism is best and can correct all of society's ills. Extreme fundamentalists who have assassinated several abortion doctors believe their act of murder is justified to save the life of the unborn. On the other hand, in France, the imposition of restrictions on public display of religion has been labeled by some as "secular fundamentalism." French officials have proposed a bill that would ban women from wearing a head scarf in public, a policy directed towards Muslim women who wear a head covering as part of their religious tradition.[22] The application of the term fundamentalist to both religious and social-political approaches and actions, in my estimation, seems appropriate. However, I will primarily concentrate on religious fundamentalists, since this group seems to be the most identifiable and forceful.

Religious fundamentalism is a rejection of and reaction to the modern concepts of secularism and humanism. The shift to secular and humanistic beliefs started during the Enlightenment era of the eighteenth century and intensified in the twentieth century. Secularism is the concept that government or other entities should exist separately from religion and/or religious beliefs. For example, the separation of church and state is a secular belief. Humanism attaches importance to human dignity, concerns, and capabilities, and particularly to reason. It emphasizes humanity more than religion and rejects the supernatural or magical elements of religion. In the twenty-first century humanism tends to strongly endorse human rights, including reproductive rights, gender equality, social justice, and the separation of church and state. Secularists and humanists have often attacked religious doctrines as scientifically unproven and incompatible with scientific principles. As a result, many fundamentalists feel assaulted by the secular and/or humanist movement and strive to stem the tide of its influence.

For religious fundamentalists, sacred scripture is considered the authentic and authoritative word of their religion's god or gods. Fundamentalist beliefs depend on the twin doctrines that their god or gods articulated their will clearly to prophets and that followers have an accurate and unfailing record of that revelation. Fundamentalists see their religion as true and others as false, usually resulting in a denouncement of alternative religious practices and interpretations. There are fundamentalist sects in almost all of the world's major religions: Christianity, Islam, Buddhism, Hinduism, Judaism, and others. Across cultures, fundamentalism is characterized by a cluster of common characteristics including a literal interpretation of scripture, a suspicion of outsiders, a sense of alienation from the secular culture, a distrust of liberal (progressive) elites, and belief in the historical accuracy of their own religious interpretation. Religious fundamentalists are often politically active, strive to shape the social order in line with their beliefs, and feel the state should be administered according to their religious principles.

Fundamentalism is a movement through which its followers attempt to rescue their religious identity from inclusion into modern, secular Western culture. They have created a separate identity based on their particular religious community and upon the fundamental or founding principles of their religion. This formation of a separate identity is deemed necessary as a defensive measure to stem the real and perceived assault from the modern world.

Many scholars see most forms of fundamentalism as having similar traits. In the United States, for example, the pattern of conflict between fundamentalism and modernism in Protestant Christianity has parallels in other religious communities as well. This is especially obvious if the mainstream society, such as the U.S., holds modern, secular, or even atheist values as the norm. The fundamentalist views are thus seen as minority views and relegated to an inferior status. Religious scholar Peter Huff wrote: "Fundamentalists in Judaism, Christianity, and Islam, despite their doctrinal and practical differences, are united by a common worldview which anchors all of life in the authority of the sacred and a shared ethos that expresses itself through outrage at the pace and extent of modern secularization."[23] Religious scholar Karen Armstrong has found that three forms of fundamentalism—Christianity, Islam, and Judaism—nearly always begin as defensive movements; usually as a response to a campaign of coreligionists or fellow countrymen that is experienced as hostile and menacing.[24]

Fundamentalist beliefs are often thought to have a direct and unbroken connection with the past. Despite the centuries that have passed since the origins of these universal religions, the fundamentalists claim that their particular religious interpretation is the one that most closely reflects the intent of the religious founders. This is not true. The fundamentalist version of their particular religion, be it Christian or Muslim, grew out of a particular history. A brief history of three fundamentalist faiths— Christianity, Islam, and Judaism—gives a clearer understanding of how they have arrived at their present stance. I have not started the history at the beginning of the religious traditions; instead I have started the history with modernization. These fundamentalist traditions are a reaction to modernity rather than an exact replication of the religion of the past. I am assuming that most readers of this book are more familiar with the Christian tradition than other religions; therefore, I will devote more to its history than the others.

CHRISTIAN FUNDAMENTALISM

We can either emphasize those aspects of our traditions, religious or secular, that speak of hatred, exclusion, and suspicion or work with those that stress the interdependence and equality of all human beings. The choice is yours..... Karen Armstrong, Twelve Steps to a Compassionate Life

Many Europeans came to North America to escape religious persecution in their native lands and practice their chosen religion freely in the new colony. Although there were attempts to establish a state-administered religion in some colonies, such as by the Puritans in the Massachusetts Bay Colony, by and large these attempts proved to be too cumbersome and were banned or were replaced with governments that practiced separation of church and state. The Enlightenment principle of separation of church and state took root in the newly-formed United States. In fact, many of the founding fathers and elites, such as Thomas Jefferson, were deists. Deists believed that religious truth in general could be determined using reason and observation of the natural world alone, without needing faith or organized religion.

By the 1830s, Deism had been marginalized in the nation and a new version of Evangelicalism became very popular. Its objective was to convert believers to the good news of the Gospel. Followers wanted a religion of the heart, not the Deist's remote religion of the head. They wanted the faithful to follow biblical authority and to personally commit to Jesus. According to Evangelical ideas, faith did not require learned philosophers and scientific experts, as was the case

84

with Enlightenment philosophers; it was a simple matter of felt conviction and virtuous living. From those settling on the frontier to the inhabitants of developing cities of the Northeast, they were ready to listen to a new kind of preacher who stirred up a wave of revivals known as the Second Great Awakening (1800-1835).[25]

Evangelical Christianity led many Americans away from levelheaded rationality to the kind of anti-intellectualism and rugged individualism that still characterizes American culture. The leaders of the Second Great Awakening were not educated men, and their rough, populist, democratic Christianity seemed far removed from the cerebral Deism of the founding fathers. Preachers held torchlight marches and mass rallies, and the new practice of gospel singing elevated audiences to the point where they openly wept and shouted for joy. Like some of the fundamentalist movements today, these congregations gave people who felt marginalized and exploited by the wealthy elites and mainstream society a means of making their voices heard. They were mistrustful of learned experts; they wanted a plain-speaking religion with no impenetrable theological arguments.[26]

Unlike many fundamentalists today, Evangelicals saw religion as a firmly rational faith and in keeping with science. They believed that God could be known through science as a matter of common sense. To them, there was only one path to truth, so theology must follow the scientific method.[27] In line with their faith in science, fundamentalists read the scriptures with an unparalleled literalism, because this seemed more rational and scientific than the older ways of reading scripture as allegory. Like scientific language, they reasoned, religious language should be clear, transparent, and have only one meaning. The Evangelicals also brought the Enlightenment concept of "belief" to the center of Protestant fundamentalism. They followed the Enlightenment *philosophes* in making the practice of morality central to religion. They declared that humans were good in exactly the same way as God. Interestingly, they enthusiastically embraced the virtues of thrift, sobriety, self-discipline, diligence, and temperance that ensured success in the expanding capitalist marketplace.[28]

Evangelicals of the 1820s threw themselves into moral crusades that fought against slavery, urban poverty, exploitation, and liquor, and campaigned for

85

penal reform, the education of the poor, and the emancipation of women. They celebrated the worth of each human being, egalitarianism, and the ideal of inalienable rights. Today, as in the 1820s, these causes are considered to be on the liberal end of the political spectrum but in the current political climate fundamentalists trend toward conservative political and social views. By the mid 1800s, perhaps as a result of the Evangelical initiative, Americans were more religious than ever before.[29]

In 1859 Charles Darwin (1802-1882) published his ground-breaking book *On the Origin of Species* in which he presented his scientific theory that all species of life have evolved over time from common ancestors, and this pattern of evolution resulted from a process that he called natural selection. At first most Christians did not appreciate the full implications of natural selection and accommodated the theory. During the late 1800s Darwin was not yet the monster that he would later become to them. In fact, Christians argued that God was at work in natural selection and that humanity was gradually evolving to a greater spiritual perfection.[30] They had not yet fully evaluated how Darwinism had undermined the theology on which their belief was based. Today we are accustomed to the tension between science and religion, but in the late nineteenth century, most religious people still respected science. Actually, the Evangelicals did not bash science, but the popularizers of Darwin went on the offensive in an antireligious battle. The real divide in the 1800s was between liberal and conservative Christians. Conservative Christians insisted on the literal truth and factual accuracy of the Bible and all its stories and statements. Liberal Christians, on the other hand, did not interpret the Bible literally and read it more as allegory and story, rather than categorical fact.[31]

In 1906, the first congregation of Pentecostals formed and rebelled against modern rationalism. Pentecostalists were reacting against the more conservative Christians who were trying to make their Bible-based religion entirely reasonable and scientific. According to Karen Armstrong, "They claimed to have experienced the Spirit in a tiny house in Los Angeles, convinced that it had descended upon them in the same way as upon Jesus' disciples on the Jewish festival of Pentecost, when the divine presence had manifested itself in tongues of fire and given the apostles the ability to speak in strange languages." At a Pentecostal service, men and women fell into trance states, were seen to levitate, and felt that their bodies were melting in inexpressible joy. Within four years, there were hundreds of Pentecostal groups all over the U.S., and the movement had spread to fifty other countries.[32] The dramatic increase of this type of faith indicated widespread rejection of the modern rational, scientific culture. It developed at a time when people were beginning to have doubts about science and technology.

Others followed a different approach to religion. A.C. Dixon, one of the founding fathers of Protestant fundamentalism in the 1920s, said his faith depended upon "exact observation and correct thinking." Religious doctrines were not theological speculations but facts. These Evangelical Christians still sought the early modern ideal of absolute certainty based on scientific verification. They would also see their experiences—born-again conversions, faith healing, and strongly felt emotional convictions—as positive confirmation of their beliefs. This claim to rationalism indicates, perhaps, a hidden fear. With the horrific battles of World War I fresh in their minds, many people had apocalyptic fantasies from Revelations and believed that the scriptures revealed that the Last Days were close at hand. Many Christians were now swayed to believe that they were on the front line of an apocalyptic war against Satan. They also no longer saw Jesus as a loving savior but rather as the foremost conservative.[33]

Armstrong writes "Every single fundamentalist movement that I have studied in Judaism, Christianity, and Islam is rooted in profound fear." She found that the first fundamentalist movement in modern times followed that pattern. Dixon and his colleagues were reacting to the widespread discontent following World War I. They were assailed by liberal Christians, and the fundamentalists retaliated. Distorting the traditions they were trying to defend, they underscored the certainty and literalism of biblical scripture. They seemed to be gaining the upper hand until a new movement set them back for a few decades.[34]

In the 1920s, the Democratic politician William Jennings Bryan (1860-1925) launched a crusade against the heretofore uncontroversial teachings of evolution in schools and colleges. Almost alone, he put Darwinism at the forefront of the fundamentalist agenda. He quoted a suspicious study that claimed evolutionary theory had played a role in Germany's determination to declare war in 1914, which had propelled the collapse of morality and decent civilization. Although his ideas were naive and incorrect, people were beginning to be wary of science and he found an agreeable audience. His lecture, "The Menace of Darwinism," drew large crowds and got widespread media coverage. At this time, the fundamentalist movement was largely limited to the northern states, but southerners had also become troubled about evolution. In response to this unease about science, legislators passed a law in several southern states prohibiting the teaching of evolution in public schools. The disquiet about evolution erupted in a public frenzy when John Scopes, a young teacher in Dayton, Tennessee, confessed that he had broken this law and in July 1925 was brought to trial. The new American Civil Liberties Union (ACLU) sent a team of lawyers to defend him, headed by the rationalist campaigner Clarence Darrow. When Bryan agreed to speak in defense of the anti-evolution law, the trial ceased to be about civil liberties and became a contest between religion and science.[35]

Like many fundamentalist disputes, the Scopes trial was a clash between two opposing points of view. Both Darrow and Bryan represented core American values: Darrow stood for intellectual inquiry and Bryan for the rights of the ordinary folk who were traditionally wary of learned experts, had no real knowledge of science, and felt that urbane elites were imposing their values on small-town America. While Darrow argued brilliantly on the stand, Bryan was a disaster. At the end of the trial, Darrow emerged as the hero of clear rational thought, while Bryan was seen as a blundering, inept relic who was hopelessly out of touch with the modern world.[36] Yet, in the long run, Bryan made anti-evolution thought a keystone of fundamentalist belief that continues today.

After the Scopes trial, fundamentalism lost much of its appeal during the Depression, World War II, and the optimistic period of the 1950s and 1960s, but it had not gone away. Followers had simply withdrawn defensively, as fundamentalists of other traditions would do in the future. In a world that seemed antagonistic to religion, they created an enclave of the faithful, forming their own churches, broadcasting stations, publishing houses, schools, universities, and Bible colleges. By the late 1970s, when they had gained sufficient strength and confidence, the fundamentalists would return to public life, launching an offensive to press the nation to accept their principles.[37]

During the time of retreat, the fundamentalists became more radical, harboring deep criticism of mainstream American culture. History would show that when a fundamentalist movement is attacked, it almost always becomes more hardline, acrimonious, and extreme. Since fundamentalism is rooted in fear of extermination, its followers see any attacks as proof that the secular or liberal world is intent on the eradication of religion. Jewish and Muslim movements would also follow this same pattern. As noted, before the Scopes trial Protestant fundamentalists fell on the left of the political spectrum, willing to work with socialists and liberals in the poverty areas of the nation's rapidly industrializing cities. After Scopes there was a distinct swing to the right, where they have remained. The mockery and contempt by the press during and after the Scopes trial reinforced, not undermined, their movement; the fundamentalists became even more confrontational in their views. Before the Scopes trial, evolution had not been an important issue, but afterwards a steadfast biblical literalism became central to the fundamentalist mind-set and creation science became the trademark of the movement. It would become difficult to discuss the issue sensibly, because evolution was no longer about scientific findings but a symbol of the deeply felt and sometimes real fear that religion would be crushed under the modern views of mainstream society. Armstrong notes, "When attacking religion that seems obscurantist, critics must be aware that this assault is likely to make it more extreme."[38]

Protestant fundamentalism made inroads into public awareness when it opposed new scientific discoveries. Fundamentalists in other traditions have been concerned by different problems and are not as fixated on "belief" in the same way. In a clear departure from mainstream or liberal Christian tradition, fundamentalists are convinced that their religious beliefs are a precise, ultimate expression of sacred truth and that every word of the Bible is literally true. They believe that miracles are an essential promise of true faith and that God will give the believer anything he asks for in prayer. If an individual's prayers are not answered, perhaps something is wrong with the individual. Fundamentalists crusade against the teaching of evolution in public schools, are staunchly patriotic but suspicious of democracy, see feminism as one of the great evils of the day, and fight against abortion and homosexuality. Like evolution, abortion has become emblematic of the murderous evil of modern society. They are intolerant of other faiths, see Jews and Muslims as fated for hellfire, and some regard Buddhists, Hinduists, and Daoists as devil worshippers.[39]

THE EXPANSION OF WORLD FUNDAMENTALISM: THE 1970s

Those who advocated for a rational, secular, modern worldview spoke too hastily of the death of religion. This became apparent when a dramatic religious uprising occurred in the late 1970s. From 1978-1979, the Western world watched as an obscure ayatollah brought down the government of Shah Muhammad Reza Pahlavi in Iran, which had seemed to be one of the most modern and stable nations in the Middle East. At the same time as governments applauded the peace initiative of President Anwar al Sadat of Egypt, observers noticed that young Egyptians were donning Islamic dress, casting aside the trappings of modernity, and engaging in a seizure of university campuses in order to reclaim them for religion in a way that was reminiscent of student rebellions during the 1960s. In the U.S., Jerry Falwell established the Moral Majority in 1979, urging Protestant fundamentalists to get politically involved and to challenge any state or federal legislation that supported a "secular humanist" agenda. In Israel, fundamentalists proclaimed Israel to be a religious state.[40]

Religious extremism emerged in regions where a secular, Western-style government had separated religion and politics. Its cohorts were resolute in dragging God and/or religion from the sidelines of modern culture and back to center field, echoing a widespread disenchantment with modern culture. People all over the world were demonstrating that they wanted to see religion more openly reflected in public life, despite the derision heaped upon them by intellectuals, the media, and politicians.

Despite their intense dislike and distrust for each other, fundamentalist movements around the world share commonalities. They are quick to denounce people whom they regard as the enemies of God. Because fundamentalists feel under attack, they are distrustful and unwilling to consider any alternative point of view; this is yet another expression of the intolerance that is a part of modernity. They take a hard line on what they regard as social morality.

Some modernizers have loudly called for the abolition of religion and have railed against it as the root of all problems; they have done so in the past and continue to do so. Fundamentalists' movements begin with what they perceive as a real attack by followers of liberal or mainstream religions or a secularist state, and more attacks simply make them more extreme. This was seen in the U.S. after media attacks in the wake of the Scopes trial; Jewish fundamentalism advanced after Hitler tried to exterminate European Jews and after the October War in 1973 when Arab armies launched a surprise attack against Israel.[41]

In their anxiety and fear, fundamentalists often distort the faith they are trying to preserve. They are convinced that they are fighting for God but they can be highly selective in their reading of scripture. As Armstrong notes, for example, "Protestant fundamentalists quote from the book of Revelation at length and are stirred by its violent end-time vision but rarely refer to the Sermon on the Mount, where Jesus tells his followers to love their enemies, to turn the other cheek, and not to judge others. Jewish fundamentalists cite extensively from the Deuteronomy sections of the Bible and seem to overlook the rabbis' command for charity. Muslim fundamentalists pointedly ignore the Qur'an's numerous calls for peace, tolerance, and forgiveness, and extremists quote its more hard line verses to defend violence."[42]

CONCLUDING INSIGHTS: THE TRADITIONAL WORLDVIEW

Even though it is usually thought that fundamentalists are set on returning their religions to their historic roots of the past, actually these movements could not have taken place at any other time than our own. As mentioned above, fundamentalism can be seen as another post-modern rejection of modernity. Fundamentalists are not conservative; indeed, many are anti-orthodox and regard the more conventional faithful as part of the problem. These movements have sprung up autonomously, and each has its own idea of religious belief. However, they bear commonalities and are similar to the pattern set by American Protestant fundamentalism, the earliest of these movements. Armstrong explains, "All are initially defensive movements rooted in a profound fear of obliteration, which causes them to develop a mistrustful vision of the "enemy." They begin as intra-faith movements, and only at a secondary stage, if at all, do they direct their attention to a foreign foe."[43]

Fundamentalists often see the choices as to the organization of their nation as limited to a modern society or one based on the traditions of an imaginary past. Since they reject a modern society, the only other choice they see is the preservation of their traditional ways. Also many people in modern nations find that traditional values give resolute comfort and reassurance in a fluctuating and inexplicable world. Therefore, many people from the Middle East to India to the United States find that the familiar traditions of the past give meaning, identity, and steadfastness to their lives. The essence of many of these traditional beliefs continues today and is zealously held by millions, if not billions, of people throughout the world.

Fundamentalists fear modernity and the disrupting influences of globalization and know that some adversaries vow to destroy religion. They have found that their religion has provided them with the sole guarantee of certainty in an increasingly uncertain and complex world. They will fight to their death to defend this certainty.

Chapter 6
The Progressive Worldview

Even the sober desire for progress is sustained by faith—faith in the intrinsic goodness of human nature and in the omnipotence of science. It is a defiant and blasphemous faith, not unlike that held by the men who set out to build a city and a tower, whose top may reach unto heaven and who believed that nothing will be restrained from them, which they have imagined to do.... Eric Hoffer

WHAT IS PROGRESSIVISM?

From the twentieth century onward, there have been influential movements that have critiqued and even rejected the modern worldview. Though the modern worldview has been battered and diminished, it continues to be pervasive and influential, while another worldview has not stepped in to claim the dominant spot. But the unraveling of the modern worldview continues to provide space for the emergence of other worldviews and movements. As we have seen, conservatives of different stripes form an uneasy coalition under the umbrella of the traditional worldview. The liberal/progressive left has formed a worldview as well, consisting of different groups and interests that I call the progressive worldview.

Progressive implies progress, the foundational belief of the progressive worldview. It is called different names, such as the left, neo-progressives, populist left, democratic socialists, and liberals. While dissimilar from each other in many important ways, these ideologies share important ideas and characteristics. Thus, the progressive label aptly fits their central belief in the perfectibility of humankind through education and creating institutions to further the cause of progress. To achieve this perfectibility, progressives say that humans must cast off the chains of religion, family hierarchies, and traditions that have hindered them from reaching their full potential. Progressives embrace continuous change and reinvention, and those on the far left may even call for a political revolution to reformulate society into their ideal version.

Progressives believe in the superiority of reason over faith and disparage the notion of divine revelation. Many reject Christianity and religion in general and work towards freeing humans from what they perceive as the evils that religion has foisted on humankind. In theory, they support the working classes, and one of their goals is to have them join the progressive cause to achieve greater income equality and respect. Many on the extreme left abhor capitalism as well as the corresponding concept of private property, which they contend leads to the concentration of wealth and inequality resulting from unfettered capitalism. They work towards the promise of world peace and support institutions to carry out this goal, such as the United Nations and a myriad of other non-governmental organizations and non-profits.

Progressives oppose social hierarchy and class distinctions and work towards social equality and egalitarianism. This allegiance to equality typically involves a concern for those in society who they perceive as disadvantaged relative to others and historically marginalized. They assert that unjustified inequalities need to be reduced or abolished. Those who have garnered more wealth than others have done so, according to some progressives, because of their social or white privilege, which should be stripped away and the wealth garnered from that privilege should be redistributed to those in need.

The goal of universal prosperity guides many progressive policies. Social justice advocates work to abolish inequalities. Social justice is a concept promoting fair and just relations between the individual and society. The concept of social justice also describes a number of movements that are working to achieve more equality in society. These movements aim towards fashioning a society in which all members, regardless of background, have basic human rights, such as health care, clean water, a quality education, and equal access to the benefits of their society.

The difference between liberals, progressives, populist left, democratic socialist, and the antifa movement is a matter of degrees. It is helpful to think of a political spectrum in which those on the political left of the spectrum want change that is immediate and sweeping. Their goal is often structural change in the existing political and economic system. Radicals often encourage the use of violence and revolution as one of the ways to promote change. At the center left of the political spectrum are liberals who advocate for incremental change and believe it should improve conditions for individuals. They believe that change should be moderate reforms of the existing system that cause minimal disruption to the everyday lives of ordinary people. Sandwiched between the radicals and liberals are progressives. I will try to distinguish between the different groups with the correct labels as best as possible. Before turning to a description of the various progressive ideas, let's look at the historical roots of progressivism, primarily in the United States, which helps give us a clearer background of this worldview.

HISTORICAL ROOTS OF THE PROGRESSIVE WORLDVIEW

Modern liberalism had its earliest beginnings during the Enlightenment period in eighteenth century Western Europe. Advocates of liberalism sought to replace traditional conservativism—in which the Catholic Church, monarchies, and an inherited nobility class held absolute rule—with a form of government in which hereditary privilege, state religion, and absolute monarchy were abolished. Instead of arbitrary rule by elites they put forth a liberal form of government which included ideas of representative democracy, the rule of law, and a written constitution. Economically, liberals sought to end mercantilist policies, royal monopolies, and barriers to trade and to replace these policies with a free trade and free market system called *laissez-faire* or free market capitalism.

The Glorious Revolution of 1688 in England, the American Revolution of 1776, and the French Revolution of 1789 heralded the armed overthrow of monarchical rule and the eventual implementation of a state governed by liberal philosophy. In the nineteenth century, the liberal revolution rapidly spread across Europe and the Western hemisphere as many new nations adopted a liberal form of government.

It was actually during the French Revolution (1789-1815) that the terms left and right were coined, referring to the seating arrangement of representatives in the governing body called the French Estates General. Representatives seated on the left generally opposed the monarchy and supported the creation of a secular republic, while those on the right supported the traditional institutions of the French monarchy, aristocracy, and Catholic Church.

The English philosopher John Locke is often credited as an important founder of liberalism as a distinct political tradition. In his book *Two Treatises on Government* (1689), he made the case that each man has a natural right to life, liberty, and property, and governments that must not violate these basic rights. The basic foundation of the liberal tradition was built upon Locke's concept of natural rights and, over time, it has emphasized expanding democracy, civil rights, secularism, gender and racial equality, free markets, and freedom of speech, press, assembly, and religion.

The Enlightenment era of the seventeenth and eighteenth centuries put forth the ideas that science and reason should replace religion as the guiding principles of a modern society. Philosophers from Voltaire and Rousseau to Immanuel Kant and Karl Marx have worked to undermine or overturn the existing order and create a "new man" not burdened by the baggage of religion, traditions, and what were considered obsolete customs of the past. These Enlightenment ideas also sparked the Populist and Progressive movements at the turn of the late nineteenth and early twentieth centuries in the United States. For example, in early nineteenth century America, men who did not own property gained the right to vote and abolitionists toiled to free slaves. Later in the nineteenth century, liberal notions spurred the suffragist movements to extend voting rights and liberties to ex-slaves and women. Liberalism was firmly entrenched on American soil.

The Progressive Movement in the United States rose to prominence from the late nineteenth century through the first decades of the twentieth century. During this time, leading intellectuals and social reformers in the United States sought to address the economic, political, and social problems arising from rapid changes brought about by industrialization and the unrestrained growth of modern capitalism. Progressives believed that as the pre-industrialized, old order ended, the creation of a new order appropriate for the industrial era was needed. They generally shared the notion that government at the local, state, and national level should be actively involved in reforming society for the betterment of all its citizens. According to progressives, the outdated order needed to be converted into a vibrant system of social change, assisted by scientific knowledge and administered by an extensive bureaucracy run by experts. They championed more transparent and democratic changes, such as the direct election of senators, open primaries, initiatives, recalls, and referendums. These changes were expensive, and to help pay for them, the Sixteenth Amendment to the constitution, ratified in 1916, added a progressive income tax to fund these additional programs.[1]

MODERN LIBERALISM

Modern liberalism in the United States can be traced to the presidency of Franklin D. Roosevelt, who won an unprecedented four terms as president and served from 1933 until his death in 1944, while the Great Depression ravaged the U.S. economy. In response to the misery and pessimism of the times, Roosevelt devised a progressive legislative program called the New Deal. His intention in formulating the New Deal was to stem the tide of the depression and prevent fascism from taking root in the U.S. Although the liberal reforms did not officially end the depression, massive government spending for World War II did, and thanks to Roosevelt's skilled leadership fascism did not take root in the U.S. While New Deal reforms ushered in a more equal society than previously seen, they also curbed the power of large corporations and represented the "common person." Even though not all the New Deal programs and remedies were successful, Roosevelt left a decisive liberal legacy and influenced many future American presidents who followed his lead in putting in place a strong centralized state to institute social change and curb the harsh tendencies of unrestrained capitalism.

The progressive legacy of the New Deal continued in the 1960s as various social movements came out of the shadows. Arguably the most significant social movement in the U.S. was that of civil rights. President Lyndon B. Johnson, a protégé of FDR, launched in 1964 his signature progressive agenda, the Great Society, dubbed by historians as the "Liberal Hour." He rapidly steered through Congress monumental liberal legislation, such as Medicare, Medicaid, Head Start, the Job Corps, the War on Poverty, and the passage of the landmark Civil Rights Act of 1964 and Voting Rights Act of 1965.

Liberalism slowed in the tumultuous 1970s, and abruptly halted in 1980 as progressive ideals fell in popularity and a conservative, Ronald Reagan, was elected president. Even Democratic President Bill Clinton shied away from the liberal mantle and called himself a New Democrat, meaning traditional liberal reforms such as those in the New Deal and the Great Society were not part of his agenda. President Barack Obama, much to the chagrin of those on the progressive left, followed the more centrist track forged by the Clinton presidency. Although both men supported reforms, they were based on incremental change within the existing system, reflective of a moderate liberal philosophy, not a progressive agenda.

Today progressivism has replaced liberalism as the preferred label for the Democratic agenda. Perhaps, Hillary Clinton, Democratic presidential nominee in 2016, was the last liberal candidate. In fact, the epic Democratic primary was a stand-off between the progressive wing of the Democratic party and the more moderate or liberal wing of the party. Although with Hillary Clinton the moderate wing won the primary, the battle between the two ideologies has continued and intensified.

POST-MODERNISM

To better understand the philosophical undercurrents of the progressive worldview today and why it is so influential, it will help to look at the formation and growth of post-modernism. Although post-modernism has heavily influenced the arts in the twentieth century, in the last several decades it has become a significant philosophy in academia and its influence has spread to other groups and institutions. Let us look at the roots of discontent propagated by post-modernism.

Post-modern literally means "after the modernist movement," but it is generally seen as a point of departure from or a rejection of the modern worldview. The post-modern perspective in the late twentieth and early twenty-first centuries has largely been applied to works of literature, drama, architecture, cinema, journalism, and design, as well as to marketing and business, and in the interpretation of history, law, culture, and religion.

Post-modernism can be traced to the Romantic poets and authors of the early nineteenth century. Poets such as William Wordsworth and Samuel

Coleridge rejected what they regarded as the Enlightenment's stifling adoration of reason and instead emphasized in their works passion, emotion, intuitive ways of knowing, and the beauty of nature.

Another contribution to post-modern thought came from the early twentieth century physicists, who challenged the rational, objective modern worldview and the mechanistic order outlined by Sir Isaac Newton in the seventeenth century. The theory of relativity, formulated by Albert Einstein in 1905, shattered Newtonian absolutes and introduced the element of uncertainty: time and space are relative to the viewpoint of the observer and only the speed of light is constant for all frames of reference in the universe. Physicist Max Planck proposed that the energy released by atomic particles did not flow smoothly but jumped in discontinuous spurts or quanta, leading to the formulation of quantum theory. Scientists also concluded that both wave and particle theories, although seemingly contradictory, coexisted logically—hence, the theory of complementarity. Instead of Newton's dependable, rational laws, there seemed to be only tendencies and probabilities; scientists could never attain more than probable knowledge and certainty was impossible.

The new field of psychology also unsettled modernists' certainty about traditional, Victorian concepts of morals and values. Sigmund Freud, the revolutionary psychologist of the time, argued that human behavior was basically irrational; the primitive unconscious was driven by sexual aggression and pleasure-seeking desires. Human behavior was a delicate and unpredictable balance between instinctual drives and the controls of rational thinking and moral values.

Twentieth century novelists responded to Freud's interpretation of the human mind as irrational by using a stream-of-consciousness technique to explore the psyche. Virginia Woolf's novel, *Jacob's Room*, consisted of a series of internal monologues, in which ideas and emotions from different periods of time randomly bubbled up. In James Joyce's novel *Ulysses*, published in 1922, conventional grammar was abandoned and replaced by a bewildering confusion of language intended to mirror post-modern life: a colossal riddle waiting to be unraveled. In his famous poem *The Waste Land* (1922), T. S. Eliot depicted a world of growing desolation and despair.

Post-modernism in the artistic realm included post-impressionist paint-
ers. They desired to know and depict an unseen, inner world of feeling and
imagination, expressing an obscure psychological view of reality as well as
evoking powerful emotions. Vincent van Gogh painted the vision of his mind's
eye in *The Starry Night* (1889) with blazing trees and exploding stars all swirling together in one great rhythmic cosmic dance. Pablo Picasso founded the
Cubist movement which depicted a complex geometry of zigzagging lines and
abstract, sharply-angled planes. And Wassily Kandinsky turned away from nature and painted form and color which represented mood and emotion, not
representation of objects as in modern paintings.

Jazz, a post-modern musical expression created by African Americans, di-
verged sharply from the classical tradition. Played by bands in contrast to the
highly-ordered symphony orchestras representative of the modern worldview,
jazz was improvisational, and the lead performer often spontaneously invented
and varied both melody and rhythm in non-standard repetitions.

Dance experienced a similar break from tradition. Classical ballet dancers, a representation of the modern worldview, performed on a separate stage
from the audience in a remote and detached style. In contrast, modern dancers
broke from the rituals of ballet and spontaneously conveyed their individual
and deeply personal emotions and passions. In jazz clubs and cabarets, dancers energetically merged into the emotional ecstasy of the music and were not
disconnected, separate performers.

Post-modern cultural thought continued in the 1970s, and by the beginning of the 1980s was well-placed in the intellectual community. During the
1970s and 1980s, according to many post-modern thinkers, tremendous technological innovations in computers and communication devices rendered the
individual mind servant to "artificial intelligence." Individual accomplishment,
effort, and identity were dwarfed and often felt obliterated by the spread of
technological advances. Influenced by these developments, post-modern
thought has a quality of arbitrariness, randomness, a lack of restraint, and the
propensity for diverse cultural strains and theories.[2] Post-modern culture is
a fragmented world of sub-cultures and small groups and has no integrating
cultural theory.

Deconstruction is the name of an approach (whether in philosophy, literary analysis, or in other fields) which insists on the careful reading of a text. It embraces self-referentiality, which regards the text as a self-enclosed, structural world of knowledge. Deconstructionists advance the idea of conflictuality, which means that within texts there are internal conflicts at work, while the process of deconstructing the text includes taking the surface meaning of the text and breaking it down. The text disintegrates because of the oppositional and conflictual nature of language, breaking itself down into several layers of meaning. According to deconstructionists, there are infinite meanings in texts, moving from the conscious layer toward the unconscious. As one focuses on the gaps between the conscious and unconscious layers, the text begins to deconstruct itself. It is not the critic who deconstructs the text but the text deconstructs itself—the observer and observed are one.[3]

Deconstructionists reject the liberal, modern, humanist tradition, which emphasized fixed meanings, a set canon of scholarly works, tradition, hierarchy, and objectivity. Instead they see only infinity of meaning. This deconstructionist theory erodes classical, rational liberalism, the cornerstone of the modern worldview and of classical liberalism.

Despite its opaque message, the impact of post-modernism has trickled down to the masses and influenced mainstream or mass culture. For example, the narratives in television dramas are often fragmented, follow a nonsequential order, and offer a vague message. Post-modernism has influenced the progressive worldview with its emphasis on identity politics and rejection of classical liberal ideas, such as speech that violates political correctness and examining all sides of an issue.

PROGRESSIVES REJECT THE NOTION OF HUMAN NATURE

Progressives, generally speaking, disregard human nature since it contradicts the philosophy of progressivism. Human nature is the fundamental dispositions and traits of humans, or the essence of being human. It reveals traits of the human psyche that are fixed but expressed in culturally different ways across time and place, such as gender differences, tendencies to embrace hierarchies and authority, propensities to establish territorial boundaries, inclinations to form tribal groups, an affinity for the sacred, and many other universal traits.

Many progressives reject human nature because they see it as an outdated concept. Instead, they claim that humans are pliable and perfectible, making our own nature through socially constructing a government or system in which each person can reach their full potential and thrive. Their idea is that if progressives create the right kind of system or government, humans can alter what corrupted us in the first place, such as incidences of social injustice, the rise of patriarchal systems, the oppression of religion, or the accumulation of capital. They believe that the human mind is malleable and determined by social and cultural constructs. For example, gender differences are socially constructed, world peace is possible, and tribal differences can be socialized away with proper education. An example on the extreme left of political thought was the Chinese communist dictator Mao Zedong, who wanted to recreate human nature. He orchestrated the Cultural Revolution, a communist revolutionary idea in which a simple, agricultural people would live in an equal and simple state. In reality, the opposite occurred.[4]

Others disagree with the progressive view that humans can be perfected. Those who believe there is a fundamental human nature, such as Robert Greene, argue that "the evidence is clear looking at our chimpanzee ancestors and the record of early homo sapiens that we do have aggressive, violent impulses, that we are pretty much irrational by nature, and that the kinds of qualities that we value can only come about through personal work, through conquest, through overcoming our tendencies that are kind of animal-like. And that rather than some government that's going to perfect us, it's the work of individuals being conscious and aware of who they are." He believes that progressives "hold up a sort of idealized mirror of who we are as if it's not a matter of effort, of coming to terms with …our ugly aspects of our nature, but rather through a new government or technological progress."[5]

Greene concludes that it is part of human nature to always want to take the path of least resistance. We look for an easy route to something that we want. He sees it as a naïve belief, as if a pill will cure your ailment or the government will cure all of society's ills. "We must understand," he continues, "that we're all flawed and we need to get over our sense of moral superiority." He sees this as the most aggravating quality in twenty-first century life—people's insane sense of moral superiority. It's so much a part of modern life and it's this need people have in times where things are a bit dark. It's this sense of, "Oh, I'm not tainted by these times that we live in, I'm superior to it, I'm superior to other people, I'm good."[6]

THE ANTIFA MOVEMENT

The antifa movement is a loose collection of far-left groups, networks, and individuals who believe in active, forceful resistance to far right-wing movements. Although the movement stretches across Europe, I will concentrate on it in America.

The current antifa movement sees itself as the successor to anti-Nazi activists of the 1930s in Germany. They claim that if ordinary Germans had more aggressively fought the Nazi party in the streets in the 1920s and 1930s, the Nazis would not have been able to come to power. The recent antifa movement began in the 1980s with a group called Anti-Racist Action. Its members confronted neo-Nazi skinheads at punk gatherings. By the early 2000s the movement was mostly dormant, until the rise of Trump and the alt-right.[7]

The antifa movement encompasses a number of different politically left-wing groups, such as the anarchist movement, and some people with mainstream political backgrounds have also joined their ranks since the election of President Trump. Socialists, communists, and even some social democrats activists tend to be anti-capitalists. They focus on fighting far-right extremists directly, rather than through electoral means. Antifa uses online tactics to fuel their cause, which include monitoring the far right on social media. They also release personal information about their opponents online. They have been able to get some alt-right supporters fired from their jobs after identifying them online and spreading information about their political leanings.

Antifa has expanded its definition of fascist to include not just white supremacists and other extremists, but also many conservatives and supporters of President Trump. Many also have an anti-government streak and see creeping authoritarianism reflected in the Trump administration. Because there is no unifying body, it is unclear how many people are currently active antifa followers. Although their numbers vary in different locales, Portland is often cited as having a large antifa group. Sometimes antifa protesters are willing to travel hundreds of miles to oppose an alt-right event.[8]

The antifa movement uses a variety of tactics to enforce its agenda, including violence and digital activism. Their aim is to disrupt what they deem as alt-right events and speakers, including shouting, chanting, and forming human chains to block right-wing demonstrators. While some antifa use their fists in violent confrontations, other forceful tactics include throwing projectiles such as bricks, crowbars, metal chains, water bottles, and balloons filled with urine and feces. They have sprayed noxious gases, slammed through police barricades, caused property damage, and harassed law enforcement officers. Those on the right often cite the violent antics of the antifa groups to put forth a victimhood narrative that has played an important role in recruiting alt-right sympathizers to their cause.[9]

The American antifa movement has copied West German anarchists in the Cold War era by dressing all in black. Most often they will cover their faces with masks or helmets in a protest march so they cannot be identified by the police or opposing groups. Known as the black bloc, this intimidating tactic allows them to move together as one nameless group. Women have traditionally been on the sidelines of the mostly male domain of direct street action, but today a significant number of women are involved in the antifa movement and have been arrested at counter-demonstrations in California and elsewhere.

THE RISE OF PROGRESSIVE POPULISM

"I'm not a liberal, I'm a progressive," Vermont Senator Bernie Sanders told a high school student in 2003 as he spoke to a classroom about the importance of civic engagement. "There's a difference. As humans, we strive to preserve our basic rights and live up to our boundless potential. That is the meaning of human progress. It is the goal of progressives to look beyond the political spectrum and welcome all those who believe in these principles and fight for them."[10]

Sanders helped fuel the most recent version of the progressive movement. He began his political career in 1981 with a successful win as mayor of Burlington, Vermont. In 1990 he was elected to the House of Representatives and to the Senate in 2006. Sanders became a household name in 2016 as he battled with Hillary Clinton for the Democratic Party's nomination for president. Although he lost the primary to Clinton, he continued to build his progressive movement with a nationwide volunteer network. At the time of this writing, he is again seeking the 2020 Democratic nomination for president.

Sanders drew on the momentum of the Occupy Wall Street movement that began on September 17, 2011, in Zuccotti Park in lower Manhattan, New York City. The protesters were incensed about the greed, corruption, and undue influence of large corporations on the government, especially the financial services sector, whose greed was exposed during the 2008 financial crisis and subsequent recession. The protesters' slogan "We are the 99%!" refers to increasing income and wealth inequality between the very wealthy 1% and the rest of the population. Sanders' 2016 campaign brought socialist ideas to the mainstream, and the public was receptive—especially white, educated young people.

Sanders differentiated his vision of the future which demanded bold, immediate changes, to the liberal mainstream's preference for incremental reforms while keeping the basic system intact. In fact, Sanders didn't call himself a Democrat but a Democratic Socialist. Generally, democratic socialism is defined as a political philosophy that advocates political democracy alongside social ownership of the means of production, with an emphasis on some form of centralized planned socialist economy. Democratic socialists claim that capitalism is incompatible with the democratic values of liberty, equality and solidarity; these ideals can only be achieved through the formation of a socialist society.

The philosophical differences between Sanders and former Secretary of State and former Senator Hillary Clinton, the eventual nominee of the Democratic Party in 2016, symbolized the splintering of the Democratic Party between the liberal and progressive wings. It pitted two candidates on different points of the political spectrum in a battle for the nomination. Both were decidedly to the left of center on the political spectrum, but Sanders was more to the left than Clinton. Sanders attacked Hillary Clinton where it hurt: on her globalization policies—trade and outsourcing—that have contributed to greater income inequality and pain for the working and middle classes. To many people, she seemed too adjoined to corporate America, which Sanders blamed for most all of society's ailments. The two candidates seemed to agree on other policies, such as immigration, identity politics, catering to the youth vote, and social issues. Sanders drilled down hard on the inequality issue and it especially resonated with college-educated youth, who saw shrinking opportunities ahead of them while tethered to student debt. This split in the Democratic Party had a negative impact on the candidacy of Hillary Clinton. The lack of enthusiasm and constant criticism of her policies and personality by progressives contributed, along with many other reasons, to her defeat in the Electoral College to Donald Trump, although she won the popular vote by three million votes.

Bernie Sanders called for building mass movements that would spark a political revolution in the United States. He especially wanted to build a labor movement that he believes has the potential to win concessions from capitalists and politicians. Neal Meyer, writing for the "Jacobin Journal," concisely explains the socialist struggle. He believes socialists can win the struggle by changing people's consciousness and by organizing and working together. He has found that the Democratic socialist movement is intent on several actions to realize its goals, such as nationalizing the financial sector so that major investment decisions are made by democratically elected governments and removing hostile elements in the military and police. He thinks it will be necessary to introduce democratic planning and social ownership, in which there will be a "correct" mix of state-led planning and publicly-owned firms, small privately owned businesses, and worker cooperatives, instead of mainly corporate ownership. What is the correct mix is open to debate in the movement. Meyer continues, "It will mean rebuilding our democracy by instituting public financing of elections, a ban on corporate lobbying and private campaign donations, and even more radical demands like writing a new constitution."[11]

The modern progressive movement after the 2016 presidential election has been fueled by fury at the presidency of Republican President Donald Trump. Progressives resent Democratic Party leaders whom they believe have presided over a losing streak in national elections and advocate for deep structural change rather than incremental reforms. Sanders' supporters and many Progressive insurgents thought Clinton's defeat, on top of losing control of Congress and most state governments, proved them right. They sought to overthrow conventional wisdom that Democrats must stay safely in the middle to compete against Republicans.[12]

Sanders' 2016 campaign inspired many followers who are now pushing for progressive candidates. Brand New Congress and Justice Democrats are just two players in a movement where different groups with different agendas jostle for donations and influence. Some, like Democracy for America and the Progressive Change Campaign Committee, were in place years before the Sanders campaign. California billionaire Tom Steyer, the Democrats' largest donor, has spent millions of his own money on NextGen America, a group that aims to mobilize young voters. The hedge-fund manager turned activist vows to build the largest progressive operation in America. One organization, Brand New Congress, formed in 2016, has strategized to run hundreds of progressive political newcomers to oust establishment incumbents, Democrats and Republicans alike. All of these political outsiders with a record of community activism ran on a single populist platform, negotiated by the Brand New Congress organization. Their most notable accomplishment was the election of Alexandria Ocasio-Cortez as a Democratic socialist to the House of Representative in 2018. She banished ten-term Democratic congressman Joseph Crowley in a surprise primary election. To this date, she is a vocal and popular representative of progressive causes. Some claim that there is a civil war in the Democratic Party. Others, such as long-time and well-respected Democrat Leon Panetta, downplay the notion of a civil war. Panetta notes, "Very frankly, it's a party of a lot of very different voices right now."[13]

Progressives vary widely in their policy platforms. Contemptuous of the Democratic Party's coziness with big-money donors, many progressives disdain corporate money in politics. Progressive candidates gleefully tout the fact that they get most or all of their donations from small donors, not corporate bundlers. However, they fail to state that most of the small donations are from well-educated, wealthy, white progressives who have more influence than lower-income moderates who donate less money to political campaigns. Many progressives favor a government-run healthcare system in the form of Medicare for All, while some lobby to end the system of private health insurance, 56 percent of which is employer-sponsored coverage.[14]

Also on the progressive table are subsidies for college tuition or even free college, an increase in the minimum wage for workers to $15 an hour across the United States, some type of immigration reform that would allow more immigrants into the country, racial and gender justice policies, and a government-run Green New Deal. Some even call for the abolition of ICE, Immigration and Customs Enforcement, decriminalizing illegal immigration, and an "open border" policy.

One of the contentious issues on the national stage is immigration. Globalizers, Republicans and Democrats, have been very supportive of high levels of immigration over the last several decades. Immigration has added many benefits to American society by making it more varied and, in my opinion, more exciting. But the steady stream of new immigrants has also helped the globalizers by providing cheap labor for their enterprises and siphoning the brightest workers from around the world to the tech industry in Silicon Valley. The needs of countries losing their most educated or industrious citizens to migration are often ignored in the debate. As countries lose citizens to migration to the U.S., they also lose out in their "investment" in their citizens' education or training, while the U.S. gains an already educated person or an industrious worker without a comparable investment.

President Trump vows to stop illegal immigration and boasts about building a wall to further separate Mexico and the U.S., spending billions of dollars for this effort. Trump supporters want to curtail if not eliminate immigration and "round-up" immigrants who are in the U.S. illegally, especially if they have a criminal record. This means approximately 11 million illegal or undocumented immigrants, although the actual number is decreasing as some immigrants return to their country of origin. This number is probably too large and costly for deportation efforts.

Between 1965 and 2000, the percentage of white progressives favoring increased immigration hovered around ten percent. But this number has swelled dramatically. From the mid-2000s to roughly 2008, the number of progressives favoring more immigration increased to the 20-30 percent range. Showing a substantial increase lately, as of 2018, it sits at over 50 percent.[15] Although the immigration issue has been passed on down the line by Democrats and Republicans far too long, Trump's immigration rhetoric has created more chaos and fostered more ill-will than necessary.

THE PROGRESSIVE WORLDVIEW TODAY

The Democratic Party is not immune to the disrupting national and global forces that are wracking the nation and world. People of different stripes are grappling with governing a future that is uncertain and contentious. Progressives on the left believe they have an answer to governing in these tumultuous times that has gained tentative but growing traction across the United States and Western Europe. A question arises as to why has there been in the last decade or so such a significant shift to the progressive left among those on the left side of the political spectrum and what are the consequences of this leftward shift. Let's first look at what groups of Americans support a progressive worldview.

Not only is the United States politically divided, Democratic Party voters in the 2018 mid-term election were as well. According to New York Times columnists Thomas Edsall, Democratic voters are split into three roughly equal groups. The first group identifies as very liberal. It is two-thirds white and the most educated of all three groups. They are the most politically engaged and play a disproportionate role in setting the political agenda. The second group says they are "somewhat liberal" and is also two-thirds white. These two groups have below the Democratic average of minority representation; roughly a quarter are African-American and Hispanic voters. I call these two groups the progressives. Those in the third group are voters who describe themselves as moderate to conservative. Interestingly, this group has the largest number of minorities; it is 26 percent black, 19 percent Hispanic, 7 percent other nonwhites, and it has the smallest percentage of whites, 48 percent.[16]

The three groups favor different sets of policies. As Edsall notes: On the left, the very progressive voters stress the environment, protecting immigrants, abortion rights, and race/gender issues, while the moderate to conservative Democrats are more concerned with job creation and lowering taxes.[17] Of very liberal Democrats, 72 percent want to protect immigrants;

only 42 percent of moderate-to-conservative Democrats share that priority. Of the two very liberal groups, 66 percent want candidates to address race and gender issues, compared with only 42 percent of the moderates. Ironically, as Edsall points out, "data demonstrates that the group containing the largest proportion of minority voters is the most skeptical of some of the most progressive policies."[18]

Other ideological gaps between the three groups of Democrats are becoming more blatant. Journalist Zach Goldberg, for example, has found that white liberals became the "only demographic group in America to display a pro-outgroup bias—meaning that among all the different groups surveyed white liberals were the only one that expressed a preference for other racial and ethnic communities above their own." These findings are particularly significant because they weaken the case that minorities across the board advocate for very liberal policies. Furthermore, Goldberg concludes that black and Hispanic Democrats are "more likely to part ways with white progressives when it comes to contemporary social and gender-identity issues, including views of the #MeToo movement." They are less likely to support these issues than white progressives.[19]

Over the last few decades, I have found that the political parties in the U.S. have drawn a line with a permanent marker between their ideologies. If any progressive, for example, deviates from the "established" stances on same sex marriage, abortion, health care, immigration, trade, taxes, foreign policy, or a host of other issues, Twitter activists spring into action to condemn their views and black-list them from the progressive purity list. The same holds true for Republican hard-liners. Neoliberal, globalization-supporting Republicans have been sharply criticized by populist right supporters. The baseline attitudes expressed by white liberals on racial and social justice questions have become decidedly more progressive, more predictable, and less flexible than in the past.

A new "woke" or enlightened ideology has entered the political landscape among white progressives. According to Goldberg it is "the rapidly changing political ideology of white liberals that is remaking American politics. As woke ideology has accelerated, a growing faction of white liberals have pulled away from the average opinions held by the rest of the coalition of Democratic voters—including minority groups in the party." The revolution in woke ideology among progressives has contributed to a torrent of consequences ranging from changes in the attitudes and outlooks voiced in media and popular culture to embracing new political rhetoric and strategies by the Democratic Party.[20]

A vast majority of white progressives emotionally identify with people of color. For example, the percentage of white liberals perceiving discrimination against immigrants more than doubled between 2000 (29%) and 2013 (57%), which is well before the Trump phenomenon. Additionally, between 2006 and 2014, the percentage of white progressives expressing strong sympathy toward illegal immigrants and their families grew from 22 percent to 42 percent. From these statistics, it is clear that the rise of woke ideology is not just a visceral response to Trump; it has been building over the past decade. Interestingly, according to Goldberg, "black and Asian Democratic liberals are significantly more supportive of restrictive immigration policies and less positive toward racial/ethnic diversity than their white counterparts." Paradoxically, the attitudes and policy preferences of white progressives are generally unrepresentative of the "marginalized communities" with whom they are supposed to be allies.[21]

Not only is the group of white, affluent, highly-educated progressives influencing attitudes of race and immigration, they are also having an outsized influence on policies and the media. Elected officials are most responsive to the voices of campaign contributors they hear from the most, and white progressives are the most politically active group. While white progressives/liberals make up 20-24 percent of the general population and only eight percent of the most leftist progressives, they are more likely to consider themselves activists, are more engaged on social media, and are one of the most affluent groups in the nation. Although a democracy is most vibrant when all voices are heard, as Goldberg points out, "The danger is that 'woke' white activists acting on behalf of voiceless minorities have had their perceptions distorted by social media-tinted caricatures that obscure more objective measures of reality and end up silencing or ignoring what the voiceless groups, themselves, have to say about what policies are in their best interest."[22]

American society is made up of a balance between the guilt, empathy, and compassion of progressives and their more in-group, hierarchy-oriented conservative counterparts. A balance of both is necessary for a just, healthy, and responsible social order. But Goldberg stresses, "The problem is when these moral emotions become hyperactive and detached from objective reality; when they motivate the division of society into allies and enemies; and when they generate a level of sanctimonious outrage and judgment that places all political dissent beyond the pale."[23]

The proliferation of digital and social media has fueled a carnival of excesses. Goldberg explains, "It cultivates an image of the world soaked in the very oppression and injustices to which the user is most sensitive and attuned—and thus one that frequently triggers liberal moral alarms."[24] The image of oppression and injustice is amplified on Twitter and YouTube feeds, and the sense of moral outrage drips from the lips of progressive commentators. But for this moral outrage to arouse thoughtful outcomes it has to be kept in perspective. Unfortunately, among many progressives America is seen only through one single lens—an unjust, racist, and homophobic nation in need of a radical revolution. Who is to lead this revolution? The educated, white progressive group self-nominates for this honor. Adding to this perception of injustice held by white progressives is the notion of white privilege which adds to feelings of guilt, anger, and an empathic desire to help the suffering of others, or at least signal to others one's moral virtue.

In the space of a few years, white liberal attitudes that have not fluctuated substantially for decades have been radically overturned. In contrast, the attitudes of white conservatives—and conservatives in general—have moved at a slower gait, if at all. Goldberg points out that for progressives "the lack of awareness of how fast and far their attitudes have shifted fosters an illusion of conservative extremism. In reality, the conservatives of today are not all that different from the conservatives of years past. And it's the frustration with white conservatives' inability or reluctance to keep pace with liberals on the path to enlightenment that is intensifying our political divide."[25] Conservatives, as we found out in Chapter 5, do not respond well to rapid social change. They trend toward normative and structural stability.

The initiatives set in motion by white progressives have provoked reactions and countermeasures from conservatives and Republicans. The imposition and spread of progressive attitudes that strive for more racial justice, awareness of white privilege, and compassionate language have had the opposite effect on those who are the target of progressive scorn. The real or perceived imposition and spread of progressive norms can actually backfire in the long term, eliciting psychological reactance—a gut resistance in the face of perceived social pressure.[26] For conservatives, this over-exposure to politically correct language by well-intentioned progressives was one of the factors that drove many of them to vote for Donald Trump in 2016.

CONCLUDING INSIGHTS: THE PROGRESSIVE WORLDVIEW

This leftward shift in outlook has yielded several paradoxes. As was pointed out in the above section, white progressives are now farther left on immigration and race and diversity issues than the typical Hispanic or African-American voter. Second, two of the greatest marks of privilege in our society are skin color and education levels, and yet in the Democratic Party it is the highly-educated whites who express the greatest alienation within the system that directly benefits them. Third, the progressive framework is egalitarian, but the shift has opened up wide opinion and cultural gaps between this highly-educated elite and less-educated groups.

Why have white progressives moved so far to the left so fast? There are several speculations. Those on the left claim that America has historically been a racist country, tracing racism's roots back to slavery and the segregated Jim Crow system put in place after slavery ended. They assert that systemic racism has never abated and continues today. Highly-educated white progressives have woken up to this fact and are out in front of other groups in facing this reality. They find it a moral obligation to fight systemic racism in whatever forms it takes. White progressives have also woken to the discrimination and misery inflicted on brown people by whites throughout the world because of colonialism, imperialism, and capitalist exploitation. Once again, they claim they have a moral obligation to right this wrong, even if means opening our borders to whomever wants to enter the country or pay reparations to African Americans whose ancestors toiled under slavery.

Other progressives cite economic issues as the key reason for the left-

113

ward tilt. They say the failures of neoliberalism (see Chapter 7) contributed to greater income inequality, outsourcing of high-paying manufacturing jobs, and the spurring of economic globalization. They believe the economic policies of democratic socialism—a higher minimum wage, more regulation of the economy, breaking-up big banks, and moving to clean energy jobs—will result in less income inequality and greater protection of the environment than a neoliberal economic system.

Those on the political center or right take a more cynical look at the reasons for the leftward shift. They observe that the creed of wokeness that is seeping into progressive circles is mostly centered in the prestigious universities and the affluent progressive enclaves along the coasts. In this take, if you're a rich, white child of privilege you have to go to extraordinary lengths to prove you're one of the good children of privilege and not one of the bad ones. White progressives embed compassionate narratives to make themselves feel good without really undoing the structures that keep them in their secure, top-tier lifestyle bubbles.[27]

The good news is that the U.S. is a well-established liberal democracy with long-standing institutions run by committed people. We have withstood deep divisions through history—slavery, the Civil War, Reconstruction, the Depression, World War II, the 1968 rebellions—that could have easily torn apart a country with less sound institutions. It is up to these institutions—the judicial branch, a free press, civic organizations, local and state governments, religious institutions, empowered ordinary citizens, and many others—to help us weather the negative storm swirling through the country that seems bent on disrupting more than building, excluding rather than including, and hating more than kindness. We have choices in what kind of worldview to construct today and in the future. We can only select the worldview that speaks to us in our present moment.

Chapter 7
The Globalized Worldview

Globalization is not a monolithic force but an evolving set of consequences - some good, some bad and some unintended. It is the new reality.... John B. Larson

INTRODUCTION: A GLOBALIZED WORLDVIEW

A globalized worldview, the fourth worldview, is sweeping the world to-day. This worldview has greatly changed the landscape in which people around the world work, play, interact, and live their everyday lives. Taking shape in the 1980s, it has greatly intensified in the twenty-first century. It reflects the many ways in which people on an increasingly populated planet have been drawn together, not only by their own movements but also through the flow of goods, services, capital, labor, technology, ideas, and information.

Globalization is a complex, multi-dimensional phenomenon that interconnects worldwide economic, political, cultural, social, environmental, and technological forces, transcending national boundaries. It refers to the worldwide compression of space and time and the reduced importance of the nation-state. Through globalization the world has become a single place that serves as a frame of reference, influencing the way billions of people around the world conduct their everyday lives.

Growing out of the modern world, a globalized worldview incorporates many of its attributes but intensifies and quickens the pace for the growth and expansion of this way of discerning the world. Arguably, globalization is most heavily influenced by the United States and is especially prevalent in intensely industrialized areas of Canada, Europe, Japan, and Australia, yet it reaches across the world into many areas of China, India, Southeast Asia,

Latin America, the Middle East, and Africa as well.

At this point, I would argue that a globalized worldview is the most all-encompassing worldview and continues its unabated outward expansion and lure. It expands and deepens the capitalist economic practices that were launched in the modern era, yet the globalized form of capitalism is flexible enough to accommodate communist nations such as China and Vietnam and former socialist nations such as India. For many people, following a globalized worldview has "opened up" the world in many positive ways—the Internet and communication networks, transportation linkages and travel opportunities, sophisticated technology, breakthrough medical discoveries, diverse entertainment options, and comfortable living standards—but for others, the destructive effects of globalization have resulted in job loss, pension reductions, a loss of community and family, social isolation, depression and hopelessness; and a debasing of values, standards, and moral conduct. There are many other people who challenge its corporate dominance, unbridled consumerism, expedient business climate, ravaged environment, and effects on the human psyche.

While people in the traditional and progressive worldviews have sets of characteristics and hold certain values, globalizers do as well. Karen Stenner describes three kinds of conservatism: authoritarian, status quo, and laissez-faire conservatism. I described the authoritarian and status quo conservatism in Chapter 4, the Traditional Worldview. In this chapter I will describe the third type of conservatism: laissez-faire conservatism.

Although this group of conservatives may identify with the traditional or progressive worldviews along with the globalized worldview, they are primarily concerned with socioeconomic status and the distribution of wealth, which is by far the most important and consistent determinant of globalized, free market values. The more privileged the globalizer's socioeconomic status in which he or she is favored by market distribution of economic rewards, the greater the opposition to government intervention in the economy. Stenner explains, "This attitude toward government intervention in the economy is largely a product of whether one would be more the beneficiary or benefactor of that intervention. This applies to a number of variables variously reflecting aspects of socioeconomic status, such as subjective social class, occupational prestige, education, and family income." She also notes that unlike the authoritarian and status quo

116

conservatives, across diverse cultures globalizers generally are more tolerant of difference and do not object to rapid social change.[1]

A GLOBALIZED ECONOMY

Global capitalism is the dominant economic system in the world, with almost all nations pulled into its economic web. National and local economies, regulated and protected by national and local governments, have been largely folded into one integrated economic system governed by capitalist principles. Business, currency exchanges, and trade policies are conducted in a global economic marketplace that ignores national boundaries. Global multinational corporations make many of the rules and conduct the business of the world marketplace. They promote a consumer-focused economy by extending their broad influence to the farthest reaches of the globe.

In the modern worldview, capitalism and communism and their variants were the two dominant economic systems to guide the economies of modern nations. With the collapse of communism in the early 1990s, the American form of free market capitalism reigned. Even the former communist nations seemed to eagerly embrace capitalism. Today, the global economy can be separated into three related dimensions: neoliberalism/state capitalism, economic globalization, and the financial sector. Let's start with an examination of neoliberalism and state capitalism.

Neoliberalism, a version of capitalism, has prevailed in the United States since the early 1980s. It is one of the ways in which the rules of the global economy operate. Although the concept is the same, it is also known as free market capitalism, free trade capitalism, supply-side economics, laissez-faire capitalism, classical capitalism, corporate capitalism, market fundamentalism, or an Anglo-American version of capitalism. "Neo" in neoliberalism means new, since it is a newer version of the classical economic system found in the nineteenth and early twentieth centuries pioneered by Great Britain called liberalism. Since neoliberalism's definition was established hundreds of years ago in the Enlightenment era, the term should not be confused with the conservative/liberal divide we see in politics today.

Neoliberalism favors free trade, privatization of commonly-held entities,

117

minimal government intervention in business operations, low taxes for businesses, and minimal public expenditure for social services. Neoliberals give several reasons for their support of their preferred economic system: self-interest motivates humans, competitive behavior is more rational than cooperation, materialism is a measure of progress, markets allocate resources most efficiently, governments should only provide infrastructure and enforce property laws and contracts, and inequality results from individuals failing to adapt to the new economic reality.

Neoliberals favor multinational corporations (MNCs), with services in at least two countries, as a form of ownership of capital in the global economy. MNCs have maneuvered to gain access to the decision-making operations of international, rule-making institutions like the World Bank, World Trade Organization (WTO) and International Monetary Fund (IMF). The World Bank loans money to nations to build large infrastructure projects, the WTO governs the rules of global trade, and the IMF supports global monetary cooperation. At this time, the rules of these three institutions favor Western countries and MNCs. Because rules made by these institutions take precedence over national laws, national enterprises are obliged to comply with them or risk economic ruin. Thus, these global institutions have generally usurped oversight of corporations from national governments. For example, national laws passed by a nation's legislative branch can be in violation of rules passed by the WTO and are, thus, subservient to WTO rules.

After the collapse of communism in the early 1990s, it appeared that the neoliberal model was becoming a global favorite. But in the 2000s, another version of capitalism—state capitalism—emerged as an attractive alternative to neoliberalism for many countries as a way to structure their economy. In keeping with their political situation, many communist, socialist, and former command economy nations favored state capitalism over the free market system. In state capitalism, government officials direct markets to create wealth as they see fit. This economic system is not merely the re-emergence of socialist central planning in a twenty-first century package, but it is a form of state-engineered capitalism particular to each government that practices it. Political scientist Ian Bremmer defines state capitalism as "a system in which the state plays the role of leading economic actor and uses markets primarily for political gain." State capitalist governments believe that public wealth, public investment, and public enterprise offer the surest path toward political stability and economic development.[2] For example, the royal family of Saudi Arabia invests the kingdom's massive oil wealth for lucrative returns. The Chinese government sends state-owned firms abroad, especially to Africa, in search of long-term access to oil, gas, metals, and minerals. China continues to have a communist form of government with many state-owned enterprises, while also following an export-oriented form of capitalism in which the government supports industries that export products to other countries. Among the world's leading state capitalist countries are China, with ties to the Chinese Communist Party; Saudi Arabia, with ties to the Saudi royal family; and Russia, with ties to the powerful current president, Vladimir Putin.[3]

A second dimension of the global economy is economic globalization. Economic globalization refers to the increasing expansion of capitalism around the world, even integrating non-capitalist economies into a world economic system. Even though countries may have different versions of capitalism, they still participate in the world economy. With economic globalization, all aspects of the economy, including trade, investment, production, technology, and labor movement, are carried out across local and national boundaries. Many national and local economies are subsumed into one integrated economic system governed by capitalist principles. There is also a growing concentration of wealth and influence in multi-national corporations, huge financial institutions, and state-run enterprises. With economic globalization has come the absorption or systematic destruction of centuries-old local/domestic economies around the world.

Certain factors are necessary for economic globalization to function. These ten factors are pieced together into an economic globalization puzzle. All of the puzzle pieces make up the full picture of economic globalization (see *The Global Economy: Connecting the Roots of a Holistic System* for more information). Nations are persuaded, some say duped, into conforming to the rules of economic globalization with the threat that if they do not participate in the global marketplace, they will be left behind in economic development.

The financial sector, the third component of the global economy, encompasses a broad range of institutions that deal with the management of money.

Among these are banks (commercial and investment), credit card companies, insurance enterprises, consumer finance companies, stock brokerages, investment funds, foreign exchange services, real estate, and others. Currently, the Industrial & Commercial Bank of China is the largest bank in the world.

Ten Pieces of the Economic Globalization Puzzle

1. Reduction of Local Economies
2. Economic Growth
3. Consumerism
4. Rule-making Institutions
5. Free Trade
6. Privatization and Commodification
7. Concentration of Corporate and State Enterprises
8. Specialization
9. Reduction of Labor's Influence
10. Military Hegemony

Financialization took off after the economic crisis of the 1970s. The U.S. government had closely regulated the financial sector since the 1930s because of the debacle of the unregulated industry in the roaring 1920s that resulted in the Great Depression of the 1930s. But many thought it was time to deregulate the financial sector, and deregulation gained steam in the 1980s. Technological advancements made it easier and more efficient to devise financial products spurring the notion, promoted by industry insiders, that deregulation was the smart thing to do.

As a result of deregulation, there was a rash of sophisticated speculative financial products, such as derivatives, and escaping governmental monitoring and regulation. The trading in speculative financial products was little more than gambling; hence, the name "casino economy." In fact, speculative finance boiled down to an effort to squeeze more "value" out of already created value, instead of creating new value.[4] In other words, the goal was not innovation to create new wealth, but to try to get more margins or value out of existing products and services. CDOs, collateralized debt obligations, were an example of this complex process that later became vehicles for refinancing mortgage-backed securities. During this time of financial speculation, instability rocked the financial sector, skipping from one crisis to another. The government had to step in several times to rescue the overheated financial sector with "bail-out" packages funded by taxpayers. Thus, there is now an increased bifurcation between the hyperactive financial economy, known as Wall Street, and the stagnant real economy, known as Main Street. This is not an accidental development; the financial sector exploded precisely to make up for the stagnation owing to overproduction in the real economy.[5]

SIX FACTORS FUELING THE GLOBAL ECONOMY

1. Consumer Capitalism

Capitalism needs constant new sources of wealth creation to expand and grow. Since the 1980s, the expansion of consumerism has been the underpinning of wealth creation in the U.S. and global economy. For example, private consumption expenditures make up about 70 percent of the U.S. Gross Domestic Product (GDP). Goods and services not only are provided to satisfy common needs but also to secure identity and meaning. Consumption is powerfully shaped by forces such as advertising, cultural norms, social pressures, and psychological associations. Sociologist Madeline Levine criticized what she saw as a change in American culture in the post-war years—"a shift away from values of community, spirituality, and integrity, and toward competition, materialism and disconnection."[6]

Capitalism has been immensely successful at producing goods and services for about 20 percent of the world's population who can afford these products, yet the other 80 percent of the world's population cannot. This is one of the many paradoxes of capitalism. It is supremely efficient at producing goods and services, but is not proficient at distributing them to those in real need. In fact, capitalism has been too successful in producing goods and services. Thus, producers have sought ways to induce consumers to buy more—more than they actually need. Enter the advertising industry. The single goal of this industry is to create gimmicks and enticements to convince consumers to purchase more and more.

2. Advertising

The advertising industry finds ways to stimulate new consumer needs and desires, creating a malaise among those whose only cure is to buy more. The traditional values of the Protestant ethic that have shaped the American value system since the country's founding include thrift, hard work and its rewards, long-term planning, rational behavior, stability, and adherence to rules and laws. The dilemma for advertisers is that a person with these values does not impulsively consume. The advertising industry figured out that it needed to change individual behaviors and values to those that are impulsive, irrational, self-centered, and reckless. Then it launched a brazen and successful campaign to do so.[7]

Adults holding to a consumerist ethic are pawns in the hands of the advertising industry. The demands of the mobile global economy have severed consumers' ties to their traditional communities; instead, their sense of belonging and identity has shifted to brands of consumer products. The brands selected by an individual or family indicate their particular income, class, and place. These are called lifestyle choices. These branded identities are superficial veneers replacing traditional family, ethnic, cultural, and national identity. Corporate names such as Nike, emblazoned on T-shirts and athletic wear, for example, identify the values of the wearer while providing free advertising for the company. Although it appears that we freely choose these identities, in reality they are reflective of the permeation of the ubiquitous commercial culture into every aspect of our lives. Advertisers happily promote this brand identification among consumers because it cuts across national and ethnic boundaries to mold a true globalization of identity.[8]

3. Economic Growth

Through the march of human history having more comforts and surplus food has made people's lives easier and more predictable. As populations have grown, so have economies. Unlimited growth made some sense decades ago when the human population of the world was relatively low and natural resources for human consumption appeared to be endless. In this "empty world" money and human labor were the limiting factors, while natural resources were abundant. In this context, there was no need to worry about environmental destruction and social disruptions, since they were assumed to be relatively small and ultimately solvable. It made sense to focus on growth of the economy as a primary means to improve human living standards.[9]

Economic growth is the process by which wealth increases over time as the economy adds new market value to goods and services. It is an essential component of capitalism, which must expand constantly to generate new wealth. Its drive to accumulate and its built-in tendency to expand distinguish capitalism from other economic systems. Innovative activity—which in other types of economies is optional—becomes mandatory under capitalism, a life-and-death matter for businesses. Through history, the creation of new technology proceeded at an even-handed pace, often requiring decades or even centuries to develop, but under capitalism, time and innovation speed up because, quite simply, time is money.

Promoting growth—achieving ever-greater economic wealth and prosperity—may be the most widely shared and forceful cause in the world today. Modern societies regard growth as their "secular religion."[10] We now live in a world relatively full of humans and the infrastructure that we have built. In this new world, human populations and labor supply are vast, while the natural resources to support human life are limited. There is a dawning recognition that the growth model eagerly adopted by modern countries is no longer working; that model is geared towards a time in the past that differs from the reality of today. And all this is happening at the expense of our natural world, which is being battered by the demand to produce more products for human consumption and absorb its wastes.

Individuals support growth policies because they accept the commonly held notion that growth will give them and the next generation a better standard of living. Governments seek growth as a remedy for just about every imaginable problem. Economists believe growth to be essential for full employment, upward mobility, and technical achievements. Politicians encourage growth because it expands the economic pie, and they can postpone hard choices.[11] Growth, development, progress, advancement, gain, success, improvement, and prosperity are deeply embedded assumptions and values that are celebrated among globalizers. Systems thinkers refer to these qualities as structural reasons for the continuation of growth.

4. Information
In a global economy, information is added to the economic mix of land, labor, and capital. Information is specific data or particular services applied to a product, service, or activity that adds monetary value. Some examples of value-added information are services from advertisers, lawyers, marketers, accountants, insurers, financiers, efficiency experts, risk analysts, and computer applications. The purpose of adding information is to maximize productivity, profitability, and efficiency, and attract recognition to a product or service in an intensely competitive world.[12] Information in the globalized economy is not just applied for societal well-being, but to maximize profit.

A sharing economy takes a variety of forms, often leveraging information technology to enable individuals, corporations, non-profits, and government with information to efficiently distribute, share, and reuse the excess capacity in goods and services. This sharing economy succeeds because of a depressed labor market, in which many people supplement their income by commodifying their property and labor in different ways. People join the sharing economy because they may have lost a full-time job, including a few cases where the pricing structure of the sharing economy may have made their old jobs less profitable or obsolete. For example, many full-time taxi drivers have switched to driving for Uber, the transportation company that develops, markets, and operates the Uber mobile app, which allows consumers to submit a trip request that is linked to their network of Uber drivers. Uber is displacing traditional economy taxi drivers and companies with mostly part-time, independent contractor workers who use their own car to transport people for extra income. The real economic benefit goes to the privately owned Uber Corporation and its shareholders, currently worth $120 billion, which takes in a big slice of the profits.[13]

5. Labor and Economic Globalization
The 1941 Stolper-Samuelson theorem explains labor trends accompanying the spread of economic globalization, as well as trade. It basically says that the effect of trade between a core (rich) nation and a periphery (poor) nation is that the wages for the unskilled labor force in the core nation will be lower because they are competing globally with unskilled workers in a periphery nation. This

theorem is currently being played out in the U.S. and other core countries. Since the 1980s, two and half billion people in China, India, Eastern Europe, and the former Soviet Union have discarded economic isolationism and joined the global economy. When the global economy added these workers, wages fell across the board. When a core, capital-abundant country (such as the U.S.) trades with a labor-abundant country (such as China), wages in the core country fall and corporate profits go up. The theorem's economic logic is simple. Free trade is tantamount to a massive increase in the core country's labor supply, since the products made by periphery country workers can now be imported. Additionally, demand for workers in the core country falls as corporations shift labor-intensive production to a periphery country. The net result is an increase in the labor supply and a decrease in labor demand in the core country; thus wages fall.[14] Economist Thomas Palley notes, "Now, this shift is coming together in the form of a 'super-sized' Stolper-Samuelson effect, and has depressing consequences for American workers."[15] Adding two and half billion people from low-wage countries to the global labor market is an unprecedented event.

Samuelson questioned the benefits of economic globalization for labor in older industrialized countries. With the emergence of China, India, and Eastern Europe, the dam of isolation holding back two and half billion workers from the global economic workforce has been removed. If two swimming pools are joined, the water level will eventually equalize. A threat to labor is competition. Manufacturing workers in core countries are already competing with technological innovations as well as labor from periphery countries, with dire consequences for manufacturing workers in the core countries. Samuelson claimed "that since U.S. labor has lost its old monopoly on American advanced know-how and capital, free trade could indeed lower the share of wages in the U.S. GDP and increase overall inequality."[16]

Outsourcing involves the contracting out of a business function to an external provider, usually to a low-wage country. One of the reasons for the rapid decline in manufacturing jobs in core countries is the outsourcing of jobs to low-wage periphery countries, such as China, Mexico, Indonesia, India, and Vietnam. The same is happening to professional and higher-paid workers in core countries with similar effects. Outsourcing is not just the province of the manufacturing sector, but includes professionals in software, banking, insurance, accounting, pharmaceuticals, and engineering. Therefore, in core countries most of the new jobs are in highly skilled occupations or domestic services and low-paying retail work.[17] The middle has been hollowed out.

6. Technology

Technological changes have ushered in faster and more sophisticated communication and transportation technologies that transcend national boundaries and more intricately connect the world than at any time in the past. These instantaneous high-speed communication devices with sophisticated computer technologies have revolutionized our relations with each other. The Internet, television, high-speed travel, cell phones, and other forms of telecommunications link the world by dissolving former barriers of time and distance and provide new connections between people. But on a downside, the extreme gap between the global rich and poor is due in part to technology and economic globalization.

A GLOBALIZED SOCIETY

Since the economy is global in scope, the class structure is as well. A global economy has changed the class structure that was formerly nation-based to one that is now globally-based. The American economy has been in the midst of a sea change, shifting from industry to services and information technology and integrating itself far more tightly into a single, global market for goods, labor, and capital. China, India, and other countries have emerged as economic competitors, capable of producing large volumes of high-value, low-priced goods and services. This transformation has been underway since the 1980s, but the pace of change has quickened since 2000 and even more so since the 2008 financial crisis.[18]

For core nations, the hollowing out of the middle class way of life has a triple-edged onslaught that favors the wealthy more than the middle and working classes: technological innovations, neoliberalism, and economic globalization. Along with the hollowing out of the American middle class, there is tak-

126

ing place a surge in the formation of a middle class in Brazil, Russia, India, China, and South Africa (BRICS), and others.

The wealthy have designed the rules of neoliberalism and economic globalization to benefit them; they encourage competition among countries for business, which drives down taxes on corporations, weakens health and environmental protections, and undermines labor rights, such as collective bargaining.[19] On the other hand, policies that favor the middle class—higher income tax rates on the wealthy, ample funding for education, low-interest loans for education, research and development that encourage job creation, a fair inheritance tax rate, tax deductions for home ownership, a safety net for economic hardships, and pensions for retirement—have all been eroding since the early 1980s.[20] Also, the formation and profitability of small businesses have been hampered by "big box" retailers, such as Walmart, and online businesses like Amazon that undercut their smaller rivals.

The global middle class consists of one billion individuals. They have average wealth per adult of $10,000 to $100,000 and own one-sixth of global wealth. Almost 60 percent or 587 million individuals in the middle segment are located in Asia Pacific, the fastest-growing economies. The middle class of this region is expected to replace indebted U.S. middle class households as the global growth locomotive.[21] The middle class has expanded in Asia Pacific countries and has shrunk in many core or Western nations and other periphery countries mostly because they simply stopped making things and started buying them from the Asia Pacific countries. Since 2000, the U.S. has lost over three million manufacturing jobs; Brazil has lost two million since 1998, and South Africa has lost nearly one million. In the past, Argentina assembled televisions; now it purchases most of them from abroad. Mozambique in Africa packaged its cashew crop thirty years ago; today the country ships its raw nuts overseas for others to package. Zambians made their own clothes in the 1980s; now they sort through bundles of clothes shipped from the U.S. and Europe. The Hunters Point neighborhood in San Francisco, California (US) manufactured the ships that delivered American-made goods to the world; now the ships docked in the Bay Area's ports are mostly from East Asia, unloading foreign-made products for U.S. consumers.[22]

Increasingly, in some countries the workplace is more central to social life than the family. Family members are spending more time at work or school, or going to and from work than in the home. Many critics contend that the workplace has evolved into a substitute family. Generally, both men and women spend more time at work than with their families, resulting in personal workplace relationships. While the workplace offers rewards, acceptance, and recognition that are often missing in family relationships, it can also be shattering to individuals if their workplace ceases operation or if they are terminated from a job. Some critics argue that work consumes so much family energy and time that in many cases family life is an empty shell. Instead of creating their own viable family life with all the accompanying trials and tribulations, many individuals turn to television, computers, their personal devices, and social media as a fantasy replacement for family life. As a substitute family, the workplace and social media fail to provide the stability, continuity, and acceptance that a healthy family traditionally furnishes. With growing temporary employment stints, job uncertainty, and telecommuting, the workplace is not a source of stability and security needed by individuals; thus, many people feel more insecure, uncertain, anxious, alienated, and fragmented.

POLITICAL GLOBALIZATION

Politically, nations are no longer the only defining political entity. The nation state still exists as a workable political organization but can no longer deal in isolation with complex problems—terrorism, environmental pollution, weapons proliferation, conflict resolution, disease control, drug proliferation, and migration—that disregard local, regional, and national boundaries and can only be addressed on a trans-national basis. Nations share their former exclusive sovereignty, in varying degrees, with other world organizations. These organizations include the United Nations (UN), World Court, the World Trade Organization (WTO), and World Bank; regional organizations such as the North Atlantic Treaty Organization (NATO) and European Union (EU); and regional trade alliances like the North American Free Trade Association (NAFTA). Human rights agencies such as Amnesty International, humanitarian agencies Red Cross and Doctors without Borders, and environmental watchdog groups like Greenpeace and Sierra Club also meet global challenges.

Multi-national corporations play a significant political role in the globalized world as well. They, in many cases, seduce local, state, and national politicians with campaign donations or outright bribes to formulate policies and laws that favor their profitable undertakings.

Sometimes nations, such as the United States, balk at giving up their sovereignty to join with others in fostering mutual world cooperation. With the upswing of the right-wing populist movements in the U.S. and Western Europe, populist supporters have been more vocal than in the past in disparaging global institutions such as the UN and emotionally calling for patriotism and allegiance to their particular nation.

Democracy is still a favored political structure and liberalism an attractive political philosophy in much of the world. Yet, since the end of the financial crisis, democracy has been under increasing assault from within and outside its borders. More authoritarian types of political configuration have made advances in countries such as Turkey, Poland, Hungary, Brazil, Russia, and others. In times of turmoil and uncertainty, as we are experiencing today, many people gravitate to the presumed order and stability of authoritarian leaders. Attempts to establish democracy in nations such as Egypt, Syria, Libya, and China have failed miserably. Yet, despite world disorder, the West still encourages democracy as a form of political organization. As well, many social justice groups fight the oligarchic tendencies of global corporations to ensure that their nations do indeed retain democratic institutions, and that the form of democracy embraced by emerging nations is not just a facade for the real corporate powers that operate behind the scenes.

In a globalized worldview, conflict and warfare are different than in the modern worldview. Conflict has become more unpredictable, random, irrational, and volatile. Wars can be sparked by many factors, among them: scarce resources like water, food, fuel, or other basic necessities; religious differences and perspectives; different worldviews; exploitation by core nations; and tensions and anxieties created by rapid social disruption with the accompanying loss of solidifying traditions and customs. Recent terrorists' attacks by marginalized people resisting modernization and globalization are examples of conflict in a globalized world. Also, within nations, such as France, the United States, and Britain, domestic terrorist groups wielding automatic assault weapons kill in an irrational frenzy of hatred towards others. These capricious acts of violence leave negative feelings of anxiety and resentment by citizens of the nation in which the violence took place.

CULTURAL GLOBALIZATION

Consumerism is touted as a new "world religion." Led by the U.S., a vast entertainment and advertising sector has perpetuated and glamorized the notion of consumerism as a form of status and as a symbol of affiliation with modern culture. Rampant consumerism has gone way beyond the basic products for a comfortable material life to a frenzied accumulation of consumer items that purportedly bring an individual psychological well-being and status recognition.

The globalized worldview is reflected in mainstream American thought in what I label the "consumer creed." The principles of the consumer creed are generally accepted by a vast majority of Americans who have energetically exported its tenets to others throughout the world, such as India and China. It includes: the desire for a comfortable life-style with a profusion of consumer comforts; an attitude of economic progress in which hard work is blessed with ample financial rewards; a right to material abundance without concern for the environmental costs or for the welfare of those who provide these goods and services; a competitive, ambitious, individualistic value system; a professional or entrepreneurial career preference where wealth is realized without regard for how it is obtained; faith in technological progress as the means to solve all problems; a disconnect between our materialistic/consumer way of life and its effects upon the environment; and the attitude that this "consumer creed" is the highest ideal and this way of life should be shared with the rest of the world. Without regard for future generations, the consumer creed has left many people discontented, alienated, unfulfilled, and in a spiritual malaise while leaving the planet environmentally ravaged.

A common language acts as a unifying factor, and English is increasingly that universal language. The world's elites speak English in part because of the influence of Great Britain in the nineteenth century and the hegemony of the U.S. in the twentieth century. English, the language of business, commerce, and education, is the unofficial language of those holding a globalized worldview.

Accompanying the sophistication and expansion of computer technology is the availability of an overwhelming amount of information. Technological and economic developments have outpaced our cultural and social responses, often leaving us confused about how to make sense of this overwhelming influx of information and rapid change. Intense debates rage among diverse religious, civic, environmental, and other concerned groups about the future; some are problematic as the dialogue descends into acts of incivility. Others see the debates as a reaction to complex changes and anxiety brought about by rapid technological changes, random acts of violence, economic developments, and future uncertainty.

One key change in communication is the deemphasizing of face-to-face, interpersonal communication. Technological devices—smart phones, texting, email, Twitter, Facebook, and on-line courses—erase the boundaries of time and space that had previously slowed and restricted communication by fostering instant communication with anyone in the world. These forms of communication connect people removed from their social and physical environment, but also separate interactions from the social spaces in which people physically exist. In this way, technological forms of communication contribute to the annihilation of the public space which had connected people with one another. For example, a huge trend in education is on-line or distance learning courses, in which students do not attend a traditional classroom but complete the subject material on the computer through an on-line program. The direct, inter-personal exchange between students and instructor is eliminated and displaced by on-line communication.[23] Our attention is no longer directed only to those within the confines of our physical space but beyond it. We can become isolated islands in the public sphere, separated from others by our technological wonders.

Many cultural expressions—music, dance, art, entertainment, literature, film, and dress—have been made into commodities for the world consumer market and follow a distinctive Western commercial bent. Dazzling sets and astonishing effects provide manufactured excitement. Mass-produced shows featuring a renowned celebrity can command premium prices for star-packed spectacles. Entertainment can range from celebrity singers to Broadway musicals and plays, comedians, musicians, music festivals, and stage acts. All have in common a hefty price that globalized viewers are willing to pay.

In the art world, sophisticated buyers with fistfuls of cash are intent upon purchasing authentic and unique art pieces that distinguish them as connoisseurs. Many are collectors of one-of-a-kind memorabilia ranging from old movie posters to out-of-print books, rare coins, comics, or antique furniture. Undoubtedly the collections bring pleasure to the collectors, but collecting still involves commodification of items and attaching monetary value to them.

Critics of the commercialized entertainment industry maintain that there is no interaction between the performer and the audience. Instead, the audience merely observes the performance and responds through admiring applause. The entertainer then packs up the show to present the exact same performance in another locale in a franchise-like duplication of artistic services. The result is a "McDonaldization" of the entertainment industry.

CONCLUDING INSIGHTS: THE GLOBALIZED WORLDVIEW

The most established, mainstream ideology in the U.S. and many parts of the world (including China) is that of the globalized worldview. The universalization and homogenization of a commodified and commercialized globalized culture has expanded since the early 1980s. This globalized culture is increasingly being accepted and replicated by many people, with businesses encouraging consumerism as an embodiment of universal culture. For example, over one million foreign students attended American universities in 2017. This education and socialization process enfolds foreign students into a globalized culture, which many enthusiastically embrace and take back with them to their country of origin. Millions of middle class Chinese and Indians enthusiastically purchase cars and other material goods that traditionally are associated with the West. Also, the ubiquitous satellite dishes perched on roofs around the world beam commercial-laden television programs direct from Hollywood and Seoul, South Korea to the homes of billions around the world. Television programs implicitly extol the values of a globalized worldview in their programming selections and blatant commercialism.

As we have seen in this chapter, the globalization worldview has both negative and beneficial aspects. One of the most disturbing aspects of a globalized worldview in my estimation is a gradual loss of cultural diversity that results in monotone cultural conformity around the world revolving around a consumerist and technological mindset. Many people are immersed in their own virtual world with little outward connection to others or nature. On the other hand, technology has enabled us to connect with others across time and space in a way that can foster greater communication in solving intractable global problems.

How do we balance the beneficial aspects of a globalized worldview with the negative? This fundamental question is what those embracing a transformative worldview will have to sort out. Let's turn to the transformative worldview chapter to find out what some people have in store for a future in which they hope to foster greater personal and global well-being for all.

Chapter 8
The Transformative Worldview

For the first time in human evolution, the individual life is long enough, and the cultural transformation swift enough, that the individual mind is now a constituent player in the global transformation of human culture. ... William Irwin Thompson

AN INTRODUCTION TO THE TRANSFORMATIVE WORLDVIEW

We are at a critical juncture in our human history. The modern worldview that has held sway for centuries is unraveling and what worldview or worldviews will replace it is still uncertain. We are living in a time of doubt, unrest, and confusion about the way forward. The worldviews that I have written about in earlier chapters—indigenous, traditionalist, progressive, and globalized—all have different visions of the best way for society to function.

The transformative worldview is another worldview that is emerging out of the fraying of the modern worldview and slowly taking shape. This chapter is a combination of my research about current trends and ideas and also commentary about what I believe are the right choices for the future. I put forward these choices because I believe they will be best for our collective personal and global well-being, as well as the environment. They are not always my own personal preferences.

At this point in time, millions of diverse people around the world are actively calling for a new worldview. Some say a different story is urgently needed to assure the continuation of our human species and life as we know it on Earth. People in varied fields—educators, religious leaders, business entrepreneurs, international political leaders, indigenous farmers, political activists, politicians, environmentalists, entertainers, scientists, working people, artists, writers, small business owners, academics, economists, concerned citizens, and many others—are contributing to the creation of what I call a transformative worldview. Those who adhere to a transformative worldview, at least in part, imagine that diverse paths are possible and attainable, and a globalized worldview or other visions of the future are not inevitable. They are promoting alternative ideas and options for a different worldview and voicing their convictions in a forceful, yet usually peaceful fashion.

Those involved in forming a transformative worldview, transformers, are drawing their ideas from diverse sources; some are positive aspects of the four other worldviews. From the modern worldview, transformers glean noteworthy accomplishments, such as the ideals of liberal democracy, the advancement of scientific inquiry, medical improvements, beneficial technological innovations, public-supported mass education, and progress in the expansion of human rights to include women, people of color, and other marginalized groups. These ideals have withstood the passage of time. Highly regarded from the indigenous worldview is the wisdom of indigenous people who call upon the council of their elders to help guide them through uncertain times. Traditionally, they have had a deep respect for nature, connecting and coexisting with it, and they treat the environment in a reverent manner. Drawing on the support and kinship of their extended family, they also value a strong relationship with territorial place.

Transformers can learn from the traditional worldview in which the values of family and community are recognized as a greater force than individualism alone. They may also draw upon traditionalists' respect for ceremony, ritual, and connection to place. Spirituality, either through organized religion or another form, is important in psychological grounding of individuals and society. From progressives, transformers may adopt their commitment to ideals, such as racial and gender equality, LBGTQ rights, and working towards reducing the impact of climate change on the planet. Transformers also utilize the stunning technological developments from the globalized worldview, especially high-speed, integrated computer networks and reasonably-priced global transportation that have provided instantaneous communication linking diverse people around the globe. Even some indigenous people in remote villages, such as the village of Vincente Guerreo in Mexico, are linked to the internet and use appropriate scientific knowledge for enhancing their own goal of self-sufficiency in food consumption. And some would say that the globalized worldview's vision of "opening up" the world to unfettered trade has benefited many people with a more materially comfortable standard of living than ever before.

All of these worldviews have some positive contributions, but transformers believe that there should be selectivity and mindfulness in fitting values of the other worldviews into a new framework. Therefore, a different worldview needs to continue to evolve and offer alternatives to prevailing notions of cultural uniformity, rigid fundamentalism, corporate dominance, consumer-driven values, selfish individualism, oligarchic concentration of wealth and power, political stalemate, and environmental destruction. Transformers have a diverse array of thoughts, beliefs, ideas, theories, lifestyles, choices, and actions that defy rigid categorization, but they do share common principles and ideals that I have placed under the umbrella of a transformative worldview.

The transformative worldview is still a minority view, as I see it, but it is a worldwide movement in which millions of people are reassessing the values of the other worldviews in order to find a more compassionate, equal, realistic, sustainable, and community-focused value system. I have organized ten characteristics that briefly describe the emerging transformative worldview in the U.S. and across the world.

The Transformative Worldview: 10 Characteristics

1. **Interdependent Ideals** focus on cooperation, community, connections, support, and altruism rather than greed, aggression, independence, and segmentation. Other characteristics include simultaneity, relationships, networks, webs, and integration.

2. **Community-Focused Social Values** draw upon the wisdom of elders and their experiential insights. Intense individualism is a learned behavior, historically created and promoted by Western

society, especially the U.S. A shift to a worldview emphasizing greater cooperative, supportive, and life-enhancing attributes is a viable and much-needed alternative.

3. **Natural Capitalism** places priority on the well-being and sustainability of the Earth, while integrating market forces to efficiently allocate resources using supply and demand principles. It includes socially responsible investing, social entrepreneurship, micro-credit banking, community development, local businesses, self-managed worker-run enterprises, cooperatives, non-profit organizations, and other forms of management in which individuals have a vested interest in profitability and outcomes.

4. **Ecological Awareness** has awakened our insight into the interdependence of everything in nature, where every event affects everything else. Humans are part of the mystery of the Universe and not isolated, separate, and superior entities.

5. **Renewable Energy** in the form of wind, solar, water, steam, and geothermal, for example, is important in countering the dire effects of climate change and stimulating sustainable economic development. The devastation caused by a fossil fuel-dependent lifestyle has galvanized world citizens to start shifting from oil and coal dependence to sustainable energy.

6. **Peace and Justice Movements** connect millions of people instantly with world-wide communication networks. These vigorous movements include democratic reforms, peace efforts, nuclear disarmament, population stabilization, human rights, animal rights, LGBTQ rights, environmental issues, educational reforms, equality, rights for indigenous people, women's and children's issues, and many others.

7. **Sustainable Agriculture** is a shift from industrial agricultural that is harmful to the environment and people's overall health to small scale agriculture that is more local and organic. Although this type of agriculture is not able to meet the world's food needs at this time,

the shift is underway and is expanding to bring its benefits to more people, rather than just the wealthy elite.

8. **Holistic Health** offers alternatives to Western medicine that is often dominated by a for-profit pharmaceutical industry and invasive medical procedures. It encourages health, well-being, a mostly plant-based diet, and a holistic way to cure diseases ranging from cancer to heart disease. This type of health care also has the potential to employ many people in an industry that benefits individuals rather than just large pharmaceutical companies and insurance providers.

9. **Spirituality** includes alternative practices that may differ from organized religious traditions. In response to the growing recognition of many people's desire for new kinds of spirituality, many traditional religions have shifted their beliefs and practices to create a more connected and personal spiritual experience rather than rote adherence to prescribed creeds and rituals.

10. **Holistic Education** is the key to ushering in alternative changes. Holistic educational practices for adult lifelong learners and youth encourage recognizing our diversity along with emphasizing unity, open-mindedness, inquiry-based learning, multiple intelligences, a global perspective, and an integrated approach.

The transformative worldview is further explained using six patterns—cultural, political, social, economic, technological, and ecological.

CULTURAL PATTERNS

Transformers embrace new and emerging transformative ideals, such as cooperation, community, and holistic thinking. Holistic means that all the traits of a culture—economic, technological, social, political, religious, ideological, and cultural—interact and reinforce each other. It also sees the world as an intricately interconnected organism; accentuates uncertainty, approximations, and relativity instead of absolutes; calls for interdependence instead of independence; and recognizes seemingly paradoxical concepts. Highly regarded are Eastern philosophies and religious thought that emphasize cyclical thinking, highlight harmony with nature, and see unity within diversity and diversity within unity.[1] A holistic perspective recognizes that nature, which has been treated for centuries as dead and mechanical, is an animate, invisible organizing force. The Earth (Gaia in ancient Greek mythology) is seen as a living organism interconnected within a web of life. This perspective counters the split between nature and humans which threatens life on Earth. A holistic view intuits that an underlying consciousness circulates within humans, life on Earth, and the Universe, connecting all into an intricate, interdependent circle of existence.

Many holding a transformative worldview continue to embrace traditional universal religions that arose in the past, such as Buddhism, Daoism, Judaism, Christianity (Protestant and Catholic), Islam, and Hinduism. Others are gravitating to alternative forms of spirituality that depart from traditional forms. A New Age movement, emerging out of the West in the 1960s and 1970s, is an umbrella term that embraces an eclectic array of spiritual beliefs and practices. It encompasses a wide range of personal development strategies and healing tactics to improve human well-being. Deepak Chopra, a spiritual teacher, states that New Age values support conscious evolution, a non-sectarian society, a non-military culture, global sharing, healing the environment, sustainable economies, self-determination, social justice, economic empowerment of the poor, love, and compassion in action.

Another type of New Age spirituality is a resurrection of feminist spirituality that encourages a connection with the sacred feminine and worship of the goddess that is said to have been suppressed by male-dominated universal religions for centuries. My cousin, a self-proclaimed practicing shaman, performs rituals for clients and friends, such as fire ceremonies, that she contends burn away negative feelings and evil entities resulting in a cleansing of the soul and renewal of positive energy.

The field of ecopsychology, connecting psychology with ecology, offers many people a way to spiritually connect with Mother Earth and remedy our alienation from nature. Ecopsychologists maintain that this emotional connection between individuals and the natural world will help inspire them to create sustainable and simple lifestyles. They support preserving nature on public lands, bringing nature into civic spaces, and connecting nature to their own personal living space. In keeping with these ideals, instead of the traditional lawn of green grass and shrubs, my neighbor has a menagerie of native plants that provide a welcome sanctuary for birds and other wildlife, all within the city limits. Using native plants encourages native pollinators, which are crucial to the survival of the plant life we depend on.

In some ways, post-modernism is part of the transformative worldview. Although I described post-modernism more fully in the progressive worldview, its rejection of the modern worldview and critique of many assumptions of power, the economy, and traditions help inform the transformative camp as well. Post-modern thinkers of the twentieth century deconstructed the objective, scientific, modern worldview that has held sway for centuries and instead posited that there is no fixed meaning, canon, tradition, or objectivity—only an infinity of meaning. This way of thinking corrodes classical, rational liberalism, the cornerstone of the modern worldview.[2] However, post-modernism has perhaps gone too far, eroding foundational belief systems that give individuals meaning, structure, and stability in their lives. Without this stability, individuals may experience alienation and anomie that can result in episodes of depression and thoughts of suicide, both of which have increased in recent years.

Aesthetic expression in a transformative worldview differs from that found in a globalized worldview. In many instances, the distance between the observer/observed or entertainer/entertained is reduced or eliminated. Instead of a person going to a concert and sitting passively as an observer, she may participate in the musical production by performing herself or helping with the production. For example, a dancer in the audience might spontaneously participate in the dancing. The professional qualities that make certain artists celebrities are blurred and the boundaries between the performer and audience fall away. A small, neighborhood performance-theater in Pennsylvania, for example, featured audience participation as they followed sing-a-long tunes reminiscent of the 1960s "Sing-a-Long with Mitch" television show. The audience was the performer.

The self-publishing book industry, which has recently skyrocketed, provides another example of this trend. The big publishing houses no longer dictate what will be available to the book-buying public. Instead, individual authors can self-publish their own books, freed of restrictions imposed by corporate publishing entities. Readers can pick from a wider assortment of books of their choosing than in the past. Also, blogs, tweets, and other forms of social media are not governed by established rules—authors can write about whatever they determine is important and readers may or may not respond to their posts.

POLITICAL PATTERNS

The contentious political arena reflects deep societal divisions today. In particular, the populist right in the traditional worldview and the progressive/populist left in the progressive worldview are the most antagonistic and vocal. Their judgments and accusations of each other are filled with vitriol and hatred. Each is assured of their own righteousness. However, I have found that some people are able to negotiate multiple worldviews and transcend the polarities that stifle and even shut down discussion and understanding. I believe their skills and abilities to understand multiple perspectives, without necessarily changing their own perspective, is a quality desperately needed in advancing a transformative worldview. But transformers must be realistic about politics; idealism alone is not enough to create meaningful change so it must be coupled with a jolt of reality as well.

Immigration is one of the most contentious issues today. Many progressives and globalizers advocate for nations without borders, allowing for the free flow of people to the place where they most desire to live. This notion is idealistic; a realistic analysis of the situation would advise caution. Since the world is divided along economic lines, it is a fact that people from poorer nations are migrating to wealthier ones, and will continue to do so. The number of people desperate to relocate to a country with more security and opportunities is much greater than the capacity of wealthier countries to absorb them. This imbalance results in heart-wrenching scenes of desperate migrants clamoring to enter rich countries through legal but usually illegal means. This clash between the idealists—the progressives—who want to save all the people of the world from the ravages of hunger, disease, and poverty versus the realists—traditionalists—who want to limit immigration to manageable levels to prevent what they foresee as future mayhem, is volatile with emotions simmering at the boiling point. At the time of this writing, the fracture between the two visions remains unresolved and intense.

The best hope lies with transformers who can negotiate with both sides to arrive at a sensible solution that is both humanitarian and realistic. An important point that has been neglected in this volatile debate is what is happening to the countries from which the migrants are fleeing. Who will be left to rebuild war-torn or fractured countries when the most industrious individuals leave? This leads to a vacuum in which organized crime and gangs can step in to torment the remaining population, often women and children.

Today there is an intense debate between globalizers and nationalists. Especially intensifying over the last one hundred years, the political configuration of most modern countries has been towards the formation of a nation-state. With a few exceptions of failed states, such as Somalia, or obstacles to state formation, such as in the case of Palestine, the whole world is politically organized into nation-states. Although their form of government and economy is different, the political structures of a nation-state are in place in all nations. One of the key ingredients for a nation to exist and thrive is the loyalty of its citizens; otherwise instability and chaos may ensue. Citizens express their loyalty to the nation through patriotism, an emotion that signifies one is a steadfast member of a national tribe. However, patriotism can shift to the extreme version in which citizens see their nation as superior to all others. Of course, Nazi Germany comes to mind as the most extreme version of this kind of intense patriotism. But in most cases pride in one's nation does not drift towards the extreme version, and when it does politicians must be astute enough to rein in these emotions before they get out of hand.

Even though the nation-state seems well entrenched as a political configuration, there is a shift among many of those in the progressive and globalized worldviews to put more authority into global institutions. These emerging political configurations are challenging or complementing the sovereignty of the nation-state. However, this trend has been disparaged by those who want to retain the primacy of the nation, its culture, and traditions. This sentiment was reflected in a surprising Brexit vote in the United Kingdom in 2016 in which a majority of voters opted to leave the European Union. Also, the rise of populists/nationalists parties in parts of Europe, Russia, Brazil, Turkey, and elsewhere signal a revival of nationalistic sentiments.

World institutions and organizations, despite detractors, have steadily gained more authority and legitimacy from the twentieth century onwards. With the blessings of progressives and globalizers, world political institutions evolved that reflected a more interdependent world. One of the first such institutions, the League of Nations, established after World War I in 1920, failed to prevent the outbreak of World War II, although its successor, the United Nations (UN), has proven to be a more effective organization and has a peace-keeping wing to enforce its objectives. International political entities today include world, regional, non-governmental organizations (NGOs), and citizen-diplomat groups. The UN and the International Court are charged with the overwhelming task of helping to stamp out terrorism, regulate arms, monitor human rights, prevent disease and hunger, and protect the environment. The WTO, World Bank, and IMF, mentioned in Chapter 7, are global institutions charged with governing the global economy.

Non-governmental organizations (NGOs) are privately created organizations with an international scope, unaffiliated with a particular nation. According to political scientist Farouk Mawlawi, NGOs are "private, voluntary, non-profit organizations whose members combine their skills, means and energies in the service of shared ideals and objectives."[3] NGOs transcend narrow national interests in dealing with issues affecting the world and include such well-known world organizations as the Red Cross, Amnesty International, Greenpeace, Doctors Without Borders, Human Rights Watch, and many others. Many of these organizations have local and state chapters encouraging ordinary citizens to participate in realizing their missions.

Regional political organizations complement national governments. A regional organization like the North Atlantic Treaty Organization (NATO) has taken on new objectives along with its primary Cold War goal of protecting Western Europe. The Organization of American States (OAS), established in 1948 with 21 members, is the oldest regional organization of states. The European Union (EU) currently has 27 member nations; it has achieved a cooperative economy, has its own currency, the euro, and has removed tariff barriers for easier trade. Formed in 2001, the African Union has 54 members on the African continent. One of its objectives is the promotion and protection of human rights, such as the right of a group to freely dispose of its natural resources in the exclusive interest of its members. In 1945, Egypt, Jordan, Iraq, Lebanon, Syria, and Saudi Arabia signed the Pact of the Arab League States and in 2011 created the League of Arab States with 22 members. The League of Arab States is separate from the Organization of the Islamic Conference, which was the second largest inter-governmental organization in 2011 with 57 member states, slightly below the UN in membership. Formed in 1967, the Association of Southeast Asian Nations (ASEAN) has ten members.

The organization, structure, and services that governments provide for their citizenry have markedly changed because of the shift by many nations from managed capitalism and socialism to neoliberalism and state capitalism. With more wealth concentrated in the hands of the elite, politicians have increasingly supported policies that favor the wealthy. Although the political organization of the U.S. is a republic with democratically elected representatives, increasingly we see that democracy is divided into two contending segments that I call elite democracy and participatory democracy. Many transformers favor a participatory democracy, in which citizens are actively engaged in governing for the benefit of all the people, not elite democracy where a few wealthy oligarchs dominate the political agenda.

Peace and justice movements have had renewed vigor since the invention of the internet and world-wide communication. There are many local peace and justice chapters that encourage local engagement. With their ability to connect millions of people instantly, the issues of peace and social and economic justice are garnering attention and action. Among some of the many causes advocated by this diverse movement are democratic reforms, countering racism, peace efforts, nuclear disarmament, population stabilization, human rights, animal rights, gay rights, equality for non-elites, indigenous people's rights, women's and children's issues, environmental causes, racial equality, and protection from hate crimes. But transformers, more so than progressives, I believe, must also emphasize responsibilities along with rights. By emphasizing both, the balance needed for a well-functioning society is maintained. These social causes are moral and ethical standards that guide a nation's policies and action. However, there are many instances when these movements may overstep boundaries of fairness and discredit their cause. For example, in early 2019 the Jessie Smollett fiasco commanded headlines for weeks on end. Smollett, a black man, was charged with instigating a fake hate crime assault by white supremacists. Progressive media jumped into tirades of racism against the presumed assailants without corroborating the story. The accusations turned out to be false, but harm had already been done and the cause of racial justice damaged.

During this divisive time, transformers must be moral and ethical guides sorting through the mounds of misinformation attempting to aggravate one side or the other. Cool heads must prevail, and a careful look at the evidence must be at the forefront before a decision of innocent or guilty wielded. Also, arbitrarily tossing about claims of racism, homophobia, elitism, and other insults too frequently diminishes their intended effectiveness. Instead of lobbing racist insults at individuals or groups, transformers can shift the focus to one of calling out the language used and why some may consider it racist or caustic. By shifting the focus to the offensive language instead of attacking the individual, transformers can get past the negative pattern of judging others by narrow standards. Pointing out specific instances of racist language also diffuses personal attacks that end up in a vitriolic back and forth tirade of accusations and denials. This example may result in more positive interaction among the feuding entities and reduce inflamed tensions.

SOCIAL PATTERNS

The negative and positive effects of rapid social changes in the twentieth and early twenty-first centuries are playing out today. On the negative side, our society is fraying at the edges because of social fragmentation and alienation. The social and economic structures that are in place in the U.S. today widen the income gap, perpetuate poverty, alienate individuals and families, foster rampant individualism, and encourage the growth of a consumer society at great cost to the environment and individual well-being. On the positive side, unemployment at the time of this writing is at a decade-long low, wages are generally up

146

across the board, and the upper 20 percent of Americans are doing very well. Yet, the malaise among Americans is palpable.

Progressives, traditionalists, and globalizers each have their own version of how society should be arranged. The values and beliefs of each of these worldviews frequently clash, as exemplified in the circus-like atmosphere that surrounded the nomination and confirmation of Supreme Court Justice Brett Kavanaugh in October 2018. Although the traditionalists won that particular battle, their views do not always prevail.

One of the issues that religious traditionalists do not agree with and have rallied against is same sex marriage and homosexuality. They say the Bible admonishes against homosexuality, and since many believe the Bible is the literal world of God they do not support its acceptance in modern society. This rebuke has not stopped the LGBTQ movement, and perhaps has even galvanized it.

For several decades, LBGTQ movements have been working towards and achieving human rights for lesbian, bisexual, gay, transgender and transsexual, and queer people around the world. The social movement advocates for the equal acceptance of LGBTQ people in all facets of society. Although there is not an overarching central organization that represents all LGBTQ people and their interests, many different organizations are active worldwide, such as the National LGBTQ Task Force. Today these movements include political activism and cultural activities like lobbying, street marches, social groups, media, art, and research. The rapid push towards equality regarding sexual orientation that gained traction during the 1990s has made great strides. For example, the legalization of same sex marriage increased from one state in 2004 to all 50 states in 2015. The movement continues today.

Going against the views of globalizers, some transformers say our social ethic drives us to pursue individual rewards, pleasures, and recognition. Unlike transformers, some progressives devalue the family as an important unit of society, but agree with them on the issue of upholding the community and commons. In a globalized and progressive worldview, children are trucked to day-care centers so that parents can earn money in the marketplace that takes them away from the home.

Even when there is enough leisure time for family or community enjoyment, it frequently revolves around the marketplace providing platforms for entertainment, especially through digital devices. It is not unusual to dine at a restaurant and look over to the next table to see the whole family, with sullen looks on their faces, glued to their cell phones. The old adage "it takes a village to raise a child" has been replaced by "it takes a mobile device to raise a child."

Many transformers believe that education is the key to ushering in social alternatives. Today the dire state of our public education system is constantly being blamed on groups or individuals: politicians blame teachers for not educating students satisfactorily, teachers blame parents for not providing a good foundation for education, liberals blame television and social media for "dumbing down" students, conservatives blame the teachers' unions for not firing "bad" teachers, and advertisers say just be "cool" and all is well. Yet the whole system is out of balance. Transformers advocate for deinstitutionalizing our educational establishments and making our schools diverse, engaging, and beneficial to all, not just an elite group. Popular among many educators (including this author) are holistic educational practices that emphasize development of the whole child, not just a test score. Educators encourage diversity, inquiry-based learning, activities that connect with our multiple intelligences, a global perspective, and a holistic approach in which relationships are primary.

Values that stress the importance of the group, rather than over-emphasizing individualism as the central cultural value, are important to many transformers. Emerging social values can be gathered from contemporary culture, from diverse ancient traditions, and from our own imaginations. For example, we can learn to draw upon the wisdom of our elders and their historical insights. Intense individualism is a learned behavior historically created and promoted by Western society, especially the United States. When these seemingly intractable problems are looked at from a holistic perspective, they can be addressed more effectively. Those who support a transformative worldview believe a shift to a worldview that emphasizes greater cooperative, supportive, and life-enhancing attributes is a viable and necessary alternative. Visionary Mary Clark notes, "We urgently need to reinstate feelings of relatedness and community into our social vision."[4]

Humans have a universal, innate sense of wanting to belong to something bigger than just themselves. The indigenous worldview provides valuable insights into making social changes in this direction. Historically, the band, group, family, village, clan, and tribe have provided mechanisms for human belonging. It is in our deep collective unconscious to live in connection with one another. Indigenous people devised complex social relationships to ensure that everyone in the band, clan, or tribe was connected to each other. For example, the lineage of each person in the tribe was explicitly spelled out, whether traced through the mother's or father's line. Also, rites of passage are part of indigenous society; different rites demarcate boys and girls as they grow from childhood to adulthood. Each rite signifies that the individual is a valued member of the group.

We have deviated from a group focus norm with modernization. Instead, there has been a shift from the community to the individual. This has intensified since the end of World War II and further intensified since the 1980s, when the ideal of the individual reigned supreme. Now rampant individualism has reached the crisis point. Social disengagement and alienation are expressed in the upsurge in the use of anti-depressants and illegal drugs, the rash of teen suicides, and an untold number of broken families. For example, there were 70,237 drug overdose deaths in the United States in 2017, with a 12.9-fold increase from 2007 to 2017.[5] We have become untethered from our innate human need—the need to belong.

For individual well-being, those supporting a transformative worldview argue that our social patterns need to change to a more equitable, nourishing, and sustainable way of life. The good news is that many people recognize this is an urgent issue and are remaking social institutions to foster more community spirit and rethinking the self-serving individualism that permeates the values and attitudes of many parts of American and world society. Many religious institutions are once again encouraging their places of worship to provide a setting for social interaction and support for their members and others in the community. Also, community gardens, farmers markets with food and entertainment, spaces for making art, neighborhood clean-up days, town halls, and co-housing living arrangements are innovative ways for people to interact and form relationships. Changing parts of the system can trigger changes in the whole system. It is a huge challenge, but once awareness is reached, change can come about. Perhaps once again we will be able to claim that it takes a village to raise a child.

ECONOMIC PATTERNS

Transformers believe in creating a more just, equitable, and sustainable economy that places less stress on an overtaxed environment. They are trying to counter the damage from the global economy and its values of greed and consumption that have been inflicted upon the human psyche. Many individuals and organizations are struggling to eliminate or rewrite free trade agreements such as NAFTA (North American Free Trade Agreement) and the WTO (World Trade Organization) that have wreaked havoc on local economies, workers, small businesses, and the environment while enriching multinational corporations and their shareholders. Instead, many people are working to reinstate bilateral trade agreements, where each trading nation makes its own mutually beneficial trade agreements.

Some transformers are working to set up alternative business forms that differ from the large corporate model, such as non-profit businesses, cooperatives, and local, community, or employee-owned enterprises. For example, a committed group of individuals in my local community are working to establish a community-owned bank in which the state and local governments deposit their excess funds. The profits from this enterprise are channeled back into the local community rather than to out-of-state investors. I enjoy frequenting a restaurant/grocery collective in Craryville, New York in which the six owners work together to provide healthy, organic food for its many customers. Many transformers struggle to break the corporate lock on the "economic imagination" and develop diverse enterprises in which workers have a stake in their workplace and sustainable practices are given utmost consideration.

Some transformers argue that we can more effectively deal with the extraordinary rate of economic change by actively participating in life choices and not permitting the "consumer creed" to dictate our options. Natural capitalism, which places priority on the well-being and sustainability of the Earth, is among the many economic changes emerging. Other significant economic changes include socially responsible investing, social entrepreneurship, micro-credit banking, community development, local businesses, worker-run enterprises, cooperatives, non-profit organizations, and disinvestment measures. For example, some people on college campuses are calling on college financial administrators to disinvest their investments from the fossil fuel industry. There are also renewed calls for stricter financial sector regulations, a cap on excessive executive compensation, breaking up large corporate holdings, and other reforms.

One alternative to the globalized economy is the redevelopment of the once-flourishing local or domestic economy, a part of the economic sector that economic globalization has ravished. Local community members, government officials, and business owners can alleviate the drain of wealth from the local economy to outside entities by returning to "economic self-determination." This return to local capitalism reduces dependency on multinational corporations while creating wealth-accumulating enterprises at the local level. Local economies can produce, market, and process many, although not all, of their own products for local or regional consumption, reducing transportation and middleman costs. Local capitalism can bring local economies into harmony with the surrounding ecosystem, foster cooperation within the community, and substitute more personalized local products for more expensive imported and often sub-standard goods. In order for such a change to occur, the real effort must come from the local community that can better utilize available resources in imaginative ways and provide more economical and high-quality food, clothing, shelter, transportation, and energy. A transfer of economic interests and activities from urban, core centers to the local community can reduce dependency on the core and revive local economic vibrancy.[6]

Concerns are arising over the fact that our industrial form of agricultural production is no longer able to meet the needs of the world's population. Along with industrial agriculture's enormous demands for irrigation water, its chemical inputs deplete the fertility of the soil and can harm beneficial insects, and its fossil fuel dependency contributes to global warming. Clear-cutting land for farm production also harms the environment by reducing the carbon sequestering properties of forests and grassland. The mass production system eliminates farmers and other related jobs in the agriculture sector. Alternatives to mass-produced, industrial agriculture are emerging, such as the rise of sustainable, organic, and local agriculture. An alternative to industrial agriculture, organic farming connects what one eats to how one lives. It also considers the effects of toxic chemicals on the people charged with dispersing them and the considerable long-term harm done to their health.

A number of communities scattered throughout the world are working to incrementally increase the number of local businesses rooted in the community. For example, in the United States, a worker-owned initiative is located in the economically hard-hit city of Cleveland, Ohio. The "Cleveland Model" involves an integrated array of worker-owned cooperative enterprises targeted at the $3 billion purchasing power of such large scale "anchor institutions" as the Cleveland Clinic, University Hospital, and Case Western Reserve University. The association of enterprises also includes a revolving fund so that profits made by the businesses help establish new ventures. A worker-owned company, Evergreen Cooperative Laundry, is a state-of-the-art commercial laundry that provides clean linens for area hospitals, nursing homes, and hotels. It includes 50 worker-owners, pays above-market wages, provides health insurance, and is still able to compete successfully with other commercial laundries. Another enterprise, Ohio Cooperative Solar (OCS), provides weatherization services and installs, owns, and maintains solar panels. Each year, two to four new worker-owned ventures are planned for opening. A 20-acre land trust will own the land of the worker-owned businesses.[7] A revitalization of the local economy does not mean isolation and a complete rejection of the global capitalist economy; it incorporates both the global and the local economy.

TECHNOLOGICAL PATTERNS

Some people supporting a transformative worldview dispute the notion that scientific progress and our faith in technological fixes can solve all complex problems and make the world a more sustainable, safer place to live. Instead, there is a tacit understanding that science, technology, and a consumer/materialistic lifestyle have certain limitations for personal well-being and dire repercussions for our human species as well as for other life forms on Earth. Most transformers realize the importance of internet and computer technology in instantaneously linking and organizing people around the world and are avid users of it, but they use caution in advocating for technology as a solution to all or even a large portion of the world's problems.

Artificial Intelligence (AI) is a topic of concern to many people. AI is the reproduction of human intelligence processes by machines, especially computer systems. There is a debate about the ethical, moral, spiritual, social, and economic implications of AI. Will AI create massive unemployment as machines take over more and more of jobs humans have performed in the past? If so, what will people do for a livelihood? Some people also consider AI to be a danger to humanity if it progresses unabated and unchecked. However, the development of AI technology seems to be proceeding with little input from people who will be most adversely affected by its development and use.

Even though technology cannot fix all problems, perhaps it can help us deal with some urgent issues. Instead of only using technology as the latest consumer fad or for our own personal entertainment, we need the wisdom to direct technology to positive ends. As we have found in our human history, humans are good at making tools. But sometimes the repercussions of our tool-making creations are not immediately apparent; atomic and nuclear bombs come to mind as inventions that have few, if any, redeeming qualities. But many inventions have been beneficial—the Internet has certainly benefited me and billions of others worldwide as well. Many new innovations are cleaning up the environment, increasing energy efficiency, and treating complex medical issues. Perhaps technology will provide the tools we need to save ourselves—but not without the vision to help us see how to use them well.

ENVIRONMENTAL PATTERNS

Transformers know that the Earth must be healthy to sustain humans and our fellow species, and not treated as just an economic commodity. This view represents a shift in attitude that has been gaining momentum throughout the world. A new ecological awareness has awakened the realization of the interdependence of all life, where every event has an effect on everything else. Humans are seen as part of the mystery of the Universe and not isolated, separate, superior entities. With this awareness comes responsibility along with an urgency to repair the damage done to the environment and halt further environmental destruction. For example, even tourism has taken an ecological turn for many travelers who opt for popular ecotourism destinations, such as Costa Rica and Belize. Ecotourism is visiting fragile, pristine, and relatively un-developed natural areas, while having a low impact on the environment. Dif-ferent than large-scale commercial tourism, ecotourism also means travelers frequent small-scale and local tourist businesses to make sure wealth generated from tourism stays in the local community. Often ecotourists will purchase carbon offsets to make sure their travel has as little impact on the environment as possible.

The human population has grown exponentially in the twentieth century and continues to be an urgent issue in the twenty-first century. The carrying capacity of the Earth is severely strained by our current population and life-style demands. (The carrying capacity is the number of people, other living organisms, or crops that a region can support without environmental degrada-tion). Will our Earth be able to sustain nine to twelve billion people, a number projected to occur around 2050? If the nine to twelve billion people projected to live on this Earth in 2050 have a lifestyle like Americans today, the capac-ity for the Earth to provide resources will be severely compromised. The twin calamities—large populations and resource-consuming lifestyles of a growing global middle and upper class—mean that humans will continue to take more resources from the Earth than are replenished every year.

Our fossil fuel-dependent lifestyle has finally roused world-wide attention, even among some Western politicians, as a shift from our addiction to oil and coal to alternative energy is slowly underway. Events such as the first Earth Day in 1970, the Rio Environmental Conference in 1992, the Kyoto Treaty in 2001, the Copenhagen Climate Conference in 2009, the United Nations Cli-mate Change Conference in 2015, and Paris Climate Accord in 2016 address the importance of a safe, healthy environment for sustainable human life. A growing number of people think saving the planet from environmental ravages is the most urgent issue our human species is facing.

An issue connected to energy, urban revitalization, is forcing many of us to rethink the car-dependent city configurations and the accompanying suburban sprawl found in the United States. Because of the excessive amounts of energy used to maintain this way of life, efforts are underway to switch to more energy efficient modes of public transportation. Also, the alienating nature of suburbs has sparked new ideas among some people to move to more community-focused neighborhoods that reduce commuting time and conserve valuable suburban land for agriculture and biodiversity. A sense of community also decreases isolation and depression among residents.

Some ecologists suggest replacing the current economic measurement method—Gross Domestic Product (GDP), that merely measures national spending without regard to economic, environmental, or social well-being—with a Genuine Progress Indicator (GPI). The GPI, created by the organization Redefining Progress in 1995, measures the general economic and social well-being of all citizens. For example, if a business is responsible for an oil spill, the costs associated with the clean-up contribute to an increase in GDP, since the clean-up costs actually grow the economy according to this measurement. But GDP ignores the environmental damage caused by the oil spill that has a negative long-lasting cost and impact. In calculating the GPI, the costs associated with the oil spill would be subtracted from the total, since it damages the environment over the long-term. When using GPI calculations, the U.S. economy has been stagnant since 1970.[8]

A growing number of ecologists see the Earth as an interconnected organism that awakens our sacred relationship with nature and positively supports our psychic well-being. This shift of consciousness revives an ancient mystical accord with nature that has sustained humans for millions of years. A modern worldview has contributed to a destructive relationship with the Earth. A more benign connection would improve human health and mental well-being as well as prevent the extinction of many endangered species that add to the diversity of life.

Even though we are overshooting Earth's carrying capacity, it is not too late to make changes. Our human capacity for thinking long-term, globally, and holistically does not have precedence, yet it is not beyond our capabilities. We can change, and we must do so. Adjusting our thinking and way of being to view the long-term consequences of our actions is paramount. Growth needs to be reconsidered as the mantra of our society; instead, practicing and acting within the limits of our Earth's capacity holds the key to our future well-being and survival.

CONCLUDING INSIGHTS:
THE TRANSFORMATIVE WORLDVIEW

The Global Wave, the fifth historical era of human development described in Chapter 2, poses a huge challenge for us—environmental degradation, a gaping socio-economic divide, unchecked individualism, a political system out of touch with reality, and worldviews unable to deal with future challenges. Our innate behaviors and historical experiences have not prepared us well for the multifaceted and grim global issues that confront us; we do not have a firm track record that can help guide us through the wilderness of urgency and complexity. Our innate behaviors as a species have equipped us to deal with a threat such as a marauding lion or the needs of our immediate 25 member group, but now we must deal with the threat of planet-wide environmental devastation and the needs of our immediate seven plus billion member group!

We often turn to our political or religious leaders as potential saviors. However, they are also overwhelmed with the issues or caught in their own intransigent, outdated worldview. Our political leaders in the U.S. are adept (somewhat) at dealing with isolated problems in a legally deliberative, cumbersome way with built-in mechanisms to stymie impulsive actions. But they have failed to provide a vision of where we need to go and what we need to do. With their enslavement to corporations for their campaign donations, their inflexible partisanship, and their entrenched worldviews, many politicians are unable to provide the leadership citizens desperately crave.

The election in the U.S. of President Donald Trump in 2016 was a rejection of many liberal democratic principles that the country and Western nations have been founded upon. Half of the voters in the U.S. elected an authoritarian-type leader who is dispensing with checks and balances carefully put in place over the years and instead put their faith in a government run, in part, by wealthy oligarchs. Trump supporters are blithely rejecting our liberal traditions just to cut through the bureaucracy and get results that mostly benefit them.

At the same time, opponents of Trump have been mired in name-calling and anger, while not addressing the hard political tasks ahead. It is much easier to criticize and point fingers than it is to be creative and negotiate real solutions. Partisanship seems more entrenched than at any time since the end of World War II. These political inactions are sure to have profound consequences.

Many religious leaders have also failed us, although many are working hard to bring about change. Many religious people, for example, have scoffed at the idea of climate change, although some evangelical leaders are now alarmed that we are contaminating God's creation and are calling for action. Other religious people continue to disbelieve the hard scientific findings of climate change. Many traditionalists are wary of progressive attempts to solve climate change through "big government" programs that they perceive as having a not-so-hidden "socialist" agenda. Progressives fail to see traditionalists' discomfort with these huge and expensive program proposals. Inaction has resulted, while the ticking time bomb of climate change continues.

The modern and globalized worldviews, the dominant views currently, are, in my opinion, incapable of addressing the challenges we face. In fact, they exacerbate the problems. Paradoxically, the competitive individualistic behaviors that served us in the modern worldview are the opposite behaviors of those we need to deal with problems such as climate change and rising inequality. These problems require collective action, long-term commitment, and cooperation among diverse people, while eschewing our addiction to immediate self-gratification and short-term solutions. The reward—saving our planet for future generations—is well worth any sacrifices we may have to make. Unfortunately, that goal seems too remote and disconnected from the everyday lives of many people who have immediate concerns, such as having enough food to put on the table.

A challenge today and in the future is how to accommodate diverse opinions without losing social and national cohesiveness. We must be able to understand and work with people holding different worldviews while also holding to our principles. It can be done. Although some of the positive dimensions of the four worldviews have already been mentioned and can be incorporated into the transformative worldview, each of the other worldviews alone has glaring detriments that are harming our planet or undermining our future life.

We need to integrate the sense of local place and the consideration of the environment that many indigenous peoples have connected with for millennia without losing our awareness that we are all global citizens. Indigenous peoples have a lot to offer us as to the importance of living simply, putting technology in its proper place, respecting Mother Earth, and seeing friendship and relationships as primary. Modern society has relegated elders to inconsequential relics of the past. Indigenous peoples, on the other hand, revere their elders and the wisdom that they share. Perhaps it is time for elders to throw off the blinders of their particular tribe, political party, class, race, ethnicity, or gender to look at the big picture of our life on Earth and share with others their experiential wisdom as to the best path to follow. A transformative worldview needs their guiding light.

The traditional, progressive, and globalized worldviews emerged out of the modern worldview. We need to move beyond the mechanistic, segmented order of the modern worldview without losing the importance of scientific inquiry, secularism, rational, logical thought, and shared patriotism. We need to assimilate the advances in technology, transportation, and communication, while rejecting the despoiling of our planet through environmental exploitation.

For a more inclusive and culturally tolerant worldview, we need to tone down the rigid dogma and intolerance of religious fundamentalism without losing the sense of shared meaning and universal values such as compassion, love, and purpose outside of oneself that traditional religion offers. Traditional conservatives have a lot to share with transformers as to the importance of traditions, religion, ceremony, and rituals to modern individuals. We cannot blithely cast off traditions without members of society feeling alienated and disaffected from the whole.

Post-modernists, part of the progressive worldview, emphasize irrational behavior, bleakness, and relative values that are failing to stir future generations. The obscurity and indeterminacy of post-modern and deconstructionist thought are providing unique perspectives about reality but do not provide enough inspiration for people to create a more just and sustainable future. We need to counter the fragmentation, pessimism, elitism, and uncertainty of post-modernism while incorporating the principles of relativity, the relationship of the observer and observed, and the capacity to probe below surface meanings.

Progressives' compassion for the poor, minorities, and oppressed people is a contribution to forming a transformative worldview. However, this compassion should also be grounded in reality rather than guilt about progressives' immense privilege or idealistic programs that are bound to fail. How to couple the enthusiasm and idealism of progressives with the realism of traditionalists is work for transformers to contemplate and act upon.

There is also a need to embrace the technological wonders of the globalized worldview that connect people throughout the world, yet get beyond the rampant consumerism and social divide that economic globalization fosters. What worldview will emerge to replace the shattered worldviews that have failed to provide a framework that will enable us to address vast global problems?

Drawbacks to the transformative worldview are that some people who claim to be transformers feel self-righteous about their "cause" and are unwilling to listen to others. This sanctimonious behavior among some has estranged many people who otherwise might be drawn to the worthy causes. While shouting their tolerance and rejection of hate during protest marches, many have shown intolerance to views other than their own, especially on college campuses. Hardly a movement that is inclusive. A willingness to listen and consider other views and people will do much to further many of the positive qualities of the transformative worldview and the dedicated people advancing its initiatives.

Those supporting a transformative worldview need not totally disregard the other four worldviews in shaping a new one, yet they need to be selective and mindful in fitting values of the other worldviews into a new framework. Even though the traditional, progressive, and globalized worldviews are currently the dominant paradigms at this point in time, the transformative worldview is gaining momentum and continues to mount a vigorous challenge to mainstream ideas while offering viable options for a sustainable and more equitable future. Which worldview or combination of worldviews will global citizens choose for our future? While some people are already taking action, others are going through a process of debate, consideration, and deliberation.

For many people, the transition to a new way of thinking and acting is difficult. But many people are inspired to make the world livable and safe for our collective children and grandchildren. Although we eagerly install fluorescent light bulbs or turn off our computers at night, deep structural, systemic changes are difficult to accomplish individually. Our worldviews are embedded in the way society is structured; it is hard to make the leap to another worldview.

Writers have written of a "tipping point," where things quickly make a dramatic shift to something different. As I finish up the editing of this book, the coronavirus is dramatically changing the daily lives of practically every person in the world. Perhaps this event will be the tipping point that signals a different worldview is around the corner. The leap to a transformative worldview is ever more urgent.

It is crucial to create a worldview that can enable us to avert environmental collapse, deal with the myriad of issues facing us today and in the near future, and forge a way of life that fosters well-being, happiness, and fulfillment. Inspired by these goals, I have written this book from a transformative worldview perspective, promoting it as a viable worldview today and in the future. After much research and reflection, I find that transformation is necessary to help us make the shift to a new way of thinking and acting that will move us into a new and more creative, tolerant, compassionate, and sustainable relationship with each other and our world.

You have been reading about different worldviews and imagining and practicing how to interact with other people holding different worldviews. My goal is not for us to forcibly convert people to a transformative worldview, but through listening, kindness, and compassionate conversations we can actively demonstrate to others that the transformative worldview is a life-enhancing future scenario in which all people have a crucial stake. It is my intention and hope that through engaging with others and seeing other perspectives, we can shift our consciousness to a transformative worldview. We all have a voice and critical stake in the future outcome. We can make that leap!

Chapter 9
Integration: Jonathan Haidt's Six Moral Foundations and the Five Worldviews

The human mind is a story processor, not a logic processor. ... Jonathan Haidt

INTRODUCTION TO MORAL FOUNDATION THEORY

The cultural divide is a collision of visions about a wide assortment of issues, ideas, behaviors, and worldviews. Ideas about what makes for a good society are not universally shared and many ideas are contentious. In previous chapters I have outlined five worldviews—indigenous, traditional, progressive, globalized, and transformative—highlighting different ways that groups of people see the world. In this chapter, I am introducing the work of psychologist Jonathan Haidt and his Six Moral Foundations Theory. I am introducing Haidt's ideas since these six moral foundations seamlessly integrate with the five worldviews. Since the progressive and traditional worldviews are generating a great deal of conflict today, I will pay more attention to these two worldviews.

Introducing Haidt's Six Moral Foundations will give us a deeper look into the workings of the worldviews, as well as bring attention to the ground-breaking work of Haidt. Integrating the two different models—Six Moral Foundations and Five Worldviews—is one way of examining the cultural divide and is also useful in finding solutions for bridging the cultural divide. A note here on terminology: Haidt often uses the terms conservative, right, and Republican to describe points on the political spectrum that I have included in the traditional worldview and the terms Democrat, left, liberal to describe what I include in the progressive worldview. I will use the terms interchangeably in this and the next chapter.

Professor Jonathan Haidt investigates how morality really works, not how it should work. While working on this question he went through his own personal transformation that changed the way he looked at the world. Although a self-identified liberal early in his career, Haidt now calls himself a centrist. He has braved considerable criticism from the left and right, but has been able to put aside his political leanings (as much as possible) to follow where the evidence takes him in the field of morality. Many of his conclusions have clashed with the entrenched "prevailing wisdom" of academia. For example, he has argued that religion is important in building cohesive societies, liberalism is based on a precariously narrow moral foundation, and humans use intuition a lot more than reason in making their moral decisions.[1]

One of Haidt's breakthrough epiphanies came while conducting research on morality in India, where he recognized the diversity of moral landscapes. He found that he "was able to see a moral world in which families, not individuals, are the basic unit of society, and the members of each extended family (including its servants) are intensely interdependent. In this world, equality and personal autonomy were not sacred values. Honoring elders, gods, and guests, and fulfilling one's role-based duties, were more important."[2] After this experience, when he looked at Americans he saw an overly individualistic and self-focused society. After more research, he later theorized that moral psychology is a series of innate moral foundations that evolution etched into our brains—psychological bases that underlie both the individual-protecting qualities that liberals value, like care and fairness, as well as the group-binding qualities favored by conservatives, like loyalty and authority.[3]

Haidt started his career when the field of psychology was in the grips of the rationalist model promoted by the psychologist Lawrence Kohlberg. Kohlbergian psychologists measured moral development as a series of increasingly sophisticated ways of reasoning about justice. A famous Kohlbergian task, for example, was the Heinz dilemma: Should Heinz steal a drug that was unavailable by legal means to save his dying wife?[4] The baby-boomers were just beginning to enter graduate school and gravitated to Kohlberg's justice-friendly take on moral psychology. Although Haidt thought Kohlberg's research was careful and honest, it was a framework that predefined morality as justice while devaluing authority, hierarchy, and tradition. As a result, Haidt believed it was predictable that Kohlbergian researchers would support worldviews that were secular, analytical, and egalitarian, and which supported the worldview of the researchers.[5] Nearly all research in moral psychology had been limited to issues of justice, rights, and welfare.

One of Kohlberg's students, Elliot Turiel, continued in what was called the "rationalist" tradition, in which morality is foremost about protecting individuals rather than defending the group. A frequently cited definition of morality comes from Turiel, who grounded his definition in the tradition of liberal political theory and defined it as "prescriptive judgments of justice, rights, and welfare pertaining to how people ought to relate to each other."[6] Turiel argued that rules that prevent harm are moral rules, and that morality is about treating individuals well— about harm and fairness, and not loyalty, respect, duty, piety, patriotism, or tradition.[7] People holding these rationalist ideas are the WEIRD (Western, Educated, Individualized/Industrialized, Rich, Democratic) individuals described in earlier chapters. These were decidedly Western ideals not universally recognized by others.

When morality is equated with the protection of individuals, the central concerns of conservatives—and of people in most non-Western (non-WEIRD) cultures—fall outside the moral domain. But Haidt found through his research in India, Brazil, and the United States that Western elites are unusual, compared to billions of other people in the world, in restricting the moral domain to an "ethic of autonomy." This ethic is based on the idea that people are autonomous individuals with personal wants, needs, and preferences, which they should be able to satisfy as they see fit. In response to these socially constructed principles, societies established moral concepts, such as rights, liberty, and justice—the basis of individual societies—which allowed people to peacefully coexist without interfering in each other's lives. In contrast to the rationalists, Haidt proposed that morality in most cultures also involves an "ethic of community" which includes obedience, duty, interdependence, and group and institutional cohesiveness, as well as an "ethic of divinity," which included purity, sanctity, and the suppression of humanity's baser instincts.[8]

Haidt entered the field of moral psychology during the rationalist wave but began to question the emphasis on the Western, modern, secular worldview that dominated the field. He came to the conclusion that "the United States and Western Europe are extraordinary historical exceptions—new societies that had found a way to strip down and thin out the thick, all-encompassing moral orders."[9] Actually, the moral domain varies across cultures: Turiel's description of morality as being about justice, rights, and human welfare worked very well for WEIRD individuals, but it, as Haidt stated, "simply did not capture the moral concerns of the less elite groups—the working-class people— …who were more likely to justify their judgments with talk about respect, duty, and family roles."[10] To better understand the entrenched Western worldview and its implication in his study of moral psychology, Haidt drew on the works of two intellectual giants of the nineteenth century: John Stuart Mill and Émile Durkheim.

JOHN STUART MILL AND CONTRACT SOCIETIES

John Stuart Mill (1806–1873), a British philosopher, economist, and civil servant, was one of the most influential thinkers in the history of liberalism. Mill laid out a philosophical response to rapid economic changes, such as the spread of industrial capitalism, and to the embrace of philosophical liberalism, such as the political creation of the nation-state. Mill's conception of liberty justified the freedom of the individual in opposition to political control by the monarchy and social and religious control by the church.

Mill was the patron saint of a contractual society. He wrote in his seminal book *On Liberty* that "the only purpose for which power can be rightfully exercised over any member of a civilized community, against his will, is to prevent harm to others."[11] He imagined a social contract invented for the mutual benefit of all individuals: all individuals are equal, and all should be left as free as possible to move, develop talents, and form relationships as they please. Mill's vision appeals to many liberals and libertarians. A Millian society at its best would be a peaceful, open, and creative place where diverse individuals respect each other's rights and band together voluntarily to help those in need or to change the laws for the common good.[12] He also passionately defended freedom of speech.

Psychologists have researched the moral mechanisms that are presumed in a Millian society, and there are two that are innate. First, people in all cul-

164

tures are emotionally responsive to suffering and harm, particularly violent harm, and so societies have norms, rules, or laws to safeguard individuals and to encourage care for the most defenseless. Second, people in all cultures are emotionally open to issues of fairness and reciprocity, which are expanded into concepts of rights and justice. Philosophical efforts to justify liberal democracies and egalitarian social contracts consistently rely on psychological mechanisms about fairness and reciprocity.[13] Three moral mechanisms put forth by Mill—care, fairness, and liberty—would become three of the individualizing moral foundations out of the six in Haidt's Moral Foundations Theory.

ÉMILE DURKHEIM

David Émile Durkheim (1858-1917) was a French sociologist who is commonly cited as the principal architect of modern social science. Much of Durkheim's work was concerned with how societies could maintain their integrity and coherence in modernity, when things such as a shared religious and ethnic background could no longer be assumed in modern multi-ethnic and multi-religious nation states. In contrast to Mill, a Durkheimian society would prize duty over rights, loyalty to one's groups over concerns for out-groups, self-control over self-expression, and deference to authority over liberty.

Durkheim said societies were not an agreement among individuals but a web of social relationships. Haidt describes these relationships "as something that [have] emerged organically over time as people found ways of living together, binding themselves to each other, suppressing each other's selfishness, and punishing the deviants and free-riders who eternally threaten to undermine cooperative groups. The basic social unit is not the individual; it is the hierarchically structured family, which serves as a model for other institutions. Individuals in such societies are born into strong and constraining relationships that profoundly limit their autonomy."[14]

Durkheim warned about the dangers of anomie or normlessness associated with individualistic societies. Anomie is the condition in which society provides little moral guidance to individuals who are likely to suffer from this lack of guidance. This state of anomie develops in response to conflict among prevailing belief systems which causes breakdowns of social bonds between an individual and the community.[15] Durkheim wrote in 1897 that "Man cannot become attached to higher aims and submit to a rule if he sees nothing above him to which he belongs. To free himself from all social pressure is to abandon himself and demoralize him."[16] A Durkheimian society, Haidt explains, "at its best would be a stable network composed of many nested and overlapping groups that socialize, reshape, and care for individuals who, if left to their own devices, would pursue shallow, carnal, and selfish pleasures."[17]

Durkheim regularly criticized his colleagues, such as Freud, who described morality and religion using only the psychology of individuals and their personal relationships. Durkheim argued that humans exist at two levels: as an individual and as part of the larger society. From his studies of religion he concluded that people have two distinct sets of "social sentiments," one for each level. The first set of sentiments, according to Durkheim "binds each individual to the person of his fellow-citizens: these are manifest within the community, in the day-to-day relationships of life. These include the sentiments of honor, respect, affection and fear which we may feel towards one another."[18] The second set of emotions binds the individual to the social entity as a whole; these manifest themselves primarily in relationships of the society with other societies. The first set of emotions leaves individual autonomy and personality almost intact. When living within the second set of emotions, by contrast, individuals are simply a part of a whole, whose actions are followed and influenced by others.[19]

Durkheim's higher-level sentiments describe the passion and ecstasy that group rituals can generate. As Durkheim put it, "The very act of congregating is an exceptionally powerful stimulant. Once individuals are gathered together, a sort of electricity is generated from their closeness and quickly launches them to an extraordinary height of exaltation."[20] This thrilling sensation can be experienced by anyone who has ever participated in a choir, protest march, religious ritual, or rock concert. Perhaps you have had one of these experiences before. I remember attending basketball games of my favorite college team, when an exceptionally exhilarating play was performed, the arena would erupt into a wild collective euphoria. I would be swept away by the excitement. As Durkheim explained, in such a state, "the vital energies become hyperexcited, the passions more intense, the sensations more powerful."[21]

Durkheim believed that these collective emotions pull humans fully but temporarily into the higher of our two realms, the realm of the sacred, where the self disappears and collective interests prevail. The dimension of the profane, in contrast, is the ordinary, day-to-day world where we mostly live, concerned about wealth, health, and reputation, but nagged by the sense that there is something higher and more transcendent. Durkheim argued that our movements back and forth between these two realms gave rise to our notions about gods, spirits, heavens, and the very idea of a detached moral order.[22]

A Durkheimian ethos needs more than the care and fairness moral foundations that support a Millian society. Drawing on Durkheim's work, Haidt shows that social conservatives rely upon the care and fairness foundations, but they also "value virtues related to three additional psychological systems: ingroup/loyalty (involving mechanisms that evolved during the long human history of tribalism), authority/respect (involving ancient primate mechanisms for managing social rank, tempered by the obligation of superiors to protect and provide for subordinates), and purity/sanctity (a relatively new part of the moral mind, related to the evolution of disgust, that makes us see carnality as degrading and renunciation as noble)."[23]

These three mechanisms—loyalty, authority, and purity—support moralities that bind humans into groups that work together to reach common goals. Such moralities make it easier for individuals to forget individual preferences and forge a mutually beneficial society that supports the well-being of the group. These were significant findings that motivated Haidt to develop a more sophisticated way of looking at morality. He no longer felt that there was one wrong side and one right side in the fierce culture wars between the right and left; he could see how both sides made their decisions and acted out behaviors. Haidt was moving from the political left to the center.

SOCIOCENTRIC CULTURES

Westerners are unusual, in the context of the world's cultures, because they think about people as bounded, unique, discrete individuals. Most societies follow the sociocentric way of ordering their society, placing the needs of groups and institutions first, and subordinating the needs of individuals. In contrast, the individualistic answer places individuals at the center and makes society a servant of the individual.[24]

The sociocentric approach to organizing society has prevailed through human history, but the individualist approach became a powerful contender during the evolution of the modern worldview and the Enlightenment (see Chapter 3). With the spread of Western influence and imperialism, the individualist approach battled to replace the sociocentric approach from the eighteenth century onward, as individual rights expanded, the nation-state political organization spread, and consumer culture became popular.[25] Drawing on these ideas, Haidt would formulate another rule of moral psychology: morality is not just about how we treat each other (as most liberals think); it is also about binding groups together, supporting essential institutions, and living in a sanctified and noble way.[26]

If measured against the Western notions of morality (justice, rights, and welfare), Christian and Hindu communities don't fare very well. They limit people's rights (especially sexual rights), favor hierarchy, install gender roles, and require people to spend time in prayer and ritual practices that seem superfluous and superstitious to modernizers. But it is unfair to levy on all cultures a definition of morality drawn from the European Enlightenment tradition. Haidt suggests an alternative definition of moral systems that is based upon what they do rather than by what they value. He defines morality as "any system of interlocking values, practices, institutions, and psychological mechanisms that work together to suppress or regulate selfishness and make social life possible."[27]

When conducting research at the University of Pennsylvania, Haidt found in his interviews of college students and working-class adults in nearby neighborhoods that the Penn students mostly held to the ethic of autonomy or an individualized culture, while the working-class adults mostly held to the ethic of community and identified a bit with the ethic of divinity. Haidt began to see that moral matrices coexist within each nation. Comparable to my definition of worldviews, Haidt found that "each matrix provides a complete unified and emotionally compelling worldview, easily justified by observable evidence and nearly impregnable to attack by arguments from outsiders."[28] He continues, "Moral matrices bind people together and blind them to the coherence, or even existence, of other matrices. This makes it very difficult for people to consider the possibility that there might really be more than one form of moral truth, or more than one valid framework for judging people or running a society."[29] When people are described as living in their own "bubble" socially sealed off from others, this means they are living in their own moral matrix.

Two kinds of moral systems suppress selfishness and other base behaviors. Some cultures try to suppress selfishness by protecting individuals directly, often using an extensive bureaucratic legal system to do so, and by educating individuals to respect the rights of other individuals. Haidt states, "This individualizing approach focuses on individuals as the locus of moral value. Other cultures try to suppress selfishness by strengthening groups and institutions and by binding individuals into roles and duties in order to constrain their imperfect natures. This binding approach focuses on the group as the locus of moral value."[30] Haidt points out that "the individualizing–binding distinction can account for substantial variation in the moral concerns of the political left and right, especially in the United States, and that it illuminates disagreements underlying many culture war issues."[31]

BUILDING THE MORAL FOUNDATIONS THEORY

In building the Moral Foundations Theory, Haidt grounded his ideas in the notion that humans' moral intuitions originate from innate psychological mechanisms that coevolved through the millennia along with cultural institutions and practices. Each influenced the other. These mechanisms are innate but they are adaptable according to specific cultural circumstances. Haidt and his colleagues continued to build the theory by surveying lists of virtues from many different cultures and time periods, along with case studies of morality from anthropology, psychology, and evolutionary theories about human and primate social organization. They found two clear moral domains: the widespread human fixation with fairness, reciprocity, and justice and the widespread human concern about caring, nurturing, empathy, and protecting vulnerable individuals from harm. These two domains were labeled the fairness/reciprocity foundation and the care/harm foundation, respectively. Haidt called these two the individualizing foundations because they are the source of the liberal philosophical tradition, with its learnable emphasis on the rights and welfare of individuals.[32] He later added liberty/oppression to this list to make three individualizing foundations.

Haidt and his colleagues found that most cultures did not limit their moral domains to just individualizing foundations but had more extensive clusters of virtues. They narrowed those virtues to three. The first moral foundation was loyalty, patriotism, and self-sacrifice for the benefit of the group. The second was obedience and respect for authority and deference to those who exhibited skilled leadership and protected the group. This foundation was linked to the research done on the evolution of hierarchy in primates and the ways that human hierarchy was dependent on the consent of subordinates. The third foundation combined virtues of sanctity and purity that served social functions, such as marking the group's cultural boundaries and suppressing the selfishness often exhibited by humanity's lascivious nature. This foundation cultivates a spiritual mindset that elevates notions of cleanliness and purity, and demotes base instincts, such as greed, lust, envy, jealousy, and anger. Haidt refers to these three foundations—loyalty, authority, and sanctity—as the binding foundations.[33]

The six moral foundations are innate in all humans but vary according to culture. Innate does not mean they are fixed and the same in all cultural situations, but it does mean they are organized in advance of experience. The experience shapes the type of cultural reaction to the innate behaviors. Haidt uses a metaphor to explain this notion: "Genes create the first draft of the brain, and experience later edits it. ... They are the psychological systems that give children feelings and intuitions [and] make local stories, practices, and moral arguments more or less appealing during the editing process."[34]

The aim of the Moral Foundations Theory is to identify the innate psychological systems that the process of evolution passed along to us and what each culture uses to construct its unique moral systems. Along with evolution, Haidt sees morality as a social construction that varies across cultures. We all live in a web of shared meanings and values that become our moral matrix and these matrices form "a consensual hallucination." He continues, "But all humans graft their moralities on psychological systems that evolved to serve various needs, like caring for families and punishing cheaters."[35] Synthesizing work from anthropology, evolutionary theory, and psychology, Haidt proposes the six innate moral foundations: care/harm, fairness/cheating, liberty/oppression, loyalty/betrayal, authority/subversion, and sanctity/degradation.

Haidt sees the six moral foundations as a way to explain politics. Each political movement emphasizes a different set of foundations, and the culture wars arise from which one they choose to emphasize. For example, liberals elevate care, followed by fairness and liberty, and rarely value loyalty and authority. In contrast, conservatives call upon all six foundations somewhat equally.[36] Haidt found that liberals and conservatives lived in their own closed world. Each of these worlds "provide a complete, unified, and emotionally compelling worldview, easily justified by observable evidence and nearly impregnable to attack by arguments from outsiders." He thinks that moral psychology can help us understand these moral matrices.[37]

APPLYING THE MORAL FOUNDATIONS THEORY

I have integrated the Six Moral Foundations Theory into my work on five worldviews because this addition expands on the complexity within each of the worldviews. In the rest of the chapter I will give examples of the five worldviews in each of the six moral foundations. However, since the cultural divide is particularly intense between the traditional and progressive worldviews, I will focus most of my comments on them.

THREE INDIVIDUALIZING FOUNDATIONS: CARE, FAIRNESS, AND LIBERTY

Care Foundation

The care foundation evolved from our long history as mammals complete with attachment systems and an ability to feel and have an aversion to the pain of others. It underlies values of kindness, compassion, nurturance, gentleness, empathy, and consideration of others. This human capacity to care, cherish, and protect others has helped produce our tremendous evolutionary success.

Progressives zero in on care of the oppressed. As Haidt notes, "If you grow up in a WEIRD society, you can detect oppression and inequality even where the apparent victims see nothing wrong...For American liberals since the 1960s, I believe that the most sacred value is caring for victims of oppression. Anyone who blames such victims for their own problems or who displays or merely excuses prejudice against socialized victim groups can expect a vehement tribal response."[38] An example of a tribal response to someone who deviated from care orthodoxy took place in the 1960s when liberal sociologist Daniel Patrick Moynihan, a Harvard University professor and public-policy expert, submitted a famous report to President Johnson using the phrase "tangle of pathology" to describe the black family. Moynihan argued that some of its problems stemmed from high rates of out-of-wedlock birth, not just from racism. Haidt explains, "That made Moynihan a pariah; other Harvard professors wouldn't let their kids play with his. Moynihan committed the cardinal sin of blaming the victim, where the victim is one of your sacralized victim groups." Haidt points out that now sociologists are gingerly saying that perhaps Moynihan was right.[39]

Care among progressives is often directed outside their own locality to groups with whom they may have little contact or connection. For example, progressives may participate in a protest march to protect immigrant rights but not live in immigrant communities, attend the same places of worship, or have their children attend the same public school. In the above example, the Harvard professors who ostracized Moynihan most likely had little personal contact with the single-parent African American families who were the focus of Moynihan's research. Care is dispensed in a more detached and separated way, instead of administering care through close, thick personal relationships rooted in community sharing.

The care foundation is also important to traditionalists, but it is more proportionately balanced with the other five foundations than it is with progressives. Traditionalists generally extend care towards those in their local community, geographic location, place of worship, those serving their country, the unborn, or law-enforcement personnel. Among the many conservative causes that reflect the care foundation include Southern States Police Benevolent Association, Wounded Warrior Project, and National Right to Life. Care is shared in a more personal type of relationship than it is with progressives who often call for depersonalized government services to dispense care to those in need.

Indigenous people care for a wide variety of people including the elderly, who are revered and honored. Elders often take a leadership role in the community and their wisdom and guidance are appreciated. Care for "mother Earth" is important as well and is expressed through ritual and ceremony. Care of the family, extended family, and tribal groups are also a reflection of their personalized caring attributes.

Care among globalizers is primarily directed to the success and profitability of their enterprises. Many globalizers claim they are responsible business people and give to charitable causes, but I have found this type of care is not a deep kind of personal care. Although I should avoid making judgment about their motivations for professing care, I have found it is often about projecting a caring public business image than a sincere devotion to those being cared for. Regardless of the motives, many small businesses give to causes that support the vitality of their local communities; and many large corporations are often generous providers of funds for worthwhile projects that extend care to a large number of people, such as the Bill and Melinda Gates Foundation, Ford Foundation, the Carnegie Foundation, the Carter Foundation, and many more.

Care among transformers can vary from supporting worthwhile causes around the world to establishing close personal relationships with family, neighbors, or people in the community. Care of the Earth is important as well, as it is with indigenous peoples. Ceremonies and rituals can signify reverence and gratitude for the Earth and all it provides for us. Care is also directed to many disadvantaged groups around the world, such as victims of natural disasters, refugees parked in temporary camps, and those who are oppressed by their governments.

Fairness Foundation

Our hunting/gathering ancestors performed the action of reciprocity for millions of years. When we help or are kind to others, we expect the recipient of the favor to return a favor. From these actions, humans have generated ideas of fairness, justice, rights, and autonomy. This moral foundation also touches on the notion of proportionality—that people take and give back to the group their "fair share."

Fairness is an important moral foundation, yet cultures around the world vary greatly in how they implement fairness. Those in the progressive and traditional worldviews interpret fairness very differently. Progressives construe fairness to mean equality, while traditionalists see it as proportionality—people should be compensated in proportion to what they contribute, even if that means unequal outcomes.[40] Progressives worry about transgender people being treated unfairly; traditionalists think it is unfair for welfare recipients to take advantage of the system. Many progressives find that equal opportunity is not enough; they want equal results. Since equal results are impossible in a capitalist society, many progressives think that socialism is a better answer to inequality. Haidt notes, "This is why rural and working-class whites vote Republican. Liberals think Republicans have somehow duped blue-collar whites into voting against their own interests, but people who get their hands dirty for a living are offended by the liberal assault on merit, and they hate freeloaders."[41]

Arguments about fairness are never-ending in part because there are different kinds, making it easy for traditionalists and progressives to talk past each other and interpret them differently. Haidt distinguishes between procedural fairness and distributive fairness.

1. Procedural Fairness is vital for a healthy democracy to function. It means open and impartial procedures must be used. Citizens must have faith in the system for it to operate, and if they have such faith they are more willing to accept outcomes that they may disagree with or that do not benefit them. As President Bill Clinton preached, we must "all work hard and play by the same rules." When citizens think the system is corrupt or rigged, they are more prone to join populist movements. For example, Bernie Sanders claimed that a rigged system cost him the Democratic nomination for president in 2016. Many of his followers agreed. On the left, Occupy Wall Street protesters drew attention to what they claimed was a corrupt financial system because of the 2008 financial meltdown. On the right, Sarah Palin and Tea Partiers directed their scorn at those associated with crony capitalism. As each side saw it, these examples were a direct violation of procedural fairness.[42]

2. Distributive Fairness refers to how we allocate the benefits and obligations of resources. Is everyone doing their fair share and getting their fair share? This type of fairness is divided into two subtypes: equality, where everyone gets the same amount, and proportionality, where rewards are in proportion to their inputs (sometimes called equity). According to Haidt, the distinction between the two types of distributive fairness explains many of today's political disagreements. Proportionately is widely accepted by all sides, but the left also endorses equality, even when it contradicts proportionality. The right prefers proportionality, even when it leads to considerable inequalities of outcome.[43]

Former President Obama, for example, shied away from talk about equality of outcomes, to the disapproval of progressives. He stated on numerous occasions: "We can restore an economy where everyone gets a fair shot, and everyone does their fair share, and everyone plays by the same set of rules." Haidt analyzes Obama's statement: "The second phrase (fair share) is a clear plea for fairness as proportionality, and the third phrase (same set of rules) is a clear plea for procedural fairness. But what should we make of that first phrase, everyone gets a fair shot? What exactly is a fair shot?"[44] Progressives and traditionalists have different interpretations of these notions, leading to a debate about the proper role of government in this matter.

For conservatives, a fair shot refers to procedural fairness. They believe it is not the government's role to make everyone equal at the start of the race, but it is the government's job to make the race fair. The conservative refrain is "if you work hard, you will succeed, if you don't you will fail." Some people succeed, others fail. If you pay your taxes, then you deserve benefits. If you don't contribute to the pool of resources, you don't deserve benefits. Equality is not a concern for them. However, Democrats have a different definition of what a fair shot means. To them, it is not just procedural fairness that is at stake, it also involves questions of distributive fairness.[45] To better understand this analysis let's look at liberty alongside fairness; but first let's consider fairness in the other three worldviews.

Indigenous peoples would subscribe to the notion of procedural fairness and also to the subtype equality in the distributive fairness category. They are fundamentally an equal society and most people receive an equal share of resources despite their contribution. For example, the elderly do not contribute their fair share of resources to the group's common pool but their contributions in the past are recognized and appreciated. However, in older traditional societies, if the elderly became a burden to the group, they might willingly take their own lives in order that more resources would be appropriated to the younger generations. Also, in older indigenous societies freeloaders were not always tolerated since their lack of contribution to the group could threaten its survival.

Globalizers ascribe to procedural fairness and need transparent rules in which all players know how the global economy operates in order for it to function smoothly. They have created institutions such as the World Trade Organization and World Bank to monitor procedural fairness. However, they would favor distributive fairness according to equity instead of equality. The global meritocracy is all about equity, rewarding those who achieve and excel, and they are not concerned with equality.

The transformative worldview would endorse procedural fairness, since most transformers favor reducing social and economic inequality without the implementation of a vast bureaucratic system required to monitor its implementation. Most transformers want political decisions to be made at a local, regional level, which can more efficiently ensure the goals of proportionately with equality as an ideal rather than an unattainable outcome.

Liberty Foundation

Americans of all stripes value liberty. The Tea Party's manifesto was "Give Us Liberty." Occupy Wall Street protesters renamed Zuccotti Park, the location of their demonstrations, "Liberty Park." Even though both sides value liberty, unsurprisingly they disagree on the main threat to American liberty. Politically, the essential element of all forms of liberalism is individual liberty. Liberals have historically taken an optimistic view of human nature and of human perfectibility; they hold the belief that people should be as free as possible to pursue their own personal development.[46] Those on the right have a bleaker view of human nature, saying that liberty will be compromised if order is not imposed on the undisciplined mobs. Those on the right say that the biggest threat to liberty is an out-of-control federal government, while the left says it is big business and the upper one percent.[47] Adding to the confusion liberty has two different and competing meanings: positive and negative, both associated with fairness.

Negative liberty refers to the freedom to be left alone. It is, according to Haidt, "the absence of obstacles which block human action ... the freedom from oppression and interference by other people." When this negative type of liberty is violated, those who are offended often elicit a psychological state called reactance, which is an angry reaction against perceived pressure or constraint. Haidt notes, "Reactance makes people do the opposite of what they were pressured to do, even if they were not inclined to act that way beforehand."[48] For example, when progressives heatedly decry Trump supporters as racist homophobes, those targeted by the insults are unlikely to have a reflective moment and say, "Yes you are right, I will change my behavior to what you think is right." Instead, the repeated charges will most likely have the unintended consequences of exacerbating dormant or unconscious racist behavior or attitudes and make them explicit.

In contrast to negative liberty, positive liberty refers to having the power and means to select one's path and achieve one's potential. But if the society you are living in offers you few options (negative liberty) what good is positive liberty? Haidt notes, "Proponents of positive liberty argue that governments have an obligation to remove barriers and obstacles to full political participation, and to take positive steps to enable previously oppressed groups to succeed."[49] Lyndon Johnson in his 1965 commencement speech at Howard University exemplified the argument for positive liberty. He began the speech with a celebration of the 1964 Civil Rights Act, which granted negative liberty to African Americans: "Freedom is the right to share, share fully and equally, in American society—to vote, to hold a job, to enter a public place, to go to school. It is the right to be treated in every part of our national life as a person equal in dignity and promise to all others."[50]

Johnson then made the transition to positive liberty in the following passage. "*But freedom is not enough*. You do not wipe away the scars of centuries by saying: Now you are free to go where you want, and do as you desire, and choose the leaders you please. You do not take a person who, for years, has been hobbled by chains and liberate him, bring him up to the starting line of a race and then say, you are free to compete with all the others, and still justly believe that you have been completely fair. Thus it is not enough just to open the gates of opportunity. All our citizens must have the ability to walk through those gates. *And this is the next and the more profound stage* of the battle for civil rights. We seek not just freedom but opportunity. We seek not just legal equity but human ability, *not just equality as a right and a theory but equality as a fact and equality as a result*.[51] (emphasis added by Haidt)

Johnson's civil rights ideas may seem appropriate to the 1960s civil rights era but do they apply to African Americans today? Once the left made the switch from negative to positive liberty, it meant they would use the power of the federal government to promote some policies that embraced fairness viewed as equality and positive liberty. Although in hindsight it seemed a compassionate act, at the time it violated many people's notions of fairness viewed as proportionality and negative liberty. Republicans seized on the unpopularity of these policies to attack liberals. Liberal programs are numerous; one deeply unpopular example was forced busing of public school students to achieve racial integration. This action violated white parents' sense of negative liberty and triggered strong reactance. Another unpopular policy was affirmative action to achieve educational equality which violated the idea of procedural fairness. Haidt remarks, "Generous welfare programs violated many people's notions of proportionality—the government seemed to give out money for nothing, which made it ever easier for men to abandon their children and pass the bill on to the taxpayers." These policies, along with other actions, combined to alienate the white working class, who had stronger values of proportional fairness and positive liberty than liberals, driving many in the working class to the Republican Party.[52] Donald Trump and his populist message were able to exploit the left on this vulnerable topic in the 2016 election.

Many indigenous people may strongly identify with positive liberty because they were treated unfairly for many years. They reason that the government owes them money for the lands they took from them, mismanagement of those lands, and health care clinics to compensate individuals for the effects of environmentally polluting their lands.

Globalizers would strongly identify with negative liberty, in that they are free to compete with others on an equal footing. But generally they would not support government programs that provide ways to foster equality of outcomes. Globalizers support the freedom to pursue a consumerist lifestyle without the restraining forces of obligation, tradition, and religion.

Transformers view liberty is an important moral foundation. They would support the idea of negative liberty as freedom to select a path that leads to personal fulfillment and personal growth. They would not be as inclined to promote positive liberty as progressives.

THREE BINDING MORAL FOUNDATIONS: LOYALTY, AUTHORITY, AND SANCTITY

How would you answer these questions: Should people be loyal to their family members, even when they have done something wrong? Do all children need to learn respect for authority? Should people do things that are disgusting, even if no one is harmed? These three items are a few of the questions asked by Haidt and his colleagues to measure the loyalty, authority, and sanctity foundations on their Moral Foundations survey.[53]

Social conservatives, whose morality rests in large part on the three binding foundations, don't see eye to eye with liberals who more closely identify with the three individualizing foundations. Basically, liberals want to make things more open with fewer rules and traditions, especially in ways that they believe will make it easier for women, African Americans, and other oppressed groups to escape from traditional confining roles. Conservatives, on the other hand, want to ensure traditions, especially in ways that they perceive will help parents, teachers, police, and other authorities maintain order. These disagreements led and continue to lead to culture war battles.[54]

Unlike older generations, the millennials score low on the three binding foundations. As Haidt notes, millennials "have been raised on a diet of tolerance, diversity, and a reluctance to make moral judgments."[55] They do not remember historical events which would have instilled in them a stronger sense of the need for national unity. Haidt continues, "Instead, technology links them increasingly to young people all around the world, making it harder to inflame them with pleas revolving around Loyalty. They have little fondness for hierarchy and tradition, so it will be hard to woo them with appeals based on the Authority foundation. And they have no visceral sense of disgust at homosexuality, and have been socialized to be as inclusive as possible, so arguments about sexuality derived from sanctity will fail to move them."[56]

Loyalty Foundation

Early humans were not individualistic seekers of personal growth but engaged with others in developing ways to enhance and ensure their survival. Loyalty was one of the most essential ethics. Haidt explains that loyalty is "based on the idea that people are first and foremost, members of larger entities such as families, teams, armies, companies, tribes, and nations. People have an obligation to play their assigned roles in these entities. Many societies therefore develop moral concepts such as duty, hierarchy, respect, reputation, and patriotism."[57] In sociocentric societies, the Western assertion that people should pursue an individualistic agenda forged by their own creative powers seems reckless, egotistical, and dangerous to conservatives. When loyalty to one's group begins to dissipate, conservatives have found that society begins to fray and loose cohesiveness, bickering intensifies, and loyalty to established norms disintegrates. Soon the social fabric that weaves the society together is weakened and institutions damaged, and the continuation of that society is in grave peril and all suffer as a result.

Indigenous peoples strongly identify with loyalty to kin, tribe, traditions, and ancestors. They have elaborate networks of social relationships to cement ties with their kin and others. They have rituals and ceremonies in which their loyalty and devotion to their ancestors and others in their social network is expressed. It is not uncommon for many of them to have a shrine in their living area that is dedicated to worshipping and remembering their ancestors.

Loyalty is not important to globalizers. Loyalty by employees to their company is a bygone value and the company is not loyal to individual employees either. The days of thanks for decades of service with a gold watch are long gone. Moving on to another company if a greater opportunity comes along is very common among individuals. Companies are unrepentant when dismissing workers who are no longer needed; especially when they are older workers whose salaries exceed what corporations want to pay.

Loyalty is important to transformers, including fidelity to family, neighbors, community, and work endeavors. Commitment and responsibility are often missing in modern and globalized societies but these values are necessary for human well-being. Transformers are intent on building and sustaining life-supporting institutions, families, and communities.

Authority Foundation

All societies have and need an authority structure to function, otherwise chaos will ensue. But liberals and conservatives have different personality traits and attitudes towards authority. Conservatives have traditionally taken a more pessimistic view of human nature than liberals, arguing that people are innately selfish and imperfect. They hold that people need the restraints of authority, religion, institutions, and traditions to know how to live civilly with each other. Some conservatives have a tendency toward authoritarianism when threats to the social order emerge, which motivates them to identify authority figures that purport to defend order. The two core aspects of conservativism are resistance to change and opposition to difference. Liberals on average are more open to experience and more inclined to seek out change and novelty both personally and politically, while conservatives have a stronger preference for things that are familiar, stable, predictable, and orderly.[58]

Haidt experienced the consequences of progressives' reluctance to assert authority when he visited the Occupy Wall Street demonstrations in 2012. While milling about he observed the night's meeting in which protesters were crafting a vision statement. He found that during the decision-making process "several people facilitate, but no one leads. The way to make yourself heard above the din is the people's mic, a system whereby one person speaks and the crowd amplifies the words. A row over internal charges of racism and sexism dogs the meeting from the start."[59] Throughout the evening, Haidt asks questions and listens to what is on the mind of the protesters. Haidt is stunned by "how messy the procedures are. When people get down to debating the manifesto, the document does not name any specific goals. One speaker reports her group could not even agree on a section about nonviolence, since there are a diversity of tactics within the movement." Without any leadership decisions could not be made, even about nonviolence.[60]

Indigenous peoples have a respect and deference for the chief as leader of the tribe. However, the chief reflects the group's interests, and is considered part of the group and not an autonomous leader. In smaller indigenous groups, a circle of elders often holds authority because of their experiences and accumulated wisdom. But usually they wield authority after skillfully gathering consensus from all or most members.

The authority foundation is important among globalizers. They follow a corporate organizational model in which there are clear levels of authority among different divisions. The board of directors and Chief Executive Officers wield a great deal of power. Actually, the profitability of companies and their obligations to shareholders exercise a great deal of authority and power within corporations.

Transformers view authority in similar ways to indigenous peoples. Elders and community and religious leaders have more authority than other group members, although consensus is important and many voices are heard before decisions are made. Once decisions are made, it is the responsibility of all group members to go along with the consensus to insure tranquility and peaceful relationships.

Sanctity Foundation

The sixth moral foundation, sanctity, is arguably the most important to humans. Through religious or spiritual faith, humans developed the "psychology of sacredness," the notion that some people, objects, days, words, values, and ideas are special, set apart, untouchable, and pure. Haidt explains that this foundation is based on the idea that "people are first and foremost, temporary vessels within which a divine soul has been implanted. People are children of God and should behave accordingly. Many societies develop moral concepts such as sanctity and sin, purity and pollution, elevation and degradation. In such societies, the personal liberty of secular Western nations looks like libertinism, hedonism, and celebration of humanity's baser instincts."[61] According to Haidt, religion is an evolutionary adaptation for binding people into groups that are better able to compete against other groups.[62]

Religion and political leadership across time and place perform the miracle of converting unrelated individuals into a cohesive group. If people are united in worshipping the same sanctified things they can trust one another and cooperate in the task of completing larger goals such as organizing a functioning society. Thus, religion serves multiple functions: connecting the individual to the sacred, providing a unifying answer to complex questions, offering a way for individuals to participate in a larger group, and giving help to those in need in times of distress. Haidt notes that "Durkheim long ago said that God is really society projected up into the heavens, a collective delusion that enables collectives to exist, suppress selfishness, and endure. The three Durkheimian foundations (loyalty, authority, and sanctity) play a crucial role in most religions."[63] When these three binding foundations are excluded from a society that society can easily disintegrate into a hollow shell filled by superfluous activities, such as shopping and playing computer games.

Religion arose as an instrument to set the rules for a smooth-functioning moral community and to bind people to its values. Haidt explains, "If people believe in omniscient gods they are less likely to cheat when no one is looking, and a common set of rules creates trust—what psychologists call social capital. This is the key to getting large numbers of people to cooperate with others who are not immediate kin."[64] Haidt continues, "The recent evolution of our species took place within a thick matrix of morality, much of it religious. We worked, lived, traded, and mated in accordance with this moral matrix, even though we had to sacrifice personal growth."[65]

The purpose of religious rituals and sacred practices is to encourage people to sacrifice and to feel they are in the presence of something profound. By religious, Haidt does not mean the "depth of conviction but depth of commitment, how enmeshed people are in their congregations. It is belonging, more than believing, that builds up social capital."[66] Religious people give more to charity and do more volunteer work than non-religious people, although much of their giving goes to their religious group. They are also more caring neighbors and citizens, and contribute proportionately more to non-religious charities, such as medical research foundations. The social capital from religious activities generates vast surpluses that spill over into society and benefit everyone.[67]

Many progressives claim to be atheists, a significant social shift from societies deeply rooted in the universal and indigenous religions that have survived for thousands of years. Haidt warns that progressive societies, for all practical purposes, "are the least efficient societies ever known at turning resources (of which they have a lot) into offspring (of which they have few)." He believes that the "left makes a great mistake in overlooking the importance of religion and of other group-derived sources of loyalty and morality."[68]

Indigenous peoples have a rich spiritual tradition that is in many ways different from the universal religions. They tend to believe that life and spirit are within what modernists think of as inanimate objects and even animals and plants. For example, they find that a mountain has a spirit present in and around it. Indigenous spiritual leaders are shamans who can manipulate spiritual energy that can be advantageous or detrimental to humans. Indigenous peoples have many rituals and ceremonies conducted by shamans or elders to connect humans to the spiritual world.

Globalizers, I would assume, do not connect with a spiritual presence or with a particular religion. Like many progressives, they may dismiss religious sentiments as superstitious, quaint, or incompatible with modern trends and lifestyles.

Religion/spirituality is important to many people in the transformative worldview. They see purity or sanctity in the organic foods they eat, in nature, and in many indigenous spiritual traditions which are being resurrected. Old rituals are being incorporated into daily routines, such as giving gratitude to Mother Earth, or practicing kindness towards everyone. Although they may dismiss the literal interpretation of ancient texts, they are eager to see and learn about patterns of ancient religions, myths, and stories that can shed light on helping to guide us in this transitory and confusing world.

CONCLUDING INSIGHTS: MORAL FOUNDATION THEORY

When looking at the political/cultural/social divide the complexity of all the different views can be overwhelming. But through the lens of the five world-views and six moral foundations, we can more clearly see how people may interpret events and issues very differently. We can better understand the ways in which diverse Americans sort ourselves into different worldviews, as if we lived in different nations with our own sets of beliefs, facts, and values. How to sort it all out? By taking a step back and not judging whether one view is right and another wrong, hopefully we may be more inspired to arrive at mutually agreeable solutions to complex problems.

Chapter 10
Bridging the Cultural Divide

Understanding the simple fact that morality differs around the world, and even within societies, is the first step toward understanding your righteous mind....
Jonathan Haidt

Bringing together information from the five worldviews and six moral foundations, this final chapter provides a foundation for understanding the cultural divide. After describing the trickster archetypal character, ten thoughts about how to better understand the divide are highlighted. Wrapping up the chapter are 15 tips on how to help bridge the cultural divide.

BEWARE OF THE TRICKSTER

We are living in uncertain times. Our divisions appear to be intractable. It is a time for us to be attuned to strange occurrences and alert to messages from questionable leaders. Tricksters are most visible when people are in conflict and trauma, whether on a global, national, local, or personal level. Now is such a time.

The trickster is a universal archetypal figure in the history of humanity. Psychologist Carl Jung coined the term archetype and defined it as universal, archaic patterns and images that derive from the collective unconscious. These are inherited potentials that are actualized when they enter consciousness as images or manifest in behaviors upon interaction with the outside world.[1] Archetypes are found in cultural and religious literature, such as myths, fairy tales, and legends. They connect all human beings and cultures around the world. Through his research, Jung found 12 primary (although there are many) mythic characters or archetypes that he believed to be inherent in the human collective unconscious. A few of the most familiar archetypes are the hero, sage, lover, explorer, caregiver, ruler, innocent, and the trickster.

Each trickster is unique to its culture, but certain characteristics bind together all tricksters. The trickster archetype can be cunning or foolish or both. He is usually a male character, fond of crossing and breaking social norms and conventional behavior, boasting, and playing tricks. He is the wise-fool who openly questions and mocks authority, pokes fun at the overly serious, creates convoluted schemes that may or may not work, plays with the laws of the universe, and is sometimes his own worst enemy. He violates principles of the social and natural order, playfully disrupting normal life and then re-establishing it on a new basis. The trickster is represented as deceitful, insidious, and thievish. In any role, he is crafty, and is portrayed as being pitted against opponents who are stronger or more powerful.

The trickster seems to be a comedy of opposites. For every good feature of his persona there is an equal and opposite feature. The trickster holds no real knowledge but practices a cunning intelligence. He takes on different personas or puts on acts depending on the audience and on what they need. He is the breaker of taboos. And he will pull off elaborate schemes to teach a moral lesson or expose human folly.[2] He is often very good with words and uses them to trick or fool others and to make up for his shortcomings, such as physical or moral weakness. He is also a mime, adept at telling people whatever they want to hear.

The trickster openly questions and mocks convention and encourages others to follow their impulses, to do what is fun or what feels good rather than what is right. He is a figure of excess, especially when it comes to eating, drinking, and sexual exploits. The trickster is fun, funny, and frustrating. He is a joker and prankster, the best of companions, but also a thief, a liar and an impostor; a figure of shadow and night. He takes what is expected and turns it upside down, usually for his own benefit. An example of a trickster in ancient mythology is the shape-shifting trickster character of Loki, Norse god of mischief and lies.

The trickster manages to impose himself, not because of his real qualities, nor by enabling the people around him, but by blurring distinctions. He creates and enjoys chaos. Rather than distinguishing between truth and lie, the trickster thrives on ambivalence. While presenting himself as the solution to a crisis, in fact, the trickster is not really interested in solving a crisis. His real interest lies in perpetuating conditions of confusion, the world he thrives in, by blurring boundaries and undermining rationality and the exercise of good judgment.[3]

Americans have recently invited the trickster archetype into our midst in the form of Donald Trump, our trickster president. Why has our society invited this trickster figure into the inner circles of power? Trump has legitimately seized power and recruited millions of followers because we are in a historical situation where fear, confusion, uncertainty, and the loss of a sense of home and place are real. Trump is far from the only trickster character around the globe, but because of the wealth and influence of the U.S. he is the most noticeable and important. Because of uncertainty today, current world politics are increasingly influenced by trickster figures.[4] The trickster thrives on comfort-induced inattention and vanity-induced unawareness, and has essentially a free hand in guiding those who refuse to ever question their motives, assumptions, and beliefs.

Both the trickster archetype and President Trump share a commitment to spontaneity and improvisation that always pushes the envelope. Trump clearly enjoys his role as cultural destroyer; he seems determined to break every rule and overturn every norm. He is more interested in images than issues. Perhaps one of the reasons he has been able to elude criticism by his supporters is that much of his behavior is primal, unconscious, and fed by archetypal forces. He is slippery and ephemeral, hard to pin down.

The trickster maneuvers to control almost all situations. Trump promises to heal and unify, to make things great again, to perform magic—all of these services, he claims, for the common good. He sells the impossible, the great illusion, but only if he is in charge; the trickster is always a one-person show. He is deceptive, a con man, and an expert in assigning blame. Things are never his fault. He rarely says he is sorry, feels little guilt, and is not ashamed of any of his actions.

Any time a utopia is being promised by political leaders, the trickster is in control. Thus, the time is ripe for a trickster figure to emerge to soothe our discomfort or enrage us to the point of despair.

LESSONS FROM THE TRICKSTER ARCHETYPE

What lessons can we learn from our love affair with the trickster? The trickster is a transformer who appears when a way of thinking becomes outmoded, needs to be torn down and built anew. He signals a wakeup call and a warning as to what is going on in the shadow lands of the American and global psyche. He prods us to question things, to not accept things blindly. The presence of the trickster signals a dangerous time, but he also signals a golden opportunity to become more conscious of ourselves psychologically, and to potentially heal our divided selves. This is the hidden meaning and value that the trickster brings to us.

Jung would point out that the trickster is a manifestation of our own collective unconscious. The archetype relates to our "shadow side," those darker aspects of ourselves that we don't acknowledge but which are often the source of creativity, and which need to be consciously integrated in order for us to function with more authenticity and purpose. Trump's ascendance is a call for the nation to take a long, hard look at what the trickster is mirroring to us. When we glance in the mirror we see an idealized version of who we are, but when the trickster holds up the mirror that image is different. We see reality, not the ideal. For better or worse, the trickster symbolically surfaces at a particular moment in our history. It is at this moment of intense divisiveness and passionate anger that the trickster shows its archetypal energies.

Trump brings to the surface many of the darker elements of American culture that we are forced to confront. Although there are many good qualities about the U.S. and its people, there is also a disturbing side of the country, the shadow that lies below the surface and that we try to keep from coming out in the open. With the election of Trump to the presidency these darker elements of our country—exploitation, greed, deceit, and discrimination— have been laid bare for all to witness. These darker elements were employed to build this country, just as Trump used them to build his personal financial empire. Although these baser qualities are part of human nature, many of us imagined that our country was different and that they were not part of our collective spirit. But these elements are part of us, and Trump has exposed this unsavory side. We are in the throes of a moral, individual, ecological, spiritual, and social

190

malaise that is weakening and threatening to destroy our moral and social fabric. Now it is up to us to mature and improve the real image of our country to one that is more like the ideal.

Neither the right nor the left have all the answers in coming to grips with the shadow side of America. They both can add valuable insights to the conversation but it also requires listening and compromise, a skill that has steadily declined over the last several decades. Perhaps the trickster is revealing a turning-point, a chaotic interim phase eventually transforming into something new.

From a historical perspective, the trickster is an agent of change, often when a society (global, national, or organizational) or person has gone too far in one direction, and discontent begins to accumulate. While we may be fearful about the future, the trickster provokes us into a shift, often a paradigm shift. The trickster—stupidly clever, maliciously reassuring, unconsciously rational—emerges to thrust us into the future.[5] An awakening is due and it will probably be painful. Chaos looms. Over the long run, however, increased participation and greater self-awareness could be very good medicine for our fractured democracy. Despite his trickery, the trickster archetype may lead us from chaos into a new cultural order.

TEN THOUGHTS ON BRIDGING THE CULTURAL DIVIDE

Bridging the cultural divide can be beneficial. We often wistfully talk about bridging this divide but when cultures are vastly different, or if people are opposed to such exchange, actually doing so is more difficult than we imagined. But the chances increase if we are able to develop astute cultural awareness, and increase our openness to dealing with major cultural differences. Improving one's openness requires both humility when learning from others and inquisitiveness. Improving one's cultural awareness helps one to deal better with the stress, cultural shocks, and tension that arise from interacting with other worldviews.

The following are ten thoughts that I have found are important in enhancing our cultural awareness and bridging the cultural divide. As in Chapter 9, I also draw on the insightful work of moral psychologist Jonathan

Haidt. Rather than practical tips, these ten thoughts are more philosophical adjustments to our ways of thinking and behaviors that I have found helpful in understanding and opening us up to cultural and philosophical differences. But practical tips are important as well, and at the end of the chapter I offer 15 practical tips.

THOUGHT #1: UNDERSTANDING OTHERS

Understanding worldviews is a resource for empathy and analyzing conflicts when fundamental differences divide groups of people. I put this as the number one way in which we can bridge the cultural divide and this book is dedicated to that goal. It is fundamental to have a deep and personal understanding of others before progress can be made. However, it is difficult. Our innate behaviors make it easy for us to communicate and connect with others in our immediate group, but when we talk with those outside our comfort group we may be on guard or uneasy about the situation. Practicing the suggestions in this chapter may help us feel more comfortable and capable as we navigate bridging the cultural divide.

What kind of dog do you want or own? If you are on the liberal end of the political spectrum you are more apt to like dogs that are gentle and caring while conservatives like dogs that are loyal and obedient.[6] This makes sense, since liberals score high on the caring foundation and conservatives score high on loyalty. This is just one example of understanding differences. The world would indeed be boring if everyone owned the same kind of dog.

Other differences abound as well. Liberals are more open to new experiences—people, food, music, travel, education—while conservatives prefer things that are more familiar to them. Haidt notes, "Liberal professors give a narrower range of grades whereas conservative professors accept inequality, and give high grades to good students and flunk the worst." He has also found that conservative and liberal traits are inherited: "About half the variation in this trait is heritable in men and somewhat less in women."[7]

Haidt and his colleagues gleaned much of their research materials from their website, YourMorals.org, where visitors answer questions about their moral preferences. Haidt found that "conservatives understand the morals of liberals, but liberals do not understand those of conservatives. When conservatives are asked to answer questionnaires as if they were liberals, they generally get the motives right. But when liberals pretend to be conservatives, they attribute incorrect, evil motives. This is not surprising; liberals think conservatives are not just wrong; they are moral inferiors."[8]

Awareness of worldviews can be a seedbed from which new, shared meanings emerge. There are several ways to help express one's worldview: examining or creating new or personal stories, designing new rituals, discovering common myths, and finding inclusive metaphors. Similarly, sharing stories of heroes and heroines helps people glimpse what is important to others and uncover values they share. In doing so, all parties reveal information about their identity, what they find meaningful, their ideas about life, and relationships. By listening deeply to other stories, individuals find it harder to sustain negative images of others, discovering instead commonalities that had previously been missed. From this base of empathy, individuals are able to explore shared values with more ease, while not losing sight of the values they do not share. As we positively engage with each other, we can learn deeply about group identities (who they see themselves to be) and meanings (what matters to them and how they make meaning). As we go through this process of discovery, places of connection and divergence become clearer.

Prejudice may be reduced as one learns and understands more about different groups of people. Prejudice is a direct result of generalizations and oversimplifications made about an entire group of people based on incomplete or mistaken information. If one has the opportunity to deeply communicate with different people, both parties are better able to understand and appreciate different points of view. However, quality of interaction not mere contact is key to bridging the cultural divide, since it is difficult for everyone to eliminate preconceived stereotypes and shift entrenched mindsets. Mingling with one another in an informal and personal way and having long enough contact situations allows different groups to feel comfortable with one another. Without this interaction they learn very little about each other and cross-group friendships do not occur. But if people at different points on the divide use contact situations to trade insults, argue, resort to physical violence, or discriminate against each other, then contact cannot be expected to reduce inter-group conflict. To obtain beneficial effects, the situation must be positive. If a positive experience occurs, prejudice often diminishes.[9]

THOUGHT #2: INTUITION, NOT REASON, DRIVES MORAL JUDGMENTS

Ever since Plato, Western thinkers have argued that reason is superior to the emotions. Haidt notes, "Almost all the greatest philosophers—Karl Marx, Franz Boas, Margaret Meade, Steven Jay Gould, and almost every social science department in the U.S.—have gone farther and claimed there is no such thing as human nature. Thus we can reason our way to utopia. …Radical reformers have to believe the mind is a blank slate if they are to write their fantasies on it."[10] But science has found that the mind is not a blank slate. Humans are guided by fear, disgust, anger, affection, sympathy, and loyalty in ways that have been sharply defined by evolution. Reason is a new arrival in our human history.[11]

People do reason, but primarily to prepare for social interaction, not to seek the truth. Haidt has found that our intuitions actually rule over reason.[12] His research helped shift moral psychology away from rationalist models that dominated in the 1980s and 1990s to an understanding of morality from an intuitive level.[13] To explain intuition Haidt devises an elephant-rider metaphor. Intuition drives the elephant's emotional processing. Thinking is the rider, affect is the elephant—the rider occasionally tells it where to go. The rider has the ability to reason and think about the future so he is useful to the elephant, but the elephant—like other animals—runs mainly on instinct. The rider is also, according to Haidt, "skilled at fabricating post hoc explanations for whatever the elephant has just done, and it is good at finding reasons to justify whatever the elephant wants to do next." One of the most important functions of the rider is to make the elephant look good. Our instincts are immediate and the rider cobbles together moral justifications only afterwards.[14]

The social aspect of moral reasoning is crucial. Moral reasoning, Haidt maintains, is "part of our lifelong struggle to win friends and influence people."[15] The real purpose of morality is to justify our own actions to others and to set up rules to compel them to act as we believe they should. Arguments are unproductive. Haidt continues, "Moral reasoning is like a dog's tail: You can't make a dog happy by forcibly wagging its tail. And you can't change people's minds by utterly refuting their arguments." If your arguments ever convince anyone, it is only after you have taken the trouble fully to understand what he or she feels and thinks. Haidt believes it is such an obvious point, yet few of us apply it in moral and political arguments because our minds so readily shift into combat mode.[16]

Most of the time, says Haidt, "if you want to change people's minds, you've got to talk to their elephants, and you don't do that with reason. You do it by showing yourself to be a warm, attractive person. When you draw someone in emotionally, his elephant begins to lean your way, and the rider starts paying attention to what you say." It is rare, but occasionally someone uses reason and arrives at a conclusion against her initial intuitions. However, "intuitions can be shaped by reasoning, especially when reasons are embedded in a friendly conversation or an emotionally compelling novel, movie, art, or news story."[17]

Moral reasoning is not about figuring out the truth. Haidt explains that if you do think this you will "be constantly frustrated by how foolish, biased, and illogical people become when they disagree with you. But if you think about moral reasoning as a skill we humans evolved to further our social agendas… and to defend the teams we belong to—then things will make a lot more sense. Keep your eye on the intuitions and don't take people's moral arguments at face value."[18]

The conclusion Haidt reached about reason and intuitions can be applied to today's political divide. In 1950, the American Political Science Association, attempting to avoid sharp polarization, presented clear policy choices from two different perspectives. Regrettably, as the political parties developed differing values and lifestyles, they also developed opposing facts. Republicans and Democrats believe different things about history, the Constitution, science, and economics.[19] Explaining this dilemma Haidt states, "The main reason Republicans and Democrats can't agree on basic economic facts is that people—including politicians and economists—seek out the facts required by their values." When faced with difficult or unclear evidence, human reasoning does not ask for the truth, but asks what evidence can be found to support a foregone conclusion. Usually, we can find such evidence.[20]

Even when an overwhelming amount of reliable research points the other way, just one study supporting your side will seem totally persuasive, and you'll find all kinds of reasons to discard the reliable science.

The fact that emotions rule over reason has important ramifications for the cultural divide. When we believe our side is right and we find reliable facts to support our conclusion, it is usually an illusion we are chasing. Our emotions are ruling and the other side sees their side as equally right because they draw on a different set of facts to support their conclusions.[21]

THOUGHT #3: MORALITY BINDS AND BLINDS

Morality binds and blinds. As we saw in Thought #2, moral arguments rarely change people's minds. Jonathan Haidt points out, "This is not just something that happens to people on the other side. We all get sucked into tribal moral communities. We think the other side is blind to truth, reason, science, and common sense, but in fact everyone goes blind when talking about what they hold sacred."[22] Both liberals and conservatives are convinced they are trying to do the right thing, but their beliefs prevent them from recognizing the other side's good will. Usually we think the other side has ulterior motives, but usually this is an error. Haidt suggests that if you "really want to open your mind, open your heart first. If you can have at least one friendly interaction with a member of the other group, you'll find it far easier to listen to what they're saying, and maybe even see a controversial issue in a new light."[23] That is the way the moral mind works. But to the extent arguments do work, they have to reach the emotions first.

THOUGHT #4: FINDING COMMONALITIES: EMPHASIZING SIMILARITIES MORE THAN DIFFERENCES

When bridging the divide between two or more worldviews, a goal is to uncover universal commonalities that all people share. The process of discovering commonalities is also a way to build bridges. A few of the universal commonalities include the need for dignity and respect, the right to advocate for a point of view without fear of violence or reprisal, love and acceptance, security and safety, protection, and incremental progress that improves lives. The universal enjoyment of music, sports, entertainment, dance, place, and family goes beyond differences and is a good topic for stories and conversations with those we perceive as different.

We have more that binds us together than divides us. Haidt notes that the key to making any group work better is to "increase similarity, not diversity, because people trust people who are like themselves."[24] For example, culturally similar Orthodox Jews run extremely profitable diamond markets efficiently and honestly because they trust each other. Members of the armed forces bond as a group because of their shared circumstances, despite ethnic or racial differences. Groups that sing songs or march together feed the notion of similarity and this increases trust. Haidt even says, "There is nothing special about race. You can make people care less about race by drowning race differences in a sea of similarities, shared goals, and mutual interdependence."[25]

THOUGHT #5: WE AREN'T ALL WEIRD

Many WEIRD (Western, Educated, Individualized, Rich, and Democratic) people, especially progressives, believe people in the United States and throughout the world share their values. WEIRD societies think of humans as autonomous atoms, whose morality can be reduced to avoiding harm. Morality in the contemporary West—at least among the educated—tends to be centered on individuals in which anything that does not hurt someone else is acceptable.[26]

Other people have moral codes in which groups, relationships, institutions, and traditions are more important than individuals, and anything that gives priority to the individual is considered dangerous. But not all Western people are WEIRD. Non-WEIRD morality thrives among many less-educated people, poor whites, some African-Americans, recent immigrants to the West, and those living in Eastern Europe, who are less likely to have lost racial or ethnic consciousness. Haidt notes, "They are more likely to think that certain things—homosexuality, incest, blasphemy, drug-taking, miscegenation, and prostitution, for example—are inherently bad whether they hurt anyone or not."[27]

It is ironic that many on the left who value multiculturalism and diversity are blind in many ways to the insularity of their own group consciousness. The progressive worldview is mostly based on WEIRD values, which often clash with the groups they believe are oppressed or who they are trying to "help." In general, conservatives have a broader set of moral foundations than progressives. Although conservatives care about individuals and subscribe to fairness, they also value the authority, loyalty, and sense of sanctity that groups need. For many traditionalists, their greatest gratifications come from losing their individual identity and cooperating full-tilt with the team, platoon, congregation, dance group, or choir. Altruism, devotion, and heroism cannot exist without groups.[28]

THOUGHT #6: KARMA AND COMPASSION

Compassion is one of the most important of the six moral foundations, since it is valued by all groups of people. It is embraced by traditionalists, but it is especially important among progressives. When understanding today's left-right divide it is essentially a battle between the law of karma and the principle of compassion. Haidt explains that conservatives generally want to live in a world governed by karma—the ancient Hindu philosophy in which people reap the fruits of their actions, both good and bad. Karma is usually thought of as a law of the universe, like the law of gravity.[29]

Conservatives have historically opposed the growth of the welfare state or government supported programs to help those at the lower rung of the economic ladder. Part of the reason for this opposition, as Haidt explains, is "the belief that it grants people a sort of karmic exemption, allowing those who are lazy or irresponsible to draw resources from those who are more industrious." The right believes that the left has used government programs to indiscriminately redistribute money, Haidt continues, thus creating an entitlement society in which almost half of the people "are dependent upon government, who believe that they are victims, who believe that government has a responsibility to care for them, who believe that they are entitled to health care, to food, to housing, to you name it."[30] Conservatives conclude that society would work better if people helped themselves instead of getting a handout, and unsuccessful people failed. This also includes unsuccessful businesses, such as the auto industry, which received government-backed loans in the 2009 recession.

Progressives, in contrast, would prefer to live in a world ruled by compassion. They are more likely to give people second and third chances, sometimes even more.[31] They are eager to create government programs to help people to, in their view, succeed. For example, many progressives are enthusiastic about passing legislative programs such as Medicare for All, forgiving student loan debt, granting free college tuition, expanding food stamps, enlarging Social Security, and providing a basic income for all people. Generally, conservatives scorn these policies.

For a well-functioning society both karma and compassion are necessary pillars. Haidt concludes, "Conservatives are right that a world in which the law of karma applies tends to work better than one in which it doesn't. Results from experimental games show that cooperation rates skyrocket when cheaters expect to be punished. But it is cruel and unfair to apply karmic thinking in an unkarmic world."[32] While the idea that unemployed people are lazy may sometimes be correct when the unemployment rate is very low, in an economy with a high unemployment rate that insinuation is not justified. In capitalist societies, hard work pays off much better than laziness, yet illness, disability, unemployment, and other kinds of bad luck can hit anyone. Capitalist societies can be unforgiving at times. Karma and compassion don't balance themselves; that's a job we must do.[33]

THOUGHT #7: TRADITIONALISTS HAVE AN ADVANTAGE

Traditionalists and progressives have different personality traits, partially inherited and also socially and culturally influenced. Conservatives tend to be cognitively fixed, favor hierarchy, and are wary of uncertainty, change, and differences. When people vote for conservative candidates they do so because the candidates often offer "moral clarity"—a simple vision of good and evil that helps alleviate the voter's deep seated fears and distrusts. Democrats, in contrast, are more open to novel experiences and more readily accept change and diversity than traditionalists. Progressive candidates appeal to voters' reasoning capabilities and offer detailed policy proposals with long-winded explorations of policy options that are superimposed on a complex and shifting world.[34]

Progressive ways of thinking—reason, logic, analysis, and objectivity—are encouraged by our educational system and are valued as superior to emotional ways of thinking. Educational tests score students' analytical abilities and those with the highest scores are awarded prestigious college slots and academic recognition. Thus, progressives often think their logical, analytical ways of thinking and being are at the top of the moral order and dismiss those who are different. This ranking of ways of thinking is discriminatory but it is so well entrenched in society that it prevails unchallenged. It also gives progressives an elitist air that traditionalists disdain.

Progressives often explain away conservative successes as aberrant and convince themselves that they hold the moral high ground. Since they have self-determined who is among the educational elite, progressives have decided that there is nothing to learn from other worldviews. This blinds progressives to the fact that, as Haidt explains, "one of the main reasons that so many Americans voted Republican over the last 30 years: they honestly prefer the Republican vision of a moral order to the one offered by Democrats. To see what Democrats have been missing, it helps to take off the halo."[35]

Republicans have become the party of the sacred, appropriating issues of God, faith, and religion, but also sacred symbols of the nation, such as the flag, military, and constitution. The progressives, on the other hand, have become the party of secular lifestyles and material interests. Haidt points out that "Democrats often seem to think of voters as consumers; they rely on polls to choose a set of policy positions that will convince 51% of the electorate to buy. Most Democrats don't understand that politics is more like religion than it is like shopping."[36]

Durkheim claims that sacredness is about society and its collective concerns. If he is right then Democrats must find a way to incorporate the sacred into their messages that goes beyond the use of words like "God" and "faith." It is hard to portray a Whole Foods store as sacred, but featuring nature as sacred is an obvious and worthy choice. Democrats could close the sacredness gap if they get beyond the idea of society as WEIRD. Instead of just a collection of individuals each with an array of rights, progressives could demonstrate that the whole of humanity is in need of care and compassion. Haidt notes, "Our national motto is *e pluribus unum* ('from many, one'). Whenever Democrats support policies that weaken the integrity and identity of the collective (such as multiculturalism, bilingualism, and immigration), they show that they care more about pluribus than unum. They widen the sacredness gap." When Republicans say that Democrats "just don't get it," this is the "it" to which they refer. [37]

Democrats often try to explain away conservative positions on guns, God, and immigration by using pop psychology, which often alienates conservatives and earns progressives the elitist label. But conservative ideas need to be understood as ways to achieve one kind of morally ordered society. Haidt questions, "how can Democrats learn to see—let alone respect—a moral order they regard as narrow-minded, racist, and dumb?"[38] Perhaps lessons from Durkheim can help progressives understand the traditionalists' wide range of moral foundations.

Bringing in the three moral foundations advanced by Durkheim—loyalty, authority, and sanctity—means that the traditionalists have an expanded moral range. Progressives need to be aware of these advantages when advancing policies and trying to win elections. In fact, it might be worthwhile for progressives to expand their moral range without betraying their principles. They might be able to improve their policies by incorporating and praising some traditionalists' insights.[39]

Patriotism and self-sacrifice, expressions of the loyalty moral foundation, result in high social and moral capital and civic well-being when done in moderation. A study by Robert Putnam—*E Pluribus Unum*— found that ethnic diversity increases anomie and social isolation by decreasing people's sense of belonging to a shared community. This is a warning sign to progressives who celebrate diversity without considering the downside. Haidt notes, "Democrats should think carefully, therefore, about why they celebrate diversity. If the purpose of diversity programs is to fight racism and discrimination (worthy goals based on fairness concerns), then these goals might be better served by encouraging assimilation and a sense of shared identity."[40]

The sanctity moral foundation does not have to be held in the grips of

201

the Christian right, progressives can harness this as well. Sanctity is about overcoming our lower, greedy, egotistical individual selves in order to live in a way that is more noble and spiritual. Many progressives, for example, criticize the vulgarity and cruelty of unrestrained free-market capitalism. There is also a progressive tradition of anti-materialism and simple living which is often linked to a reverence and connection with nature and our higher spiritual selves. Haidt adds, "Environmental and animal welfare issues are easily promoted using the language of harm/care, but such appeals might be more effective when supplemented with hints of purity/sanctity."[41]

The authority moral foundation is highly admired by traditionalists but is the most difficult of the six moral foundations for progressives to identify with. This foundation is important, even though progressives tout their leaderless organizations and profess to question authority everywhere. In fact, this authority rebellion can be traced back to the 1960s hippie counter revolution. Haidt notes, "Democrats can ask what needs this foundation serves, and then look for other ways to meet them. The authority foundation is all about maintaining social order, so any candidate seen to be soft on crime has disqualified himself, for many Americans, from being entrusted with the ultimate authority."[42] Durkheim offers some insights into this foundation: in order for functional groups to operate there must be some costs imposed on cheaters and slackers. Haidt continues, "You can do this the authoritarian way (with strict rules and harsh penalties) or you can do it using the fairness/reciprocity foundation by stressing personal responsibility and the beneficence of the nation towards those who work hard and play by the rules. But if you don't do it at all—if you seem to tolerate or enable cheaters and slackers—then you are committing a kind of sacrilege."[43]

Progressives need to understand the full spectrum of American moral concerns if they are to succeed in the political arena. Loyalty, authority, and purity moral foundations are powerful tools in this political struggle. Progressives are very concerned about social justice and fairness for oppressed groups. But this divisive struggle should be balanced by a clear commitment to the whole nation. Haidt notes that "America lacks the long history, small size, ethnic homogeneity, and soccer mania that holds many other nations together, so our flag, our founding fathers, our military, and our common language take on a moral importance that many liberals find hard to fathom. Unity is not the great need of the hour; it is the eternal struggle of our immigrant nation." Until Democrats understand the importance of these three binding moral foundations, they will be vulnerable to the seductive but false belief that Americans vote for Republicans primarily because they have been duped into doing so.[44]

THOUGHT #8: PRESERVE MORAL CAPITAL

Moral communities are fragile, they are hard to build and easy to destroy. When we think about very large communities such as nations, the challenge is incomprehensible and the threat of moral entropy is intense. Traditionalists understand the importance of moral capital. Haidt defines moral capital as "the resource that sustains a moral community. More specifically, moral capital refers to the degree to which a community possesses interlocking sets of values and practices that mesh well with evolved psychological mechanisms and thereby enable the community to regulate selfishness and make cooperation possible."[45] As we have found, human societies have two ways to support selflessness: Durkheim's model of binding foundations and the Millian model of rules and laws to suppress human selfishness.

What does it take to sustain moral capital? If you believe that people are inherently good, as progressives usually do, and that they flourish when constraints and divisions are removed, then it may be sufficient to just link people together in healthy and trusting relationships. This will lead to good behavior. But conservatives view human nature differently. They firmly believe that people need external constraints in order to behave properly, cooperate, and prosper. These external constraints include not only laws and rules, but institutions, customs, traditions, communities, education, and religions as well.[46]

Conservatives fear that if you abolish all groups and disband all internal structure, you destroy your moral capital. According to Haidt, "Large-scale human societies are nearly miraculous achievements. Our complicated moral psychology coevolved with our religions and our other cultural inventions (such as tribes and agriculture) to get us where we are today. We need groups, we love groups, and we develop our virtues in groups, even though those groups necessarily exclude nonmembers."[47]

The danger of moral entropy is especially acute in diverse societies. Haidt issues a warning to progressives: "If you destroy all groups and dissolve all internal structure, you destroy your moral capital. [If] you do not consider the effects of your changes on moral capital you're asking for trouble."[48]

"Liberals need to be shaken," Haidt tells us. They "simply misunderstand conservatives far more than the other way around. This, I believe, is the fundamental blind spot of the left." He goes on to add, "It explains why liberal reforms so often backfire, and why communist revolutions usually end up in despotism. Left-wing reformers often overreach, change too many things too quickly, and reduce the stock of moral capital inadvertently." But he inserts advice for conservatives as well, "Conversely, while conservatives do a better job of preserving moral capital, they often fail to notice certain classes of victims, fail to limit the predations of certain powerful interests, and fail to see the need to change or update institutions as times change."[49] A balance of the two is necessary.

Moral systems help people trust each other and work together. Loyalty, authority, and sanctity have a crucial role to play in a thriving society. According to Haidt, "The left has learned nothing from the grisly failure of communism, and continues to destroy moral capital by pushing diversity, feminism, atheism, equal outcomes, and hedonism, not only in the West but in societies that are still attached to tradition."[50] Haidt continues, "These systems are valuable even if they make no sense to outsiders. They are not rules about justice or rights; they may not be sets of rules at all. They are relationships, practices, traditions, expectations, and rituals that have grown up over time and in which people find the place that suits them. They are not mere social conventions that can be swept aside like old rubbish."[51]

THOUGHT #9: YIN AND YANG

The Asian religions realized that societies flourish when they incorporate all six moral foundations to some degree. That is why yin and yang are friends; they are both necessary for the smooth functioning of human societies. Two gods in Hinduism represent these principles—Vishnu, the preserver, stands for conservative principles; and Shiva, the destroyer, stands for progressive principles.

They work together and one does not dominate the other.[52]

A way to see America's current political divide is through the lens of the Chinese philosophy of yin yang (陰陽). This ancient way of life describes how seemingly opposite or contrary forces may actually be complementary, interconnected, and interdependent, and how they may give rise to each other as they interact with one another. Many tangible dualities such as light and dark, fire and water, and expanding and contracting, are thought of as physical manifestations of the duality symbolized by yin yang. Intangible dualities are part of yin yang as well, such as freedom and limits, authority and submission, responsibility and rights, autonomy and dependence, and liberal and conservative. Each of these pairs represents two sides of the same coin. To maintain a good life an individual and a society need to find a balance between opposing forces, a balance that is hard to preserve, that teeters on a razor's edge.

All societies have to balance the interests of the individual and the group but American society has recently gotten out of balance. WEIRD people put the individual first, which is a very recent development and far from universal. When people really are unconnected individuals, cooperation fades.[53] Haidt believes progressive values have come to dominate, which has thrown off the sense of balance necessary for healthy human societies to thrive. He writes that "the most effective way to design an ethical society is to make it so that everyone's reputation is always on the line, so that bad behavior will have bad consequences."[54]

THOUGHT #10: SELF REFLECTION

He who knows only his own side of the case, knows little of that. Our opponents could be right for all we know or care, because they may know a fact or offer an argument we've never thought to consider. And even if they aren't right, specks of truth may exist among their falsehoods which can guide our minds in new directions.... John Stuart Mill, On Liberty

The liberal philosopher, Mill, once explained that unless we carefully study the views of those with whom we disagree, we will never really know what they're right or wrong about. Social change starts with individual change. If we are unable or unwilling to shift our ways of thinking to understand others and their perspectives then we are doomed to have a polarized nation. Life is a series of compromises and to think otherwise is naïve. It is much tougher to have our sets of principles and to work them in with other ideas than it is to stubbornly hold to our sacred views. Therefore, we need to look inward and take the more complicated but more rewarding empathetic effort of understanding the experiences of people different from us. Our culture does not promote inward reflection; instead it seeks answers outside of us, through some self-help guru, through something on YouTube, through joining a cause, or by joining a protest march. Problems are someone else's fault and "they" are responsible, not us.

Turn inward and look at yourself and come to terms with who you are. Come to terms with your past and your own flaws and sort out yourself, and finally start to see who you truly are. You're never going to see completely who you are; you're always going to remain a mystery. But through a self-discovery process, you can become somebody who can use empathy, who has the ability to withhold judgment and accept people for who they are as opposed to continually moralizing and wishing people were different than they are. Don't assume that just because you feel something that it is right. You can have a much smoother path through life, and you'll be much calmer and more peaceful without emotional baggage dragging you down. But it starts with looking inward and questioning yourself, and not assuming that everything you feel or think is right.

15 TIPS FOR BRIDGING THE CULTURAL DIVIDE

Given the divisiveness of the country today you may be at a quandary about how to interact with people who have different worldviews. This is particularly troublesome with those whom you are close to. The proverbial Thanksgiving dinner comes to mind with Uncle Ned spouting off about his political views while you sit cowering in the background trying valiantly to keep the peace and not stir up more animosity. You may decide to keep your Thanksgiving politics-free. Agree ahead of time not to talk about politics at the table. Use the time to

206

get to know each other on a different level. Ask each other about childhood memories or express gratitude for all you have in your life. Remember that you have a wonderful meal in front of you and are lucky enough to be sharing it surrounded by people important to you. Acknowledge that while your dinner guests may have different views, you still have things in common. Strive to find and discuss these commonalities. For example, you all may agree that you want the best for your country, even if you disagree on how to get there.

Along with the ten thoughts, I list below 15 short tips about bridging the divide. I am sure you can think of more as you go about the important task of navigating, understanding, and bridging the cultural divide. They are not in any particular order.

1. **Listen first, and then respond.** Don't be distracted thinking about your answer while the other person is speaking. Be courteous and hear them out. Try to understand their point of view. Then take a moment to gather your thoughts and respond. Don't interrupt, allow people to finish their thoughts and sentences. You'll get your turn. One voice at a time. Don't debate. Think about the values and beliefs that are important to them and that lead them to feel the way they do. If someone makes a snide comment about your political beliefs, you may say: "Even though I don't agree with your political beliefs, I respect and try to understand them. I would hope that you would try to do the same for me."

2. **Find common ground.** Next time you find yourself next to someone different from you, try to start a conversation. First, find something you have in common to establish trust. You will be surprised how many things you may have in common—family, pets, place, nature, entertainment, sports, places you have lived or visited, and so on. You may say, "I live in Albuquerque, New Mexico, have you ever visited our state?" Keep it positive and sincere.

3. **Be positive, show interest.** When you do bring up more controversial issues, try to start with some praise or a sincere expression of interest. "Uncle Ned, you have spent a lot of time researching ____ topic, tell me more about what you have learned." You may decide to interject thought-

provoking questions to continue the conversation.

4. **Find common projects or goals.** When groups with differences work together on a common project or pursue a common goal they often subordinate their differences by focusing on the common work of achieving positive results. They pool their energies and resources together, sharing a common effort.

5. **Avoid a winner vs. loser mindset.** When interacting with people who are different, avoid looking at a disagreement with the mindset that there will be a winner and a loser and you are determined to be the winner. Instead focus on what both parties want and how you can achieve a positive outcome for everyone involved. This is called a compromise, a word not valued very much in today's heated climate.

6. **Leave your ego at the door.** When you navigate issues and challenges without taking things personally everyone benefits. So many of our struggles involve outsized egos, each trying to prove they are right. Let the ego go, you will find it is easier said than done but the outcome is worth the effort.

7. **Walk in another person's shoes.** Put yourself in their situation, walk in their shoes, what is their life like? Be open to other opinions. This may come as a shock, but you don't know everything. Neither do I. Listen without judgment. Be open to new ideas, perspectives, insights, and information. Read biographies, watch programs about other people, find out what makes them tick.

8. **Choose your words carefully.** Avoid making judgments and using inflammatory words. Begin sentences with the word "I." When you start a sentence with "You", people automatically become defensive. You are racist, lazy, stupid, ignorant, and the list goes on. Avoid emotional words when describing your position or opinion. This is not a soap opera. Try not to cry!

9. **Ask good questions.** The core reason for the conflict may be buried. You will only get to the heart of the matter and be able to work through it if you can politely uncover the root of the issue. Avoid interrogating and go for curiosity instead; there is a difference.

10. **Compassionate conversation.** Slow down the conversation. This will enable you to digest what is being discussed without having to rush to answer and possibly misspeak. Forget about raising your voice. If someone else raises their voice, lower yours. It's a powerful communication tool that can ease tension.

11. **Work with facts.** Don't make assumptions. But realize that facts themselves are not impartial and unbiased. Note that facts can be interpreted differently and are filtered through your worldview.

12. **Admit when wrong.** Own up to your mistakes, apologize, and move on. This is what adults do.

13. **Smile and use humor.** The expression you wear on your face can be more powerful than your words. Humor cuts across differences, if used appropriately. Humor is one of my favorites!

14. **Show compassion.** Empathy, congeniality, and thoughtfulness (Emotional Intelligence) are critical life skills and necessary when interacting with people different from you.

15. **Thoughtfully interject your ideas.** Although it is wise not to interrupt, if whomever you are talking to is dominating the conversation, you might thoughtfully interject, "You have been talking about _____ a lot more than I have. I don't think that is fair (everyone wants to be fair). I would like to add my 2 cents." They will usually comply with your wish. State your ideas in a thoughtful way. It has worked for me every time.

CONCLUDING INSIGHTS: BRIDGING THE CULTURAL DIVIDE

Each individual's reality is filtered through different lenses, and learning about these different lenses can help us improve communication and relations with people who are similar to and different from us. Haidt reminds us that we are all trapped in our own moral matrix.[55] But we have choices. Shall we choose to remain happily delusional about our own worldview, or learn about other worldviews and step out of our own bubble to see others in a different light?

The good news is that the U.S. is a well-established liberal democracy with long-standing institutions run by committed people. We have withstood deep divisions through history—slavery, the Civil War, Reconstruction, the Depression, World War II, the 1968 rebellions—that could easily have torn apart a country with less sound institutions. It is up to these institutions—judicial branch, press, civic institutions, local/state governments—and empowered ordinary citizens to help us navigate the negative aspects of the storm that seems bent on disrupting more than building, excluding rather than including, and hating more than kindness.

What will be the dominant worldview during this time that I call the Global Wave? Will enough people follow one particular worldview, creating a tipping point in which it begins to holistically affect all the technological, social, political, economic, and religious patterns in our society? I like to think that if enough people become familiar with the transformative worldview, it will prevail. Working with others to build a transformative worldview seems to me very important at this critical time in our history. In any case, we all have a stake in the outcome of the interplay of worldviews.

Endnotes

PREFACE

1 Zito, Salena. "Taking Trump Seriously, Not Literally," *Atlantic Magazine*, Sept. 23, 2016. https://www.theatlantic.com/politics/archive/2016/09/trump-makes-his-case-in-pittsburgh/501335/

CHAPTER 1. WHY ARE WE SO DIVIDED?

1 Haidt, Jonathan. "America's Painful Divide," *Saturday Evening Post*, Sept./Oct. 2012. https://www.saturdayeveningpost.com/2012/08/americas-painful-divide/
2 "American Memory," *Library of Congress* and "What is the American Dream?," *Wikipedia, The American Dream.* https://en.wikipedia.org/wiki/American_Dream#cite_note-LOC-1
3 Haidt, "America's Divide," *Saturday Evening Post.*
4 Haidt, "America's Divide," *Saturday Evening Post.*
5 Haidt, "America's Divide," *Saturday Evening Post.*
6 Haidt, "America's Divide," *Saturday Evening Post.*
7 Graham, Michael. "Planned Parenthood's absolutism," *Week*, Federalist.com, Mar. 16, 2018, 12.
8 Choma, Russ and Kroll, Andy. "The NRA Raised a Record Amount of Money in 2016," *Mother Jones*, Jan. 4, 2018. https://www.motherjones.com/politics/2018/01/nra-donald-trump-guns-fundraising/
9 Haidt, "America's Divide," *Saturday Evening Post.*
10 Appiah, Kwame Anthony. "People don't vote for what they want. They vote for who they are," *Washington Post*, Aug. 30, 2018. https://www.washingtonpost.com/outlook/people-dont-vote-for-want-they-want-they-vote-for-who-they-are/2018/08/30/fb5b7e44-abd7-11e8-8a0c-70b618c98d3c_story.html?utm_term=.558699f885f9
11 Haidt, "America's Divide," *Saturday Evening Post*

CHAPTER 2. WORLDVIEWS: OUR WINDOWS TO THE WORLD

1 Meadows, Donella and Dennis and Randers, Jorgen. *Limits to Growth: The Thirty Year Update*, White River Junction, Vermont: Chelsea Green Publishing Company, 2004, 4.
2 Goekler, John. "Teaching for the Future: Systems Thinking and Sustainability."

Green Teacher 70, Spring 2003, 8-14.
3 LeBaron, Michelle. "Cultural and Worldview Frames," *Knowledge Based Essay*, Aug. 2003. http://www.beyondintractability.org/essay/cultural_frames/
4 Mudde, Cas and Kaltwasser, Cristóbal Rovira. *Populism: A Very Short Introduction,* Oxford: Oxford University Press, 2017.
5 Friedman, Uri. "What is a Populist?" *The Atlantic*, Feb. 17, 2017. https://www.the-atlantic.com/international/archive/2017/02/what-is-populist-trump/516525/
6 Friedman, "Populist?" *The Atlantic*.
7 Molloy, David. "What is populism, and what does the term actually mean?" *BBC News*, Mar. 6, 2018. https://www.bbc.com/news/world-43301423
8 Friedman, "Populist?" *The Atlantic*.
9 Stenner, Karen. "Three Kinds of Conservatism," *Psychology Inquiry*, (20), 2009, 142. https://www.researchgate.net/publication/274444535_Three_Kinds_of_Conservatism
10 Stenner, "Conservatism," *Psychological Inquiry*, 143.
11 Stenner, "Conservatism," *Psychological Inquiry*, 154.
12 Stenner, "Conservatism," *Psychological Inquiry*, 157.
13 Mudd and Kaltwasser, *Populism*.
14 Mudd and Kaltwasser, *Populism*.
15 LeBaron, "Cultural and Worldview Frames," *Knowledge Based Essay*.
16 LeBaron, "Cultural and Worldview Frames," *Knowledge Based Essay*.
17 LeBaron, "Cultural and Worldview Frames," *Knowledge Based Essay*.

CHAPTER 3. THE MODERN WORLDVIEW

1 Wallerstein, Emmanuel. "Introductory Essay to Essential Wallerstein," *Yale University Faculty Page*.
2 Lenski, Gerhard and Jean. *Human Societies: An Introduction to Macrosociology,* New York: McGraw-Hill, 1982, 341.
3 Lenski, *Human Societies*, 342-344.
4 Lenski, *Human Societies*, 342-344.
5 Haidt, Jonathan. *The Righteous Mind*, New York: Vintage Books, 2012, 113.
6 Haidt, *Righteous Mind*, 114.
7 Haidt, *Righteous Mind*, 114.

CHAPTER 4. THE INDIGENOUS WORLDVIEW

1 "Who should own Native American artifacts?" *Annenberg Classroom*, ret. 8/16/16. http://www.annenbergclassroom.org/speakouts.aspx?name=who-should-own-native-american-artifacts&AspxAutoDetectCookieSupport=1
2 "Peoples of the world," *National Geographic Society*.
3 "United Nations Declaration on the Rights of Indigenous Peoples," *United Nations*

UNPFII. http://www.un.org/esa/socdev/unpfii/documents/DRIPS_en.pdf

4 "Indigenous Peoples and the United Nations System," *Office of the High Commissioner for Human Rights*, United Nations Office at Geneva. http://www.unhchr.ch/html/racism/indileaflet1.doc. and "Indigenous issues." *International Work Group on Indigenous Affairs*. http://www.iwgia.org/sw155.asp.

5 *The United Nations*. http://www.un.org/

6 "Indigenous Peoples, Indigenous Voices," *United Nations Permanent Forum on Indigenous Issues*, ret. 5/20/16. http://www.un.org/esa/socdev/unpfii/documents/5session_factsheet1.pdf

7 Carver, Courtney. "Story of the Mexican Fisherman," *Be More With Less*, ret. 8/19/16. http://bemorewithless.com/the-story-of-the-mexican-fisherman/

8 "Collective property in South America, challenges and prospects," *LandPortal.info* ret. 12/8/16. https://landportal.info/debates/2016/collective-property-south-america-challenges-and-prospects

9 Menchu, Rigoberta (trans. Ann Wright). *I, Rigoberta Menchu: An Indian Woman in Guatemala*, New York: Verso Press, 1984, 2.

10 Menchu, *I, Rigoberta Menchu*, 134.

11 Menchu, *I, Rigoberta Menchu*, 24-25.

12 Menchu, *I, Rigoberta Menchu*.

13 "Indigenous Peoples, Indigenous Voices," *United Nations Permanent Forum on Indigenous Issues*, ret. 5/20/16. http://www.un.org/esa/socdev/unpfii/documents/5session_factsheet1.pdf

14 Ibid.

CHAPTER 5. THE TRADITIONAL WORLDVIEW

1 Kuehnelt-Leddihn, Erik von. "Leftism Revisited: from de Sade and Marx to Hitler and Pol Pot," *Good Reads Quotes*.

2 Kirk, Russell. *The Conservative Mind: From Burke to Eliot*, Washington, D.C.: Regenery, 1953, 7–8.

3 Scruton, Roger. "How to Be a Conservative," *Goodreads*. https://www.goodreads.com/work/quotes/41955792-how-to-be-a-conservative

4 Scruton, Roger. *How to Be a Conservative*, London: Bloomsbury, 2014, 139-141.

5 Heer, Jeet. "The Whitewashing of George H. W. Bush," *The New Republic*, Dec. 3, 2018. https://newrepublic.com/article/152493/whitewashing-george-h-w-bush

6 Scruton, Roger. *Conservatism: An Invitation to the Good Tradition*, New York: All Points Books, 2018.

7 Stenner, Karen. "Three Kinds of Conservatism," *Psychology Inquiry*, (20), 2009, 142-159. https://www.researchgate.net/publication/274444535_Three_Kinds_of_Conservatism

8 Stenner, "Conservatism," *Psychology Inquiry*, 142-159.

9 Scruton, *How to Be Conservative*, 137.
10 Graham, Jesse, Haidt, Jonathan, and Hosek, Brian. "Liberals and Conservatives Rely on Different Sets of Moral Foundations," *Journal of Personality and Social Psychology*, June 2009, 1029-46. https://fbaum.unc.edu/teaching/articles/JPSP-2009-Moral-Foundations.pdf
11 Graham, Haidt, and Hosek, "Liberals and Conservatives," *Journal of Personality*.
12 Spencer, Richard. "The Conservative Write," *Taki's Magazine,* August 6, 2008. https://takimag.com/article/the_conservative_write/#axzz4JRcIyz7D
13 Hawley, George. *Making Sense of the Alt-Right*, New York: Columbia University Press, 2017 and Niewert, David. *Alt-America: The Rise of the Radical Right in the Age of Trump*, London and New York: Verso, 2017.
14 Wendling, Mike. *Alt-Right: From 4chan to the White House,* London: Pluto Press, 2018.
15 "Alt Right: A Primer about the New White Supremacy," *Anti-Defamation League*, ret. 12/2717 and "Alt-Right," *Southern Poverty Law Center*, ret. 12/2717. https://www.adl.org/resources/backgrounders/alt-right-a-primer-about-the-new-white-supremacy
16 Wendling, Mike. "Trump's shock troops: Who are the 'alt-right'?" *BBC News*, Aug. 26, 2016. https://www.bbc.com/news/magazine-37021991
17 Atkinson, David C. "Charlottesville and the Alt-Right: A Turning Point?" *Politics, Groups, and Identities*, 2018, 309–315. doi: 10.1080/21565503.2018.1454330
18 "The alt-right is fractured, more violent headed into Trump's second year," *Newsweek*, Jan. 21, 2018, ret. 1/21/18. https://www.newsweek.com/alt-right-fractured-violent-headed-trump-second-year-785552
19 Gray, Phillip W. "The Fire Rises: Identity, the Alt-Right and Intersectionality," *Journal of Political Ideologies* 23 (2), 2018, 141–156. doi:10.1080/13569317.2018.1451228
20 Beauchamp, Zack. "Study: 11 million white Americans think like the alt-right," *Vox.com*, 2018. https://www.vox.com/2018/8/10/17670992/study-white-americans-alt-right-racism-white-nationalists
21 Beit-Hallahmi, Benjamin. "Fundamentalism," *Global Policy Forum*, May 2000.
22 *New York Times Opinion*, Dec., 19, 2003. http://www.nytimes.com/2003/12/19/opinion/19iht-edscarf_ed3_.html
23 Huff, Peter. "Parallels in Muslim, Christian, and Jewish, and Christian Fundamentalism." http://www.worldandi.com/subscribers/feature_detail.asp?num=24175
24 Armstrong, Karen. *The Case for God*, New York: Alfred A. Knopf, 2009, 271.
25 Armstrong, *Case for God*, 235.
26 Armstrong, *Case for God*, 236-238.
27 Armstrong, *Case for God*, 236-238.
28 Armstrong, *Case for God*, 238.
29 Armstrong, *Case for God*, 239.
30 Armstrong, *Case for God*, 247-249.
31 Armstrong, *Case for God*, 249 and 254.

32 Armstrong, *Case for God*, 269-270.
33 Armstrong, *Case for God*, 270.
34 Armstrong, *Case for God*, 271.
35 Armstrong, *Case for God*, 272-273.
36 Armstrong, *Case for God*, 273.
37 Armstrong, *Case for God*, 274.
38 Armstrong, *Case for God*, 275.
39 Armstrong, *Case for God*, 293-294.
40 Armstrong, *Case for God*, 292.
41 Armstrong, *Case for God*, 295.
42 Armstrong, *Case for God*, 295.
43 Armstrong, *Case for God*, 293.

CHAPTER 6. THE PROGRESSIVE WORLDVIEW

1 Schambra, William A. and West, Thomas. "The Progressive Movement and the Transformation of American Politics," *Heritage Foundation*, July 18, 2007. https://www.heritage.org/political-process/report/the-progressive-movement-and-the-transformation-american-politics
2 Kantor, Norman F. *The American Century: Varieties of Culture in Modern Times*, New York: Harper Perennial, 1997, 425-431.
3 Kantor, *American Century*, 454-455.
4 Holiday, Ryan. "Stop Assuming that Everything You Feel or Think Is Right"—An Interview with Robert Greene, *Quillette*, Jan. 1, 2019. https://quillette.com/2019/01/01/stop-assuming-that-everything-you-feel-or-think-is-right-an-interview-with-robert-greene/
5 Ryan, "Stop Assuming," *Quillette*.
6 Ryan, "Stop Assuming," *Quillette*.
7 "Seven Things You Need to Know about Antifa," *BBC*. https://www.bbc.co.uk/programmes/articles/X56rQkDgd0qqB7R68t6t7C/seven-things-you-need-to-know-about-antifa
8 "Who Are the Antifa," *Fighting Hate for Good*. https://www.adl.org/resources/backgrounders/who-are-the-antifa
9 "Who Are Antifa," *Fighting Hate*.
10 Kayes, Sammy. "Principles of a Modern Progressive Movement," *Progressive Times*, Jan. 23, 2017. https://medium.com/tptimes/principles-of-a-modern-pro-gressive-movement-a2c3f9e5d25a
11 Meyer, Neal. "What Is Democratic Socialism?" *Jacobin Journal*, July 10, 2018. https://jacobinmag.com/2018/07/democratic-socialism-bernie-sanders-social-democracy-alexandria-ocasio-cortez
12 Stein, Letitia, Cornwell, Susan, Tanfani, Joseph. "Inside the progressive move-

ment roiling the Democratic Party," *Reuters*, Aug. 23, 2018. https://www.reuters.com/article/us-usa-election-progressives-specialrepo/inside-the-progressive-movement-roiling-the-democratic-party-idUSKCN1L81GI

13 Ibid.

14 Katier, Keith. "Two New Federal Surveys Show Stable Uninsured Rate," *Health Affairs*, Sept. 13, 2018, ret. 1/7/19. https://www.healthaffairs.org/do/10.1377/hblog20180913.896261/full/

15 Goldberg, Zach. "America's White Saviors," *Tablet*, June 5, 2019. https://www.tabletmag.com/jewish-news-and-politics/284875/americas-white-saviors

16 Edsall, Thomas B. "The Democratic Party Is Actually Three Parties," *New York Times Opinion*, July 24, 2019. https://www.nytimes.com/2019/07/24/opinion/2020-progressive-candidates.html?module=inline

17 Edsall, "Democratic Party," *New York Times Opinion*.

18 Edsall, "Democratic Party," *New York Times Opinion*.

19 Goldberg, "America's White Saviors," *Tablet*.

20 Goldberg, "America's White Saviors," *Tablet*.

21 Goldberg, "America's White Saviors," *Tablet*.

22 Goldberg, "America's White Saviors," *Tablet*.

23 Goldberg, "America's White Saviors," *Tablet*.

24 Goldberg, "America's White Saviors," *Tablet*.

25 Goldberg, "America's White Saviors," *Tablet*.

26 Goldberg, "America's White Saviors," *Tablet*.

27 Brooks, David. "How White Democrats Moved Left," *New York Times Opinion*, July 25, 2019. https://www.nytimes.com/2019/07/25/opinion/white-liberal-democrats.html

CHAPTER 7. THE GLOBALIZED WORLDVIEW

1 Stenner, Karen. "Three Kinds of Conservatism," *Psychology Inquiry*, (20), 2009, 142-159. https://www.researchgate.net/publication/274444535_Three_Kinds_of_Conservatism

2 Bremmer, Ian. *The End of the Free Market: Who Wins the War Between States and Corporations?* New York: Portfolio, 2010, 33 and 40.

3 Bremmer, *Free Market*, cover jacket, 21 and 42.

4 Bello, Walden. "The Global Financial System in Crisis," *Speech at People's Development Forum*, University of the Philippines, Mar. 25, 2008. http://www.waldenbello.org/index2.php?option=com_content&task=view&id=86&pop=1&page

5 Bello, Walden. "A Primer on the Wall Street Meltdown," *Focus on the Global South*, 2008. http://www.waldenbello.org/index2.php?option=com_content&task=view&id=98&pop=1&page

6 Levine, Madeline. "Challenging the Culture of Affluence," *Independent*

School, 2007, 28-36. http://www.nais.org/publications/ismagazinearticle.
cfm?ItemNumber=150274

7 Barber, Benjamin R., *Consumed: How Markets Corrupt Children, Infantilize Adults, and Swallow Citizens Whole*, New York: Norton & Co., 2007.

8 Barber, *Consumed*, 167.

9 Costanza, Robert. "Toward a new Sustainable Economy," *Real World Economics Review*, Mar. 26, 2009, 1, in *Common Dreams*.org. www.commondreams.org/print/40015

10 Speth, James Gustave. *The Bridge at the Edge of the World: Capitalism, the Environment, and Crossing from Crisis to Sustainability*, New Haven: Yale University Press, 2008, 46-47.

11 Meadows, Donella and Dennis and Randers, Jorgen. *Limits to Growth: The Thirty Year Update*, White River Junction, Vermont: Chelsea Green Publishing Company, 2004, 6.

12 Carnoy, Martin, Castells, Manuel, Cohen, Stephen S., and Carduso, Fernando Henrique. *The New Global Economy in the Information Age: Reflections on our Changing World*, University Park, PA: The Pennsylvania State University Press, 1993, 1-3 and 5-6; and Perelman, Michael. *Class Warfare in the Information Age*, New York: St. Martin's Press, 1998, 16.

13 "Uber May be Worth $50 billion. Really?" *CNN Money*, (July 8, 2015), ret. 7/8/15. http://money.cnn.com/2015/05/11/investing/uber-50-billion-valuation/index.html and Guadalupe Gonzalez. "Uber Eyes $120 Billion IPO in 2019," *Inc.* ret. August 13, 2019. https://www.inc.com/guadalupe-gonzalez/uber-eyes-120-billion-ipo-2019.html

14 "Economics," *About*.com. http://economics.about.com/od/economicsglossary/g/stolper.htm and Palley, Thomas. "Labor Threat," *Tom Paine*, Oct, 4, 2005, 1. www.zmag.org/content/print_articles.cfm?itemID=8867&section ID=1

15 Palley, "Labor Threat." *Tom Paine*.

16 Samuelson quoted in Palley, "Labor Threat," *Tom Paine*, 2.

17 Chanda, Nayan. *Bound Together:How Traders, Preachers, Adventurers, and Warriors Shaped Globalization*, New Haven: Yale University Press, 2007, 294.

18 Peck, Don. "Can the Middle Class be Saved," *The Atlantic*, Sept. 2011, 63. http://www.theatlantic.com/magazine/print/2011/09/can-the-middle-class-be-saved/8600

19 Stiglitz, Josephy E. "Of the 1%, for the 1%, by the 1%," *Vanity Fair*, May 2011. http://www.vanityfair.com/society/features/2011/05/top-one-percent-201105

20 Jeter, Jon. *Flat broke in the free market*, New York: W.W. Norton & Co., 2009, xiii.

21 Pizzigati, Sam. "Mapping Global Wealth," *OtherWords*, Oct. 2010. https://otherwords.org/mapping_global_wealth/

22 Jeter, *Flat Broke*, xiii.

23 Barber, *Consumed*, 102.

CHAPTER 8. THE TRANSFORMATIVE WORLDVIEW

1 Capra, Fritjof. *The Turning Point: Science, Society, and the Rising Culture*, Toronto: Bantam Books, 1982, 21-53.
2 Kantor, Norman F. *American Century: Varieties of Culture in Modern Times*, New York: HarperCollins Publishers, 1997, 425-431.
3 Mawlawi, Farouk. "New Conflicts, New Challenges: The Evolving Role for Non-Governmental Actors," *Journal of International Affairs*, Winter 1993, 392.
4 Clark, Mary E. *Ariadne's Thread: The Search for New Modes of Thinking*, New York: St. Martin's Press, 1989, 490-492.
5 "Overdose Death Rates," *National Institute on Drug Abuse*, ret. 9/19/19. https://www.drugabuse.gov/related-topics/trends-statistics/overdose-death-rates
6 Berry, Wendell. "Decolonizing Rural America," *Audubon*, (Vol. 95, No. 2), March-April, 1993, 105.
7 Alperovitz, Gar. "America Beyond Capitalism," *Dollars & Sense*, 2004. http://www.dollarsandsense.org/archives/2004/1104alper.html
8 "Genuine Progress Indicator," *Redefining Progress*. http://www.rprogress.org/sustainability_indicators/genuine_progress_indicator.htm

CHAPTER 9. INTEGRATION: JONATHAN HAIDT'S SIX MORAL FOUNDATIONS AND THE FIVE WORLDVIEWS

1 Taylor, Jared. "Why Everyone Else is Wrong," *American Renaissance*, Aug. 31, 2012, (review of J. Haidt, *The Righteous Mind*). https://www.amren.com/features/2012/08/why-everyone-else-is-wrong/
2 Haidt, Jonathan. "What Makes People Vote Republican," *Edge*, Sept. 8, 2008. https://www.edge.org/conversation/jonathan_haidt-what-makes-people-vote-republican
3 Parry, Marc. "Jonathan Haidt Decodes the Tribal Psychology of Politics," *The Chronicle of Higher Education*, Jan. 29, 2012. https://www.chronicle.com/article/Jonathan-Haidt-Decodes-the/130453
4 Parry, "Haidt Decodes," *Chronicle Higher Education*.
5 Haidt, Jonathan. *The Righteous Mind*, New York: Vintage Books, 2012, 10.
6 Turiel, Elliot. (1983), quoted in Haidt, *Righteous Mind*, 3.
7 Haidt, *Righteous Mind*, 11.
8 Haidt, *Righteous Mind*, 116 and Graham, Jesse, Haidt, Jonathan, and Hosek, Brian. "Liberals and Conservatives Rely on Different Sets of Moral Foundations," *Journal of Personality and Social Psychology*, June 2009, 1029-46. https://fbaum.unc.edu/teaching/articles/JPSP-2009-Moral-Foundations.pdf
9 Haidt, *Righteous Mind*, 14.
10 Haidt, "Vote Republican," *Edge*.
11 Mill, John Stuart. quoted in Haidt, "Vote Republican," *Edge*.

12 Haidt, "Vote Republican," *Edge*.
13 Haidt, "Vote Republican," *Edge*.
14 Haidt, "Vote Republican," *Edge*.
15 Anomie, *Wikipedia*, ret. Sept. 6, 2019. https://en.wikipedia.org/wiki/Anomie
16 Haidt, "Vote Republican," *Edge*.
17 Haidt, "Vote Republican," *Edge*.
18 Durkheim, Emile. Quoted in Haidt, *Righteous Mind*, 261.
19 Durkheim. Quoted in Haidt, *Righteous Mind*, 261
20 Durkheim. Quoted in Haidt, *Righteous Mind*, 262.
21 Durkheim. Quoted in Haidt, *Righteous Mind*, 262.
22 Haidt, *Righteous Mind*, 262.
23 Haidt, "Vote Republican," *Edge*.
24 Haidt, *Righteous Mind*, 17.
25 Haidt, *Righteous Mind*, 17.
26 Haidt, "Vote Republican," *Edge*.
27 Haidt, "Vote Republican," *Edge*.
28 Haidt, *Righteous Mind*, 125.
29 Haidt, *Righteous Mind*, 129-130.
30 Graham, Haidt, Hosek, "Liberals and Conservatives," *Journal of Personality and Social Psychology*.
31 Graham, Haidt, Hosek, "Liberals and Conservatives," *Journal of Personality and Social Psychology*.
32 Graham, Haidt, Hosek, "Liberals and Conservatives," *Journal of Personality and Social Psychology*.
33 Graham, Haidt, Hosek, "Liberals and Conservatives," *Journal of Personality and Social Psychology*.
34 Graham, Haidt, Hosek, "Liberals and Conservatives," *Journal of Personality and Social Psychology*.
35 Parry, "Haidt Decodes," *Chronicle Higher Education*.
36 Parry, "Haidt Decodes," *Chronicle Higher Education*.
37 McNerney, Sam. "Jonathan Haidt and the Moral Matrix: Breaking Out of Our Righteous Minds," *Scientific American*, blog, Dec. 2011. https://blogs.scientificamerican.com/guest-blog/jonathan-haidt-the-moral-matrix-breaking-out-of-our-righteous-minds/
38 Taylor, "Why Everyone Else," *American Renaissance*.
39 Parry, "Haidt Decodes," *Chronicle Higher Education*.

CHAPTER 10. BRIDGING THE CULTURAL DIVIDE

1 "Jungian Archetypes," *Wikipedia*, ret. 10/5/19. https://en.wikipedia.org/wiki/Jungian_archetypes
2 "Carl Jung's Archetype: The Trickster," *School Work Helper*, ret. 10/15/19. https://

schoolworkhelper.net/carl-jungs-archetype-the-trickster/

3 Forlenza, Rosario and Thomassen, Bjorn. "Decoding Donald Trump: The Triumph of Trickster Politics," *Public Seminar*, Apr. 18, 2016. http://www.publicseminar.org/2016/04/decoding-donald-trump-the-triumph-of-trickster-politics/

4 Ibid.

5 Mackay, James. "Why Donald Trump Now," *Tavistock Institute*, Dec. 2018. https://www.tavinstitute.org/news/why-donald-trump-now/

6 Taylor, Jared. "Why Everyone Else is Wrong," *American Renaissance*, Aug. 31, 2012, (review of J. Haidt, *The Righteous Mind*). https://www.amren.com/features/2012/08/why-everyone-else-is-wrong/

7 Taylor, "Why Everyone Else," *American Renaissance*.

8 Taylor, "Why Everyone Else," *American Renaissance*.

9 "Gordon Allport's Contact Hypothesis," *Facing History and Ourselves*, ret. 9/30/19. https://www.facinghistory.org/sounds-change/gordon-allports-contact-hypothesis

10 Taylor, "Why Everyone Else," *American Renaissance*.

11 Taylor, "Why Everyone Else," *American Renaissance*.

12 Parry, Marc. "Jonathan Haidt Decodes the Tribal Psychology of Politics," *The Chronicle of Higher Education*, Jan. 29, 2012. https://www.chronicle.com/article/Jonathan-Haidt-Decodes-the/130453

13 McNerney, Sam. "Jonathan Haidt and the Moral Matrix: Breaking Out of Our Righteous Minds," *Scientific American*, blog, Dec. 2011. https://blogs.scientificamerican.com/guest-blog/jonathan-haidt-the-moral-matrix-breaking-out-of-our-righteous-minds/

14 Taylor, "Why Everyone Else," *American Renaissance*.

15 Taylor, "Why Everyone Else," *American Renaissance*.

16 Taylor, "Why Everyone Else," *American Renaissance*.

17 Taylor, "Why Everyone Else," *American Renaissance*.

18 Taylor, "Why Everyone Else," *American Renaissance*.

19 Haidt, Jonathan. "Your Personality Makes Your Politics, *Time*, Jan.9, 2014. https://science.time.com/2014/01/09/your-personality-makes-your-politics/

20 Haidt, "Personality Makes Politics," *Time*.

21 Haidt, "Personality Makes Politics," *Time*.

22 Haidt, Jonathan. "America's Painful Divide," *Saturday Evening Post*, Aug. 21, 2012. https://www.saturdayeveningpost.com/2012/08/americas-painful-divide/

23 Haidt, "Painful Divide," *Saturday Evening Post*.

24 Taylor, "Why Everyone Else," *American Renaissance*.

25 Taylor, "Why Everyone Else," *American Renaissance*.

26 Taylor, "Why Everyone Else," *American Renaissance*.

27 Taylor, "Why Everyone Else," *American Renaissance*.

28 Taylor, "Why Everyone Else," *American Renaissance*.

29 Haidt, "Personality Makes Politics," *Time*.

30 Jonathan Haidt, "Romney, Obama and the New Culture War over Fairness," *Time*, Oct. 12, 2012. http://ideas.time.com/2012/10/08/the-new-culture-war-ove-fairness/

31 Haidt, "Personality Makes Politics," *Time*.

32 Haidt, "Personality Makes Politics," *Time*.

33 Haidt, "Personality Makes Politics," *Time*.

34 Haidt, Jonathan. "What Makes People Vote Republican," *Edge*, Sept. 8, 2008. https://www.edge.org/conversation/jonathan_haidt-what-makes-people-vote-republican

35 Haidt, "Vote Republican," *Edge*.

36 Haidt, "Vote Republican," *Edge*.

37 Haidt, "Vote Republican," *Edge*.

38 Haidt, "Vote Republican," *Edge*.

39 Haidt, "Vote Republican," *Edge*.

40 Haidt, "Vote Republican," *Edge*.

41 Haidt, "Vote Republican," *Edge*.

42 Haidt, "Vote Republican," *Edge*.

43 Haidt, "Vote Republican," *Edge*.

44 Haidt, "Vote Republican," *Edge*.

45 Haidt, "Painful Divide," *Saturday Evening Post*.

46 Haidt, "Painful Divide," *Saturday Evening Post*.

47 Haidt, "Painful Divide," *Saturday Evening Post*.

48 Taylor, "Why Everyone Else," *American Renaissance*.

49 Haidt, "Painful Divide," *Saturday Evening Post*.

50 Taylor, "Why Everyone Else," *American Renaissance*.

51 Taylor, "Why Everyone Else," *American Renaissance*.

52 McNerney, "Moral Matrix," *Scientific American*.

53 Taylor, "Why Everyone Else," *American Renaissance*.

54 Taylor, "Why Everyone Else," *American Renaissance*.

55 McNerney, "Moral Matrix," *Scientific American*.

Selected Bibliography

Alperovitz, Gar. "America Beyond Capitalism," *Dollars & Sense*, 2004. http://www.dollarsandsense.org/archives/2004/1104alper.html

Appiah, Kwame Anthony. "People don't vote for what they want. They vote for who they are." *Washington Post*, Aug. 30, 2018. https://www.washingtonpost.com/outlook/people-dont-vote-for-want-they-want-they-vote-for-who-they-are/2018/08/30/fb5b7e44-abd7-11e8-8a0c-70b618c98d3c_story.html?utm_term=.558699f885f9

Armstrong, Karen. *The Case for God*. (New York: Alfred A. Knopf, 2009).

Atkinson, David C. "Charlottesville and the Alt-Right: A Turning Point?" *Politics, Groups, and Identities*, 2018, 309–315. doi: 10.1080/21565503.2018.1454330

Barber, Benjamin R., *Consumed: How Markets Corrupt Children, Infantilize Adults, and Swallow Citizens Whole*. (New York: Norton & Co., 2007).

Beauchamp, Zack. "Study: 11 million white Americans think like the alt-right," *Vox.com*, 2018. https://www.vox.com/2018/8/10/17670992/study-white-americans-alt-right-racism-white-nationalists

Bello, Walden. "A Primer on the Wall Street Meltdown," *Focus on the Global South*, 2008. http://www.waldenbello.org/index2.php?option=com_content&task=view&id=98&pop=1&page

_____ . "The Global Financial System in Crisis," *Speech at People's Development Forum*, University of the Philippines, Mar. 25, 2008. http://www.waldenbello.org/index2.php?option=com_content&task=view&id=86&pop=1&page

Berry, Wendell. "Decolonizing Rural America," *Audubon* (Vol. 95, No. 2), March-April, 1993, 105.

Bremmer, Ian. *The End of the Free Market: Who Wins the War Between States and Corporations?* (New York: Portfolio, 2010).

Brooks, David. "How White Democrats Moved Left," *New York Times Opinion*, July 25, 2019. https://www.nytimes.com/2019/07/25/opinion/white-liberal-democrats.html

Capra, Fritjof. *The Turning Point: Science, Society, and the Rising Culture.* (Toronto: Bantam Books, 1982).

Carver, Courtney. "Story of the Mexican Fisherman," *Be More With Less*, ret. 8/19/16. http://bemorewithless.com/the-story-of-the-mexican-fisherman/

Chanda, Nayan. *Bound Together: How Traders, Preachers, Adventurers, and Warriors Shaped Globalization.* (New Haven: Yale University Press, 2007).

Choma, Russ and Kroll, Andy. "The NRA Raised a Record Amount of Money in 2016," *Mother Jones,* Jan. 4, 2018. https://www.motherjones.com/politics/2018/01/nra-donald-trump-guns-fundraising/

Clark, Mary E. *Ariadne's Thread: The Search for New Modes of Thinking.* (New York: St. Martin's Press, 1989).

Costanza, Robert. "Toward a new Sustainable Economy," *Real World Economics Review,* Mar. 26, 2009, 1, in *Common Dreams*.org. www.commondreams.org/print/40015

Edsall, Thomas B. "The Democratic Party Is Actually Three Parties," *New York Times Opinion*, July 24, 2019. https://www.nytimes.com/2019/07/24/opinion/2020-progressive-candidates.html?module=inline

Friedman, Uri. "What is a Populist?" *The Atlantic*, Feb. 17, 2017. https://www.theatlantic.com/international/archive/2017/02/what-is-populist-trump/516525/

Goekler, John. "Teaching for the Future: Systems Thinking and Sustainability," *Green Teacher 70*, Spring 2003, 8-14.

Goldberg, Zach. "America's White Saviors," *Tablet*, June 5, 2019. https://www.tabletmag.com/jewish-news-and-politics/284875/americas-white-saviors

Graham, Jesse, Haidt, Jonathan, and Hosek, Brian. "Liberals and Conservatives Rely on Different Sets of Moral Foundations," *Journal of Personality and Social Psychology*, June 2009, 1029-46. https://fbaum.unc.edu/teaching/articles/JPSP-2009-Moral-Foundations.pdf

Graham, Michael. "Planned Parenthood's Absolutism," *Week*, The Federalist.com, Mar. 16, 2018.

Gray, Phillip W. "The Fire Rises: Identity, the Alt-Right and Intersectionality," *Journal of Political Ideologies* 23 (2), 2018, 141-156. doi:10.1080/13569317.2018.1451228

Haidt, Jonathan. "America's Painful Divide," *Saturday Evening Post,* Sept.-Oct. 2012. https://www.saturdayeveningpost.com/2012/08/americas-painful-divide/

_____. "Romney, Obama and the New Culture War over Fairness," *Time*, Oct. 12, 2012. http://ideas.time.com/2012/10/08/the-new-culture-war-over-fairness/

_____. *The Righteous Mind: Why Good People are Divided by Politics and Religion.* (New York: Vintage Books, 2012).

_____. "What Makes People Vote Republican," *Edge*, Sept. 8, 2008. https://www.edge.org/conversation/jonathan_haidt-what-makes-people-vote-republican

Hawley, George. *Making Sense of the Alt-Right.* (New York: Columbia University Press, 2017).

Heer, Jeet. "The Whitewashing of George H. W. Bush," *The New Republic*, Dec. 3, 2018. https://newrepublic.com/article/152493/whitewashing-george-h-w-bush

Holiday, Ryan. "Stop Assuming that Everything You Feel or Think Is

Right"—An Interview with Robert Greene, *Quillette*, Jan. 1, 2019. https://quillette.com/2019/01/01/stop-assuming-that-everything-you-feel-or-think-is-right-an-interview-with-robert-greene/

Jeter, Jon. *Flat broke in the free market.* (New York: W.W. Norton & Co., 2009).

Kantor, Norman F. *The American Century: Varieties of Culture in Modern Times.* (New York: Harper Perennial, 1997).

Katier, Keith. "Two New Federal Surveys Show Stable Uninsured Rate," *Health Affairs*, Sept. 13, 2018, ret. 1/7/19. https://www.healthaffairs.org/do/10.1377/hblog20180913.896261/full/

Kayes, Sammy. "Principles of a Modern Progressive Movement," *Progressive Times*, Jan. 23, 2017. https://medium.com/tptimes/principles-of-a-modern-progressive-movement-a2c3f9e5d25a

Kirk, Russell. *The Conservative Mind: From Burke to Eliot.* (Washington, D.C.: Regenery, 1953).

LeBaron, Michelle. "Cultural and Worldview Frames," *Knowledge Based Essay*, August 2003. http://www.beyondintractability.org/essay/cultural_frames/

Lenski, Gerhard and Jean. *Human Societies: An Introduction to Macrosociology.* (New York: McGraw-Hill, 1982).

Levine, Madeline. "Challenging the Culture of Affluence," *Independent School*, 2007, 28-36. http://www.nais.org/publications/ismagazinearticle.cfm?ItemNumber=150274

McNerney, Sam. "Jonathan Haidt and the Moral Matrix: Breaking Out of Our Righteous Minds," *Scientific American*, blog, Dec. 2011. https://blogs.scientificamerican.com/guest-blog/jonathan-haidt-the-moral-matrix-breaking-out-of-our-righteous-minds/

Meadows, Donella & Dennis, Randers, Jorgen. *Limits to Growth: The Thirty Year Update.* (White River Junction, Vermont: Chelsea Green Publishing Company, 2004).

Menchu, Rigoberta (trans. Ann Wright). *I, Rigoberta Menchu: An Indian Woman in Guatemala.* (New York: Verso Press, 1984).

Meyer, Neal. "What Is Democratic Socialism?" *Jacobin Journal*, July 10, 2018. https://jacobinmag.com/2018/07/democratic-socialism-bernie-sanders-social-democracy-alexandria-ocasio-cortez

Molloy, David. "What is populism, and what does the term actually mean?? *BBC News*, Mar. 6, 2018. https://www.bbc.com/news/world-43301423

Mudde, Cas and Kaltwasser, Cristóbal Rovira. *Populism: A Very Short Introduction.* (Oxford: Oxford University Press, 2017).

Niewert, David. *Alt-America: The Rise of the Radical Right in the Age of Trump.* (London and New York: Verso, 2017).

Palley, Thomas. "Labor Threat." *Tom Paine,* Oct. 4, 2005. http://www.zmag.org/content/print_article.cfm?itemID=8867&sectionID=1

Parry, Marc. "Jonathan Haidt Decodes the Tribal Psychology of Politics," *The Chronicle of Higher Education*, Jan. 29, 2012. https://www.chronicle.com/article/Jonathan-Haidt-Decodes-the/130453

Peck, Don. "Can the Middle Class be Saved," *The Atlantic*, Sept. 2011, 63. *http://www.theatlantic.com/magazine/print/2011/09/can-the-middle-class-be-saved/8600*

Schambra, William A. and West, Thomas. "The Progressive Movement and the Transformation of American Politics," *Heritage Foundation*, July 18, 2007. https://www.heritage.org/political-process/report/the-progressive-movement-and-the-transformation-american-politics

Scruton, Roger. *Conservatism: An Invitation to the Good Tradition.* (New York: All Points Books, 2018).

_____. *How to Be a Conservative.* (London: Bloomsbury, 2014).

Spencer, Richard. "The Conservative Write," *Taki's Magazine*, August 6,

2008. https://takimag.com/article/the_conservative_write/#axzz4JRcIyz7D

Speth, James Gustave. *The Bridge at the Edge of the World: Capitalism, the Environment, and Crossing from Crisis to Sustainability*. (New Haven: Yale University Press, 2008).

Stein, Letitia, Cornwell, Susan, Tanfani, Joseph. "Inside the progressive movement roiling the Democratic Party," *Reuters*, Aug. 23, 2018. https://www.reuters.com/article/us-usa-election-progressives-specialrepo/inside-the-progressive-movement-roiling-the-democratic-party-idUSKCN1L81GI

Stenner, Karen. "Three Kinds of Conservatism," *Psychology Inquiry*, (20), 2009, 142-159. https://www.researchgate.net/publication/274444535_Three_Kinds_of_Conservatism

Stiglitz, Josephy E. "Of the 1%, for the 1%, by the 1%," *Vanity Fair*, May 2011. http://www.vanityfair.com/society/features/2011/05/top-one-percent-201105

Taylor, Jared. "Why Everyone Else is Wrong," *American Renaissance,* Aug. 31, 2012, (review of J. Haidt, *The Righteous Mind*). https://www.amren.com/features/2012/08/why-everyone-else-is-wrong/

Wallerstein, Emmanuel. "Introductory Essay to Essential Wallerstein," *Yale University Faculty Page.*

Wendling, Mike. *Alt-Right: From 4chan to the White House*. (London: Pluto Press, 2018).

Zito, Salena. "Taking Trump Seriously, Not Literally," *Atlantic Magazine*, Sept. 23, 2016. https://www.theatlantic.com/politics/archive/2016/09/trump-makes-his-case-in-pittsburgh/501335/

About the Author

D r. Denise R. Ames' varied life experiences—scholarly research, teaching, reflections, and extensive travels—have contributed to her balanced and thoughtful perspectives about the topics she teaches and writes about. The current cultural divide, the subject of this book, has been particularly troublesome to her, but fascinating to dig into as well.

Dr. Ames grew up in close proximity to a large, extended family in the factory town of Rockford, Illinois, riding and training Arabian horses. Upon graduating college, Dr. Ames taught social studies in secondary schools in the South for several years. Upon returning to Illinois, she started a family, managed the building of seven houses, and owned a small retail business. She returned to graduate school at Illinois State University and taught there as well. After moving to Albuquerque, New Mexico in 2000, she taught at a community college and started an educational non-profit in 2003.

Dr. Ames took her bachelor's degree in history education from Southern Illinois University, and master's degree and doctorate in history education with a world history focus from Illinois State University.

For over 35 years, Dr. Ames has taught at secondary schools, universities, a community college, professional development trainings, and lifelong learning classes and workshops. Her teaching topics range from academic subjects such as world history, global issues, United States history, Western Civilization, world humanities, cultural studies, and global business issues to secondary social studies pedagogy and global issues, to lifelong learning topics.

In 2003, Dr. Ames founded the Center for Global Awareness, a non-profit educational organization that develops books and educational resources with a global perspective and holistic approach for students and educators grade 9 through university. She has written seven books for the non-profit—*Five Worldviews: How We See the World, Human Rights: Towards a Global*

Values System, Waves of Global Change: A Holistic World History (two editions), *Waves of Global Change: An Educator's Handbook for Teaching a Holistic World History, The Global Economy: Connecting the Roots of a Holistic System, Connecting the Roots of a Global Economy: A Brief Edition,* and *Financial Literacy: Wall Street and How it Works.* She has also written numerous blogs, lesson plans, articles, newsletters, and teaching units for the non-profit and clients.

Dr. Ames is now moving to lifelong learning for adults. She is developing a program called TURN—transformative understanding and reflection network—that encourages lifelong learners to see things with new eyes, shift perspectives, and open up to new possibilities for the purpose of personal and global well-being. She teaches classes and workshops on TURN topics— cross-cultural awareness, indigenous wisdom, a transformative worldview, learning from the past, mythic journey, and transformative travel. Occasionally she lectures about historical topics on cruise ships.

World cultures and history are Dr. Ames' lifelong interest and study. Her extensive travels have taken her to all 50 states in the United States and to over 50 countries around the world. Many of her travels have been education-related and have served as research for her books, blogs, articles, and resources.

Along with her professional interests, Dr. Ames has two adult children and three grandchildren. She particularly enjoys traveling, hiking, yoga, reading, playing with her grandchildren, writing, and visiting with family and friends. She currently resides near the campus of the University of New Mexico with her partner Jim in sunny Albuquerque, New Mexico, USA.

Index

A
alt-right, 78-81, 103-104
American Dream, 2-4
antifa movement, 94, 103-104
authoritarian, 28-29, 45-46, 73-74, 79, 103, 116, 129, 156, 181, 202
authority/subversion, 9, 179, 181-182

B
binding foundations, 170, 179, 183, 203
bounded assumptions, 32
bubble, 2, 7, 14, 114, 169, 209

C
capitalism, 1, 38, 42-44, 82, 94-97, 105, 116-119, 121, 123, 138, 145, 150, 164, 174, 202
care/harm, 9, 169, 171-172
Clinton, Hillary, i, iii, 2, 4, 26, 98, 105-106
common people, 23, 25-26
communism, 42-43, 45, 117-118, 204
conservatism, 5, 25, 73-74, 79, 116
consumerism, 13, 38, 71, 116, 120-121, 130, 132, 159
cultural divide, iv-v, vii-viii, 4, 6-9, 11, 161, 171, 187, 191-193, 196, 206-207, 209

D
democracy, 2, 4, 7, 26, 29, 89, 95-96, 105-107, 111, 114, 129, 136, 145, 174, 191, 210
democratic socialism, 43, 105, 114
Durkheim, David Émile, 164-167, 183, 200-203

E
ecopsychology, 140
elders, 54, 59, 136-137, 148, 158, 162, 173, 182, 184
empathy, 8-9, 11, 169, 171, 192-193, 206, 209
Enlightenment, 40, 44, 48, 82, 84-85, 95-96, 99, 112, 117, 168
environment, 24, 34, 46-47, 54, 73, 109, 124, 116, 130, 131, 135-138, 140, 144, 146, 150-158
equality, 3, 24, 34, 38, 44, 79, 82, 84, 94, 96, 105, 136, 138, 145, 147, 162, 174-179
equity, 34, 175, 176, 178
ethos of progress, iv-v

231

Evangelical, 1, 84-86, 157

local capitalism, 151
loyalty/betrayal, 9, 171, 180-182

M

Make America Great Again, 4, 77
Menchu, Rigoberta, 62-67
Mill, John Stuart, 30, 164-166, 205
Modern Wave, 18, 37-38, 53
modern worldview, 14, 37-50, 53, 90, 93, 98-101, 117, 129, 135-136, 141, 155, 157, 158, 168
modernizers, 57, 59, 62, 91, 168
moral capital, 201, 203-204
Moral Foundations, 9-10, 161-162, 165, 167, 169-171, 179, 185, 187, 198, 201-204

N

national narrative, 2-4, 6
negative liberty, 177-179
neoliberalism, 43-44, 73-74, 114, 117, 118, 126-127, 145

O

Obama, Barack, i, 2, 14, 76, 77, 98, 175
Occupy Wall Street, 105, 174, 176, 181

P

political conservatism, 69-70, 73
populism, 25-29, 75, 77, 104
populist left, 23, 93-94, 142
populist right, 23, 32, 69, 72-79, 110, 142
positive liberty, 177-179
post-modern, 91, 98-101, 141
procedural fairness, 174-176, 178
progressive worldview, 23, 25, 33, 93, 95, 98, 101, 109, 113, 116, 141-142, 147, 158, 161, 171, 198
proportionality, 174-175, 178
Protestant fundamentalism, 85, 87, 89, 91

R

reactance, 113, 177-178
Renaissance, 38-41

S

T

U

W

Y